THE WELL-CONNECTED COMMUNITY

A Networking Approach to Community Development

Third edition

Alison Gilchrist

T0373348

P

First published in Great Britain in 2019 by

Policy Press
University of Bristol
1-9 Old Park Hill
Bristol
BS2 8BB
UK
t: +44 (0)117 954 5940
pp-info@bristol.ac.uk
www.policypress.co.uk

North America office:
Policy Press
c/o The University of Chicago Press
1427 East 60th Street
Chicago, IL 60637, USA
t: +1 773 702 7700
f: +1 773-702-9756
sales@press.uchicago.edu
www.press.uchicago.edu

British Library Cataloguing in Publication Data
A catalogue record for this book is available from the British Library

Library of Congress Cataloging-in-Publication Data
A catalog record for this book has been requested

978-1-4473-4779-8 paperback
978-1-4473-4780-4 ePub
978-1-4473-4788-0 ePDF

Cover design by Andrew Corbett
Front cover image: Launch of summer youth activities. Thanks to Tonge with the Haulgh Big Local (Bolton, UK).

Printed and bound by CPI Group (UK) Ltd, Croydon, CR0 4YY

This edition is dedicated to my mother,
Toonkey Gilchrist (1927–2017), who encouraged
and inspired my interest in networking.

Contents

List of tables, figures and boxes

Tables

Figure

Boxes

Preface to the third edition

'Tis true, there's magic in the web of it.
(Shakespeare, *Othello*, Act 3, scene 4)

This book is about the value of connections and the work that is done to establish and maintain them. In the 15 years since the first edition, networking is significantly more commonplace, deliberate and computer mediated. It is now firmly acknowledged as essential to effective community development work. But the organisational and demographic environment in which community workers and activists operate is becoming increasingly dynamic, complex and diverse. Practitioners need to be ever more agile in working across boundaries. In a constantly changing and interacting world, uncertainty requires individuals and society to be more 'elastic' by 'letting go of comfortable ideas and become more accustomed to ambiguity and contradiction' (Mlodinow, 2018). Networking can help us to find this capacity in ourselves and with others.

Being 'well connected' is recognised as a source of strength. However, we have more to learn about the emotional ramifications and attitudes that can nourish or corrode connections. It takes both time and trust to build loving and respectful relationships. This applies equally to the development of community links and the informal arrangements that underpin cooperation across the public, private, voluntary and community sectors.

The past ten years since 2009 have given us a deeper and more sophisticated understanding of networks: their impact in people's lives and their contribution to society. The 'praxis' of networking is also more fully acknowledged, with an explicit emphasis on the need for reciprocity (Offer, 2012) and the value of courteous hospitality. As the latest research on empowering communities asserts, 'We are social beings and the connections we make with each other help us to realise our potential and power' (Baker and Taylor, 2018, p 35). The value of networking for developing strong and active communities is recognised now more than ever.

The theories and evidence offered in this book are rooted in research but draw heavily on phronetic knowledge: knowledge that is derived from practice and experience. The ideas have been distilled from personal reflections, action research, workshops, informal conversations, government reports and the academic literature. They are applicable to policy and practice, as well as intended to encourage critical reflection using the questions posed at the end of each chapter.

The significance of informal interactions and interpersonal networks for community life has been understood for decades. The earliest research in sociology and ethnography identified patterns of cooperation and communication that are characteristic of most societies (Sennett, 2012). The usual connotation of 'community' as a 'warm' and fuzzy concept must, however, be tempered by acknowledging that most communities harbour rivalries and internal schisms between different factions and interest groups. These are focused on different social identities and political ideologies. They may also reflect inequalities of various kinds, as well as mutual antipathies.

The informal and serendipitous nature of networks has gained prominence (Gilchrist, 2016), while evidence has accumulated to add to our awareness that 'it's not what you know, but who you know' in opening up opportunities, accessing resources and maintaining 'liveable lives' (Anderson et al, 2015). My doctoral research (Gilchrist, 2001) represented an early attempt to validate and make visible the networking skills and strategies used by people who work effectively with communities. Since then, there has been widespread recognition that lateral, often boundary-spanning, connections brokered and nurtured by intermediaries and community connectors are essential features of network governance models, partnership working and different forms of community development.

Loose networks, based on trust and shared norms, that *bond* groups together and *bridge* across sectoral and community boundaries enable valuable and fairly reliable exchanges and interactions that do not require costly or time-consuming organisational structures. In the past ten years or so, since 2010, there has been rising concern that society is becoming more fragmented, resulting in social isolation and mounting tensions between diverse groups.

There is now an explicit acknowledgement of the value of relationships for individuals' wellbeing as well as for the wider society. A relatively new term, 'community capital', has been coined, and developed through research, to underscore the shared nature of this asset. Collective dividends are reported for 'well-connected communities' in terms of community resilience, active citizenship and economic engagement. Funders have designed networking into their 'offer', allocating time and resources to encourage residents from the targeted areas to meet and share experiences, thus enhancing cross-community learning and peer support. Similarly, the training provided for community organisers' programmes places great emphasis on the organiser's role in facilitating and maintaining community networks for social change, building on the work of Anklam (2007), Vandeventer and Mandell (2007), Holley (2012) and Plastrik et al (2014).

While networks tend to be favourably viewed as vehicles for mobilising and sharing information, they can be exclusive and have their downsides regarding the abuse of power. This has been accentuated by insights into the sometimes detrimental effects of social media. We have a better understanding of how these webs of mutual influence and peer-to-peer communication propagate damaging effects of peer pressure and perpetuate unconscious biases through algorithmic processes that create 'echo chambers' of opinion. For this reason, it is vital to understand how networks are deliberately nurtured to encourage mutual relations and useful boundary-spanning connections, especially those that challenge discrimination and power differentials.

This facet of working with communities is the primary focus of this book. Networking has received increasing recognition as a vital aspect of community development practice, although it has sometimes been disparaged as overly transactional and self-interested. Creating common ground for collaboration and effective communication is regarded as involving a valuable set of capabilities for working across various kinds of edges and divides. It involves appreciating different perspectives and synthesising a range of ideas and interests as well as challenging oppressive and out-dated attitudes.

The growing interest in co-production and network governance as models for joint working between service providers and community members recognises the intangible value of the connections between participants and practitioners (Boyle et al, 2011; Durose and Richardson, 2015). There is therefore a need to invest in and nurture these by taking time to establish good relations, build rapport and avoid 'netsploitation' (Davies and Spicer, 2015).

Diversity and economic inequalities affect local communities, reducing a shared sense of belonging and creating competing equality claims and new intersected forms of social and ethnic identity (Afridi and Warmington, 2009; Hill-Collins, 2009; Hirsch, 2018). Many traditions and older versions of solidarity have withered away, undermining cohesion in some places and altering how people connect with work colleagues and neighbours. Communities are deemed to be more fractured, with social isolation and loneliness regarded as growing problems (Jopling, 2017). Associated mental health difficulties have given rise to befriending schemes and activities-based projects. A pioneering approach has been trialled by several local authorities using social impact bonds and social prescribing to invest in various programmes for improving the connectedness of older people and people suffering from various life-limiting conditions (Kimberlee, 2016).

The practices and habits of connecting have been dissected and promoted as essential to effective and sustainable community work in a variety of circumstances. While noting caveats and drawbacks, Russell (2015) argued for strategies that foster, but do not abuse or exploit, personal connections. Hobsbawm (2017) has warned against hyper-connectivity. Too much time spent online, dealing with cyber-relations and managing one's social media profile and content, lowers the frequency of face-to-face interactions and diminishes the scope for consolidating real-world relationships.

At the same time social infrastructure has deteriorated, with a loss of communal spaces and community hubs due to closure or marketisation (Hastings et al, 2015; Price, 2015; Soteri-Proctor, 2017). Nonetheless, grassroots initiatives continue to spring up, although they increasingly depend on purely voluntary effort rather than funded community development support (Scott, 2010).

The field of social network analysis has benefited considerably from the development of software designed to trace patterns of connection, communication and cooperation, for example within civil society, organisational ecosystems or neighbourhoods. It is likely that ever more sophisticated programmes will reveal significant correlations and links that will enhance our knowledge of the benefits *and* the hazards associated with 'well-connected communities'. Those of us who work with communities can be more committed, but perhaps more circumspect, in how we encourage networking.

In Britain community development has to some extent been marginalised or co-opted as a means for public authorities to engage with communities and encourage voluntary effort in the delivery of services, resulting in a delicate balancing act between state responsibilities and community interests. This has proved a mixed blessing. In many ways it has highlighted the role of community practitioners, those who work at the interface between statutory bodies and citizens, in ensuring that the users of services can be involved in decision making and the co-production of agreed outcomes. On the other hand, it has led to a practice often lacking an understanding of power and devoid of any recognition that community voices may legitimately oppose as well as support more powerful interests.

However, the rise of outsourced contracting and the decline of generic community development and the large-scale disappearance of core-funding for voluntary sector infrastructure organisations have restricted collaboration and liaison at local levels. Many organisations, especially the well-established national charities, became ensnared in this agenda, leading to a divergence across a spectrum ranging from large, hierarchical organisations through to precariously funded community groups (Milbourne, 2013; Rochester, 2013; Deakin, 2014). Some writers have argued that a hybrid model of organisation has evolved, neither private nor voluntary, but incorporating elements from each (Billis, 2010).

This has made it more difficult to nurture interpersonal and community links. Economic strategies driven by neoliberalism and austerity policies have led to dramatic cuts in government spending, stimulating a search for alternative means of maintaining public services and community facilities, for example through self-help, third sector commissioning, volunteering and social action (Rees and Mullins, 2017; Lindsey and Mohan, 2019).

This third edition has been updated to reflect developments in government thinking in the UK and the impact of austerity cuts. Recent years have witnessed a decline in the use of the term 'community development', accompanied by a reduction in the number of fieldwork professionals and the availability of training and support for activists and practitioners (ESB, 2017). A variety of types and models of community work have emerged, notably community organising, and there has been a renewed emphasis on strengths-based or asset-based approaches. Accelerating globalisation has led to added social pressures and opportunities for learning from the global South.

For those living in the UK, neoliberal economic strategies and the impact of the Brexit referendum have sharpened tensions between different ethnic groups and classes. This is having a disproportionate impact on those already disadvantaged in the economic and welfare system, exacerbating already soaring levels of disaffection, poverty and inequality (Clark and Heath, 2014; Alston, 2018; Civil Society Futures, 2018). Despite impressive dedication from many small charities and faith-based organisations, these hard times have badly undermined social relations and disrupted community networks (Lawrence and Lim, 2015). The very concept of 'community life' has been challenged (Elgenius, 2018, p 55). However, it seems that people are redesigning communities in ways that are less local and less formal, reconfiguring their relationships around joint interests and new modes of socialising. These may be looser but are just as significant, with mutual affinity and convenience rather than proximity and necessity becoming the basis for creating 'hidden solidarities' using a variety of social identities and connective technologies (Lawrence, 2018, p 240).

I hope that this third edition reflects these insights and experiences. It has been substantially updated to take account of recent developments in theory, policy and practice. It affirms the continuing importance of networking for community development and the need for this to be grounded in core values of equality, empathy and empowerment. The fundamental purpose and structure of the book has not changed: my main argument remains that effective and inclusive networking is skilled, strategic and often serendipitous.

Acknowledgements

I am grateful to numerous colleagues throughout my working life as a community worker who have stimulated my thinking and offered interesting examples from practice. I owe special appreciation to Mandy Wilson and Kevin Harris for their assistance with this edition. Many thanks are given to Ken Taylor and Nigel Coe for proofreading.

Others include Kim Adams from Easton Community Association, along with Jenny Fisher and Catriona May at the Community Development Foundation (CDF), who provided valuable support, critiques and encouragement.

Most recently, the backing from colleagues, notably Catherine Durose, of INLOGOV at the University of Birmingham, along with a small grant, have proved invaluable in enabling me to finish this third edition.

Members of the Panel Study (1996–98): Frances Brown, Teri Dolan, Pete Hulse, Caroline Kay, Linda McMann, Susan Moores, Anne Pendleton, Gary Smith, Greg Smith, Keib Thomas, Chris Trueblood, and Mike Waite.

Bristol Festival Against Racism: Lil Bowers, Lindy Clifton, Peter Courtier, Rosetta Eligon, Mike Graham, Steve Graham, Minoo Jalali, Richard Jewison, Jane Kilpatrick, Batook Pandya, Ray Safia and Balraj Sandhu.

Structure of the book

Chapter 1 begins with an examination of what we mean by the term 'community' and considers various models developed to understand different experiences. The section on social capital has been considerably expanded to include a consideration of collective efficacy, community cohesion and integration. Chapter 2 explores how networks contribute to community life, individual wellbeing and collective survival strategies. It considers how 'community' has been treated as a dimension of policy in the UK and illustrates this with some examples from recent programmes.

Chapter 3 provides some definitions of community development and offers a historical account of different models of community development, mainly as they have emerged in the UK but with reference to more global perspectives. Chapter 4 sets out the strands that comprise community development interventions and reviews two major programmes currently being implemented.

Chapters 5 and 6 are concerned with the structure, features and functions of networks in society and in organisations. They examine how interpersonal linkages affect the flow of power and influence in decision making, how community cohesion is enhanced through cross-community 'bridge building' and how emotions and shared understandings underpin strategies for collective action and political alliances.

In Chapters 7 and 8 I present the findings from research on the role and practice of community workers, intermediaries, activists and leaders. Community workers use and support networks to promote collective empowerment and to help different agencies to work better together. Specific skills and strategies are identified as well as a number of valuable traits and attitudes. I argue that 'networking the networks' and actively nurturing the more difficult connections in communities is our distinctive contribution. I therefore introduce the term 'meta-networking' as a way of making visible this important community development role.

Chapter 9 considers how and why networking benefits communities and those that work with them. The concept of the 'well-connected community' is presented as a way of thinking about 'community' as the emergent property of complex and dynamic social systems. It is a means of conjuring order out of chaos, building resilience and devising innovative solutions to intractable problems. Recent applications from the social sciences using complexity theory have been added, as have developments in social media and information technology.

Chapter 10 explores key issues and dilemmas associated with a networking approach to community development. It sets out the implications of this model for practitioners, some of them already familiar, such as accountability, role boundaries and 'burnout'. Chapter 11 draws the book to a conclusion by setting out a model of the 'well-connected community', with some recommendations for ensuring that networking practice is both effective and ethical, suggesting how 'good practice' can be supported by funders, managers and policy makers.

Alison Gilchrist,
Independent community development consultant
April 2019

1

Community connections: value and meaning

When the stranger says: what is the meaning of this city?
Do you huddle together because you love each other?
What will you answer? 'We all dwell together
To make money from each other'? or 'This is a community'?
T.S. Eliot, Chorus from 'The rock', 1934

Despite its varied definitions and applications, community development is fundamentally about the development of 'community'; but what do we mean by 'community'? It makes sense to begin by examining what we know and understand about the concept. This book is based on a belief that the experience of community is generated by and manifest in the informal networks that exist between people, between groups and between organisations. Community provides a crucial dimension to our lives and is a persistent theme within policy making. Throughout history, people have lamented the decline or eclipse of community (Stein, 1960) and the associated weakening of local social ties.

The idea of community is generally regarded as a force for good: a means of survival and progress. Lack of community is considered a present-day 'social evil', confirming an apparent yearning for community spirit and mutuality (Duerden, 2018). A survey carried out in the UK indicated that the presence of strong community spirit came fourth in people's wish list for what made an ideal place to live (Nextdoor, 2016). The majority in this sample also reported that they felt there had been a loss of 'community belonging', as compared with their grandparents' generation, resulting in a sense of loneliness and vulnerability in the face of criminal or anti-social behaviour. But, as Lawrence (2018) suggests, we are facing a strange paradox between people wanting to be more connected at community level, on the one hand, while also choosing to live independently in single households and zealously guarding their right to privacy. Bauman (2000, 2003) contends that community can be seen as 'liquid', accommodating the lumps and bumps of existing circumstances and flowing with prevalent trends and discourses, notably a Western or contemporary desire for freedom and autonomy. Without becoming cynical, it is important to remember that references to community values and identities have also been used to impose responsibilities, deny rights, generate conflict and resist change (Day, 2006; Somerville, 2016).

Nevertheless, community has proved elusive and notoriously difficult to define and to study. Indeed some writers advise against using the term at all 'because its overtones seem too simply favourable, [leading] to an underestimation of the harsher tensions and sanctions of [some] groups' (Hoggart, 1957). Early sociologists struggled to devise an operational use of the term. Some, like Stacey (1969), have argued that it should be replaced with a seemingly more scientific-sounding phrase, 'local social system'; and this approach will be explored later. Surveys on the characteristics of a 'good' community consistently reveal that people value a wide range of community and support groups, alongside a set of residents who are good neighbours and will help each other (Adams and Hess, 2006). Nearby networks of family and friends contribute to feelings of community, sustained through recurrent, often 'mundane and everyday interactions between people in localised settings' (Robertson et al, 2008).

This chapter considers some of the benefits and limitations of community networks. It looks briefly at evidence and theories concerning community life from anthropology and sociology before exploring the ways in which networks operate to the advantage of communities and, conversely, the ways in which they distort or suppress choices and opportunities. The model of the well-connected community argues that community development has a role to play in helping people to make connections that are useful and empowering and, in particular, it addresses how to overcome or dismantle some of the obstacles that prevent people from communicating and cooperating with one another. First, however, how do networks contribute to community life? What have community studies revealed about people's everyday interactions and relationships? How is the term 'community' used and how does it compare to the idea of 'social capital'? Chapter 2 will consider what relevance this has for public policy.

Community theory and studies

In his classic inventory of anthropological and sociological definitions of community, Hillery (1955) identified a core feature to be regular, mostly cooperative, interaction among a set of people over time. Labelling a set of people a 'community' generally implies that they have some common interest or bond (Taylor et al, 2000; Meijl, 2011). It also raises expectations of loyalty, support and affirmation. Early sociologists such as

Tönnies (1887) and Durkheim (1893) emphasised the emotional aspects of local life, arguing that mutual understanding, shared experiences and solidarity are what distinguish *Gemeinschaft* (community) from *Gesellschaft* (society). In modern parlance, community comprises the informal interactions and connections that we use to coordinate everyday life. These links enable us to exchange resources and ideas for mutual benefit and to share experiences in ways that are usually supportive. Indeed, the experience of 'community' emanates from ordinary and routine interactions and relationships between people who feel a sense of belonging or shared fate. These patterns of exchange and linkages are by no means random, nor are they formally organised, developing organically according to local traditions, 'on the ground' conditions and personal affinities. Expediency and serendipity play a part, as do long-standing customs and practice. The evolving webs of connection operate through informal conventions, reflecting social or family roles, human propensities to 'flock together' (known as homophily), geographical factors such as spaces and places for gathering, local economics and the availability of community-level infrastructure, such as clubs, social venues, faith bodies, open spaces or regular cultural events. Personal, collective and organisational networks are clearly key to understanding how community operates, and how it differs from, and complements, the more formal institutions of the state and civil society.

Historically, the prefix 'community' was used to soften the edge of state interventions, implying user-friendly, accessible services or partnership arrangements for the delivery of welfare to those sections of the population said to have issues that are particularly difficult to address. In policy and practice, 'community' is invoked as both an agent and an object for interventions devised to remedy perceived deficits and alleviate deprivation (Day, 2006) or to encourage adjustment to changed circumstances. When used as a collective noun, 'community' has connotations of separation; of 'them and us' and tends to refer to people who are disadvantaged by poverty, oppression and prejudice. In government policy and programmes, this underpins the deficit model of community development and regeneration and is associated with targeting so-called deprived areas, as indicated by locality-based measures of health, educational attainment, income and access to amenities. Many communities are resilient, vibrant and resourceful but have been devastated through de-industrialisation. They have experienced chronic under-investment and are often labelled as 'hard-to-reach', 'left behind', 'excluded' or 'deprived', usually due to an ignorant or reluctant mainstream failing to provide appropriate resources or skills to meet their needs and aspirations effectively (Craig, 2018). Although the term 'community' is seen by some as a euphemism for poverty, this deficit model is being increasingly challenged by 'strengths-based' community-led approaches. Nonetheless, old paternalistic connotations linger, especially in the mindsets of governments, charitable foundations and well-meaning professionals (Emejulu, 2015).

Community in history, sociology and anthropology

Anthropological research shows that collective organising characterises all human societies. Studies of humans and other higher primates suggest that we share an inherent sociability, a genetically ingrained propensity to connect and to cooperate as tribes. Indeed it has been suggested that this ability to coordinate activities with people beyond the immediate family group was what gave *Homo sapiens* an evolutionary advantage over Neanderthals in the struggle for survival in the harsh climate of the European Ice Age over 30,000 years ago (Dunbar, 1996; Gamble, 1999). This enabled us to settle in a wide range of environments by maintaining strong networks to adapt as 'generalist specialists' (Hill et al, 2009; Roberts and Stewart, 2018) in what Nowak and Highfield (2011) call the 'snuggle for existence'. Some suggest that our big brains developed because they proved useful to track and maintain social connections (Dunbar, 2010).

Local loyalties and shared cultures

The distinction between society and community inspired the research field known as community studies (see Nisbet, 1953; Bell and Newby, 1971; Crow and Allan, 1994; Day, 2006). Interpreting the use of symbols, rituals and shared spaces has been of particular significance in understanding the functioning of different communities. Initially, community studies focused on specific areas, reporting on how institutions and traditions shaped community life. The geographical dimension of community was paramount in defining the people being observed, such as the residents of a particular estate, small town or island (Frankenberg, 1966). Locality was regarded as an important facet of people's identity and there was a strong emphasis in these studies on the positive aspects of community life – the solidarity, the mutual support and the ways in which people cooperated in their routine, as well as ritual, activities. Attachment to place, such as a neighbourhood or village, seems to be associated with strong social networks. Where there is high population turnover, for example due to rented housing provision or migration, this tends to undermine feelings of trust, personal security and cohesion (Livingstone et al, 2008). Recent research indicates that transience continues to be a barrier to collective action and community empowerment (Baker and Taylor, 2018).

This geographical model of community still holds sway in many people's minds and has strongly influenced government area-based initiatives such as 'place-shaping' strategies for devolution and social action. Policy makers assume that people are more likely to become engaged in local decision-making processes if they feel they have a stake in the area where they live (Lyons, 2007; Taylor, 2008). However, people's social networks usually extend beyond geographical proximity, often based on work, faith or hobbies (Webber, 1963; Wellman, 1979). Communities are actively constructed by their members, rather than merely arising from local circumstances. Featherstone et al (2012) propose replacing old-fashioned notions of community with a form of dynamic and 'progressive localism' that emphasises responsible citizenship exercised through 'loose and pragmatic' networks whose connections are being constantly reimagined and reconfigured, and which create new spaces of convergence and inclusive hospitality (Baker, 2018, p 267). Cultural traditions and symbols are used to assert community identity, expressed through ceremonial activities, music and flags or their equivalent (Cohen, 1985; Back, 1996). This is about conventions and customs, often linked to religious or sporting occasions, but also about the ways in which people go about their everyday lives – their hairstyles, dress codes, language and so on. Such 'badges of belonging' reinforce community boundaries and can help identify 'friends' and 'foes' through multifaceted 'webs of significance' (Geertz, 1973). These act as a social resource, reducing the stress of determining how to act and what to expect, but can sometimes constrain aspirations or choices (Green and White, 2007).

Global perspectives

The predominantly Western model of the free and independent individual seems strange to other cultures that have a more collectivist way of life and find great value in the web of relationships that connect people to places, to each other and to the wider world of land and objects. In Japanese, the symbol for human being combines the characters for 'person' and 'between' – implying that human existence is primarily recognised through interactions and how we are perceived by others. This finds strong echoes in the Maori words *'whanaungatanga'* meaning relatedness among people (Meijl, 2011) and *'whakapapa'* meaning the connectedness of everything (Russell,

2004). These terms are fundamental to how indigenous society is organised in New Zealand and how it views humans' place in the world. The well-known Xhosa principle of '*ubuntu*' conveys a similar meaning of community, often translated as 'I am because we are'. As Archbishop Desmond Tutu explained, 'It embraces hospitality, caring about others ... We believe a person is a person through another person, that my humanity is caught up, bound up and inextricable in yours' (cited in du Toit, 1998, p 89). There is a Chinese proverb that describes hell as a place where the spoons are six feet long so that nobody can feed themselves, while heaven also has six-foot spoons but people cooperate to feed one another.

Mutual collaboration and the advantages of collective action are core values that make life meaningful and survivable. They convey a sense of community and suggest a shared commitment to others. A recent global survey of emotional life indicates that Latin American countries score highly in the index of positive experiences because they have strong social and family networks, and that this holds true even for conflict situations (Gallup Poll, 2017). The importance of diversity is well understood in Southern and Eastern cultures; as Gandhi asserted in his teachings, 'civilisation should be a celebration of differences'. There is an African saying that 'It takes a whole village to raise a child', and an Akan proverb contends that 'in a single polis there is no wisdom'.

Social identity

Most people regard community as a 'good thing' that needs to be revived and restored. It provides a sense of belonging and often forms part of our social identity. But, as Sen wrote, 'We are all members of several communities, and our ties with them can increase or decrease. It is both illogical and dangerous to corral people as if they could belong to only one community' (Sen, 2006, p 160). Many people see their networks as flexible and strategic, contingent on social and political contexts, as well as their personal circumstances and choices. Some religious and ideological sects have established enclosed communities, intended to protect adherents from the perils of contemporary life (in whatever era) by rooting them in moral or spiritual certainties (Jones, 2007). But most of us belong to communities that are open to outside influence and continually changing. Many have embraced globalisation, recognising that the networks of dependency and interactions that develop through migration and cultural exchanges represent a vibrant and enriching dimension of communities in the modern world (Mayo, 2005; Craig, 2012).

Not only do individuals acquire different ways of thinking about their own lives and the world around them, but they are able to gain a sense of their own identity. The feedback and advice provided through personal networks allow people to form judgements about themselves in comparison with others and to keep track of their own reputations. Psychologists believe that people's sense of identity is socially constructed within informal groups and networks, including sometimes absorbing oppressive attitudes and 'put downs' (Tajfel, 1981; Abrams and Hogg, 1990). The extent to which social media interactions can magnify negative judgements, with damaging emotional effects, has been widely reported (O'Keeffe and Clarke Pearson, 2011). Ethnic identity is not inherited but, rather, constructed through narratives and rituals passed down through successive generations or waves of migration (Barth, 1998). This sense of community or shared fate is an important ingredient in people's willingness to undertake collective action.

Models of 'community'

Williams (1976, p 65) noted that community remains a 'warmly persuasive word … [that] never seems to be used unfavourably'. There are many different ways of thinking about community and each of us has a sense of how our networks shape and constitute our personal communities, or 'tribes'. For now, these are the major models currently being used.

Social capital

'Community' has similar connotations to the more modern, and currently popular, term 'social capital', first coined by Hanifan (1916), who described it as 'those tangible substances [that] count for most in the daily lives of people: namely good will, fellowship, sympathy, and social intercourse among the individuals and families who make up a social unit'. The idea of social capital was rediscovered several decades later, notably by Jacobs (1961), Bourdieu (1986), Coleman (1990), Putnam (1993) and Woolcock (1998, 2001). Jacobs referred to it as a 'web of public respect [which constituted] a resource in times of personal or neighbourhood need'. Social capital recognises that the relationships of everyday life between neighbours, colleagues and friends, even casual acquaintances, have value for the individual and for society as a whole (Putnam, 2000; Dekker and Uslaner, 2001; Middleton et al, 2005).

The French sociologist Bourdieu was critical of the function of social capital in society because he was concerned with how inequalities in wealth and power were perpetuated through culture and connections (Bourdieu, 1986). He regarded social capital as a source of privilege that benefited the upper echelons, but had little relevance for other sections of society except to exclude them from opportunities for advancement. This notion of elite networks based on 'who we know and how we use them' (Heald, 1983) will be explored further in Chapter 3. Broadly speaking, social capital can be defined as a collective resource embedded in and released from informal networks (Lin, 2002).These are based on shared norms of trust and mutuality that bestow advantage on individuals and communities: 'better connected people enjoy better returns' (Burt, 2000, p 3). Measures of social capital have tended to focus on three different (and not necessarily causally related) aspects:

- levels of trust between people and social institutions;
- participation in social and civil activities; and
- networks of personal contacts.

Putnam is generally credited with popularising the concept of social capital and highlighting its implications for government. His approach has a particular resonance with liberal communitarian models of social and family responsibility and therefore has wide appeal to politicians and policy makers. Putnam describes social capital as the 'connections among individuals – social networks and the norms of reciprocity and trustworthiness that arise from them' that are created and maintained through associational life, extended families and community activity (Putnam, 2000, p 19). He argues that this may be due to the anticipated 'shadow of the future', cast by the likelihood that transgressions of social norms or dishonesty will attract shame and sanctions from within one's networks (Probyn, 2004). Putnam's (2000) research on levels of social capital appears to demonstrate strong correlations with economic prosperity, stable governance and social cohesion.

Understandably, this has appealed to a wide range of national and global agencies concerned with economic development and political stability. The World Bank has been especially keen to invest in community empowerment and adult education programmes that build social capital as a strategy for combating poverty and supporting regeneration (Woolcock, 1998; Narayan, 2002; Alsop et al, 2005; Kane, 2008). Most international programmes for poverty eradication, for example sponsored by the World Bank or United Nations agencies, require forms of community participation as a means of building social capital, as well as ensuring some kind of contribution from the beneficiaries (Bowen, 2008; Kane, 2008).

Putnam acknowledges that social capital is closely related to our experience of community, reflecting general levels of trust and interconnectivity within society: 'a well-connected individual in a poorly connected society is not as productive as a well-connected individual in a well-connected society. And even a poorly connected individual may derive some of the spill-over benefits from living in a well-connected community' (Putnam, 2000, p 20). Just like the concept of community, social capital reflects shared norms and values that are affirmed through sustained interaction and cooperation.

Woolcock (2001), building on Putnam's model and echoing Granovetter's (1973) distinction between 'strong' and 'weak' ties, suggests that there are different kinds of social capital:

- bonding: based on enduring, multifaceted relationships between similar people with strong mutual commitments such as among friends, family and other close-knit groups;
- bridging: formed from the connections between people who have less in common but may have an overlapping interest, for example, between neighbours, colleagues or different groups within an area;
- linking: derived from the contacts between people or organisations beyond peer boundaries, cutting across status and similarity and enabling people to gain influence and resources outside their normal circles.

These distinctions between types of social capital are not always clear cut in reality, since the boundaries and divisions within society are not themselves immutable or easily defined (Bruegel, 2005). Nevertheless this three-fold model is useful for thinking about the nature and purpose of different kinds of relationships. Community development is primarily concerned with the latter two forms of social capital – bridging and linking (Wakefield and Poland, 2005). Bridging capital can be seen as important for collective organising, managing diversity and maintaining community cohesion (Fieldhouse, 2008). Linking capital is needed for empowerment and partnership working. The networking approach used to develop the well-connected community emphasises the role played by community workers in helping people to build bridges and make links that they might otherwise find difficult.

Although the idea of 'community as social capital' begs many questions (Taylor, 2011), community networks do seem to represent a significant collective resource. The term 'community capital' is sometimes used to refer to the combined agglomeration of natural, human, social, financial and built assets that may be collectively available to members of a community, held in reservoirs of goodwill and mutual assistance that are created by networks of reciprocal interactions (Knapp et al, 2013).

Community psychology and multi-actor ecosystems

Another way of considering the meaning of community is to think about what is going on in people's minds (perceptions, attitudes and emotions) and in the dynamics between us (power relations, communication, behaviours and interactions). Sarason (1974) argued that a sense of community arises from the myriad interactions between individuals and their social context, including those who form their immediate networks. In essence, community comprises the 'perception of similarity to others, an acknowledged interdependence with others, a willingness to maintain this interdependence by giving to or doing for others what one expects from them, the feeling one is part of a larger dependable and stable structure' (Sarason, 1974, p 175).

In sociology and community psychology, communities have long been envisaged as ecologies of interdependent forces and actors, a complex system of large networks with individual members feeling connected and willing to sacrifice their own advantages for the greater good (Park, 1929; Kelly, 2006). While this may seem somewhat naïve, community psychology represents an important turn towards a more holistic approach that uses multiple inter-professional interventions to address social issues and seeks to promote changes that will benefit all members of a community (Kagan et al, 2011; Jason et al, 2016), mainly by mobilising local and professional knowledge to solve underlying problems. The psychologist Bronfenbrenner (1979) was an early proponent of the systems approach to communities, emphasising the significance of interacting components and the yearning for commonality. From an ecological perspective, a crucial component of community is 'biodiversity', with different species sharing a common environment, each with their evolutionary niche. Complex communities have been observed in many ecosystems, including in evidence from some of Earth's earliest fossils. They 'comprise species competing for numerous different resources or species that create niches for others' (Darroch et al, 2018). The same can apply to human society as Capra recognises in his model of the 'web of life':

> [I]n ecosystems, the complexity of the network is a consequence of its biodiversity, and thus a diverse ecological community is a resilient community. In human communities, ethnic and cultural diversity plays the same role. Diversity means different relationships, many different approaches to the same problem. A diverse community is a resilient community, capable of adapting to changing situations. However, diversity is a strategic advantage only if there is a truly vibrant community, sustained by a web of relationships. If the community is fragmented into isolated groups and individuals, diversity can easily become a source of prejudice and friction. (Capra, 1996, p 295)

Ideas associated with systems thinking and complexity theory are beginning to inform our understanding of community as a dynamic mesh of nested and interconnected ecosystems (May, 2001; Easley and Kleinberg, 2010; Britton, 2017). Government too has begun to adopt this approach, with the latest strategy for civil society stating that 'community will be seen as a "system" of inter-connected parts, each of which impacts the others' (Cabinet Office, 2018, p 106).

This view of communities as diverse, dynamic and adaptive uses complexity theory to understand why local connections and small-scale interactions lead to major changes. It is a model that is being used in practice to understand the complexity of situations for development interventions that create conditions for social change and community health and that encourage community enterprise (Neely, 2015).

Box 1.1: Participatory city

The London Borough of Barking and Dagenham has set up an initiative to promote friendship and social enterprise, 'everyone, every day and everywhere'. It aims to establish a 'large-scale, fully inclusive, practical participatory ecosystem' by maximising the use of local assets, such as shared space and community facilities. To this end it has created a web-based forum to guide people to these locations and facilitate the exchange of skills and resources among local residents and entrepreneurs.

The programme uses a business model and draws on twin principles of environmental sustainability and economic development, promoting innovation, local sourcing and mutual assistance. It deliberately seeks to foster a culture of networking that builds bridging social capital and peer-to-peer connectivity.

Projects are encouraged that act as 'plug-in' points that are explicitly accessible and transparent, where residents from the many different ethnic communities living in the borough can meet for specific activities (often around food or making things).

See: www.participatorycity.org/

Below the radar: micro-level organising

Since the second edition of this book was published, more has been learned about the sphere of associational life that is sometimes referred to as forming the backbone of the community sector or its heart and soul (McCabe and Phillimore, 2017, p 61). The energy and efforts of 'low-flying heroes' (MacGillivray et al, 2001) are responsible for much of these 'under the radar' activities and micro-social enterprises that go largely unnoticed by policy makers yet are a vital, albeit unregulated, dimension of civil society. Although this micro-level of informal do-it-yourself social action has been investigated and championed by some (Rochester, 1999; Richardson, 2008; Soteri-Proctor, 2011), its existence remained until recently somewhat 'in the shadows' (Chanan, 1992; 2003; McCabe, 2018). Small-scale charities, clubs and community-led groups, such as food banks or street associations, tend to be run by energetic volunteers and are reliant on donations, fund-raising activities or seed-corn grants (McCabe and Burnage, 2015). Although small and self-organised, they are not isolated and appear well-connected at local level (Soteri-Proctor, 2017). This and their independence mean that they can remain flexible and responsive to changing circumstances. As the National Coalition for Independent Action (NCIA) observed in their review of semi-formal self-organising 'community service groups' and 'voluntary action associations', '[t]he purpose, ways of working and range of idiosyncratic activities are a crucial aspect; however, these may be fuzzy, informal and hard to pin down precisely' (Aiken, 2014, p 8).

Despite facing innumerable challenges as a consequence of the recession that began in 2008, many community groups have demonstrated defiant resilience in the face of cuts and growing demand, even while infrastructure support, including informal in-kind assistance from local councils, has dwindled. The impact of neoliberalism, austerity and the waning of community development as a paid occupation has led to more activist-led approaches and this layer of self-organisation is, unsurprisingly, regarded as an essential plank of the government's strategy for the future of civil society in the UK (Cabinet Office, 2018). Emejulu (2015) has examined these recent discourses, comparing the impact of neoliberalism in the US and UK post-recession settings, and has found contemporary community development practices to exhibit an unhelpful, patronising slant towards communities. She highlights the tensions between the rhetoric of community development values with the reality of what's happening on the ground as played out in the micro-politics of state-sponsored interventions, leading her to call for a democratic renewal through political education and for more respect for the work of unpaid community leaders.

As Wilson (2018) has observed, reflecting on the last ten years of community work in the UK, 'Community-led development has to negotiate the fine grain of micro-politics and may require support.' These complicated and multitudinous interactions and exchanges form the bedrock of community life. Attempts to harness this 'under the radar' volunteering and community action are well meant but sometimes clumsy. Making the links between these very informal frontline micro-organisations and more formal infrastructure organisations that could potentially offer 'on tap' advice and support requires sensitivity and the skills of buddying and friendly mentoring (Taylor and Wilson, 2015).

Commoning

Partly due to recent financial crises, there has been an upsurge in independent collective action and social enterprise, organised in geographical localities but also around shared identities and interests (NCIA, 2015). This has led to a burgeoning revival of the notion of 'commoning', defined as uncoerced participation and voluntary association that takes place in 'social spaces outside the home and away from family and independent of political states and economic markets' (Bollier and Helfrich, 2012). Commoning has been rediscovered as a model for an alternative community economics, based on collective ownership as groups of people come together to set up, for example, schemes for shared housing (Kratzwald, 2016) and water supplies (Clark, 2018). It could be argued that attempts to transfer assets and establish 'friends of' groups to run what had hitherto been municipal facilities (libraries, parks, swimming pools and so on) have pirated the politics of commoning to paper over austerity cracks in public provision and can instead be seen as a transfer of financial liabilities and management burdens (Wilson, 2018).

This resurgence of commoning reflects commitments in community development to claim and cherish shared values such as cooperation, social justice and fairness (Esteva, 2014; Laerhoven and Barnes, 2014). These 'commonance' models promote consensual decision-making and draw much of their inspiration from global movements against capitalism, such as Occupy. More formal arrangements have evolved, increasingly web based, to facilitate such peer-to-peer exchanges, including TimeBanks, Tool Link, Freegle, Streetbank and LETS, as well as apps designed to encourage 'urban commoning' or collaborative consumption (Botsman and Rogers, 2010).

Conclusions

The idea of community continues its grip on private sentiments and public policy. It signifies a valued dimension of society, and community involvement has become a preferred means of addressing 'wicked issues' and policy problems, locally, nationally and even globally. However, communities take many forms and operate across various areas and levels. In addition to the more traditional models of local, geographically defined communities, we now need to consider other ways people connect with one another to form:

* communities of identity (to share cultural activities and experiences);
* communities of interest or passion (to pursue or resist shared fates);
* communities of purpose (to achieve a common goal);
* communities of practice (to exchange experience and learning);
* communities of inquiry (to collectively investigate an issue);
* communities of support (to provide mutual aid and encouragement);
* communities of circumstance (to deal with temporary, sometimes unplanned, situations).

These may overlap and be more salient for people at different times in their lives or for different purposes, as will be considered in the next chapter.

QUESTIONS FOR REFLECTION AND DISCUSSION

✧ What communities do you feel part of?

✧ Do you participate in community life? Why?

2

Community networks and policy dimensions

I refuse the prison of 'I' and choose the open spaces of 'We'.
Toni Morrison, *Mouth Full of Blood*, 2019

Community brings many benefits to us as individuals and for society. This chapter looks at how community networks support collective arrangements that enable people to live and work together. It will also explore the negative aspects of community networks that can lead to stress, exclusion and corruption. Networks enable us to meet personal and social challenges, seize opportunities and deal with some of the problems facing communities in this increasingly global, yet fractured, world. Over the years, governments of all persuasions have sought to harness the power and knowledge to be found in communities, and the chapter considers how policy making has incorporated these functions to the advantage of both state and society.

Survival and resilience

Low-income communities, struggling with hardship and uncertainty, are often praised for their resilience, despite what Dobson (2018) calls 'frenetic neglect'. But resilience doesn't necessarily challenge social injustices; for those affected, it tends to be associated with communities 'getting by' and 'just about managing' (Hickman et al, 2014). The Joseph Rowntree Foundation's (JRF) 'liveable lives' research revealed the patterns and traditions of often mundane, subtle and unnoticed 'everyday help and support' in three neighbourhoods of Glasgow (Anderson et al, 2015). There were a number of components to this arrangement, not least the levels of trust and solidarity. Residents felt that the city's reputation for friendliness gave them a 'licence' to act in kind and generous ways, maintaining a 'moral economy' (Anderson et al, 2015, p 41) of mutual sociability involving favours, swaps and helping hands that enabled people to 'stick together' while valuing both privacy and reciprocity. The authors argue for a 'social mindfulness' of informal helping and greater awareness that networks may need constant maintenance and occasional repair, especially in places where there are low cohesion and poor public amenities (Anderson et al, 2015, p 56). At the individual level of what Brownlie (2014) calls ordinary relationships (as opposed to professional ones), people seem to benefit and find solace from the advice and support of others simply 'being there' in times of trouble, the kind of 'emotional labour' often undertaken by women that helps people to cope with trauma and get on with their lives (Guy et al, 2008; Hochschild, 2012). A study in Sheffield found that areas that had 'gathering places' and regularly shared local information demonstrated greater resilience, suggesting that local networks among residents and between agencies are important to helping communities to adapt to changing circumstances and to accommodate uncertainty (Platts-Fowler and Robinson, 2013).

Studies of everyday life identify the many ways in which shared spaces, and the activities that occur within them, are shaped by informal behaviours (Vaneigen, 2006). Mostly, these small acts are about conviviality and survival, construed as kindness, neighbourliness, friendship, mutual aid and vigilance (Beck and Purcell, 2015). 'People who can draw on extended families and wider networks of friends are more likely to be resilient to shocks that might push others further into difficulty' (Bacon, 2013, p 10). An approximate reciprocity allows people to trade in favours, support and practical assistance through swaps and shares, without needing formal contracts or payments. This casual, but often sensitively honed, help contributes to making lives 'liveable' in vital but often intangible ways. Action research projects to investigate and foster kindness suggest that as a society we can shape social infrastructure and landscapes to make it easier to habitually express goodwill and thoughtful support (Anderson et al, 2015; Hall and Smith, 2015; Ferguson, 2016, 2017).

Numerous community studies have highlighted the importance of social connections in helping people to cope with adversity and, to access resources and opportunities beyond the immediate circle of acquaintances or what Morgan (2009) refers to as 'known strangers'. Informal networks enhance people's ability to overcome difficulties and disasters by keeping hope alive and bolstering wellbeing, even in the face of long-term social exclusion and crises (Cattell, 2001; Matthews and Besemer, 2014). Communities with strong social networks are more likely to recover from catastrophe than those where networks are obliterated or non-existent. Strategies for community resilience and recovery are most effective if statutory bodies and non-governmental organisations work through local networks to support relief efforts rather than attempting to control interventions. As well as communities appearing to crystallise from sudden disaster, they also coalesce around experiences of systematic discrimination and exclusion. This has been especially important in situations where communities have been disrupted by civil war or migration (Hall, 1990; Andrew and Lukajo, 2005). Work with refugees fleeing persecution and armed conflict emphasises the importance of helping people to deal with trauma and dislocation by rebuilding social networks that are culturally appropriate, restoring personal and social resilience (Miller and Rasco, 2004; Phillimore et al, 2017; Piacentini, 2017, 2018).

For some marginalised and disadvantaged groups, these informal and semi-formal collectives are a matter of survival: a means to overcome barriers and challenge discrimination. For example, Gypsy, Traveller and Roma (GTR) communities experience prejudice and institutional procedures that prevent them from accessing services and all sorts of opportunities, including education and employment (Cemlyn et al, 2009). Traditionally, and probably as a consequence, GTR livelihoods are often maintained through informal channels, further disadvantaging them in the labour market. Historically, black and minority ethnic communities in this country have encountered institutional and interpersonal racism, and so have been forced to set up their own arrangements for socialising, finding accommodation and religious worship. Most migrant communities initially organise through informal, ethnic-specific networks, even though these may restrict opportunities while providing a vital safety net for 'getting by' rather than 'getting on'.

Neighbourliness and mutual assistance

Small and routine acts of neighbourliness help to maintain loose and interdependent ties within localities, improving people's sense of safety and strengthening community spirit (Henning and Lieberg, 1996). Research in the Netherlands indicates that this is enhanced in localities with more than one meeting place, and where there are both opportunities and incentives for people to invest in local relationships (Völker et al, 2007).

Many people get involved in community activities in order to meet people and gain a sense of belonging. For some, this is about self-help and survival, enabling people to cope during times of adversity and to secure a decent quality of life for themselves and their families (Burns et al, 2004). Community networks supply practical assistance with a variety of tasks (Williams and Windebank, 2000, 2003; Williams, 2004). They operate as a collective mechanism for sharing risk and resources in situations of scarcity and uncertainty (Stack, 1974;

Werbner, 1988). The Pakistani clan-like *biraderi* offered similar support to newly arrived migrants and continue to exert their influence on patterns of loyalty and exchange (Anwar, 1985), although perhaps to a diminishing degree (Shaw, 2002).

Transnational communities created by global migration rely on family and informal social networks to survive and these embryonic support groups are often the precursors of civil society organisations for those who settle (Theodore and Martin, 2007). These 'networks of necessity' (Hunter and Staggenborg, 1988, p 253) are crucial mechanisms for the survival and sustenance of poor and other segregated groups. Several semi-formalised models for saving and lending exist in different communities, such as the '*pardner*' clubs and '*hawala*' systems used to share and transfer money without recourse to formal contracts or banking systems. These are often based on kinship, caste and trading networks that support reciprocal arrangements for childcare, money-lending and similar exchanges, helping migrants to smooth their settlement in Britain (Kottegoda, 2004). Both have deep roots in former slave communities and were used by early immigrants to the UK from the Caribbean and South East Asia. Although only loosely regulated, they rely on informal peer pressure and the honour system for enforcement.

Box 2.1: Awra Amba village

Awra Amba is an experimental community in northern Ethiopia that voluntarily rejected dependency on aid and resolved to become self-reliant through establishing a community cooperative to spin, weave, produce and sell cloth products. After several years of hard work the village is earning enough through its social enterprise to invest in social security and welfare services that they make available to others nearby, including health and educational facilities. This has allowed them to renew and consolidate relationships with neighbouring communities who regard the Awra Amba example as an inspiration and positive model for their own development.

The community is democratically run through several committees responsible for different aspects of village life, with major decisions taken by referendums. 'The teahouse is the heart of the village where people meet, gossip and debate about everyday things as well as big philosophical matters' (Journard, 2010).

As well as pioneering a model for economic self-sufficiency, Awra Amba's founder, Zumra Nuru, was determined to achieve a utopian vision of gender equality and secularism, in marked contrast to the rest of the country. The villagers also have a commitment to sharing their experiences with the wider world through an interactive project that documents and shares their activities

See: http://visitawraamba.com/

Community cohesion and managing difference

Anderson (1983) talks about nationhood as an 'imagined community', invoked through symbols, anthems and shared narratives to summon a 'fictive unity' in which differences are acknowledged rather than feared or reviled. The 'community' dimension of society can also be used as a mechanism for integration and cohesion. Community cohesion is able to transcend ostensible differences in origin and interests, but also reflects local circumstances and pressures (Hussein, 2007; Khan, 2007; Phillips, 2007). Networks help to build relationships within and across communities, to span boundaries and to develop a consensus around equality and justice that can inform future strategies for integration and collaboration. Ideally, community offers a simple affirmation of mutuality, in which individual relationships form and diversity can flourish.

Since the period of significant migration in the 1950s, UK policies for integrating people from these different backgrounds have moved through stages of assimilation (expecting newcomers to fit in by adopting British styles of living), multiculturalism (encouraging communities to express their different traditions and preserve religious practices) and, most recently, community cohesion (Flynn and Craig, 2012). Community development has been involved in each of these phases, working to improve 'race relations' and promote equality by combating racial discrimination and xenophobia and celebrating diversity. This has included the formation of separate (ethnically based) associations or projects, dealing with conflicts and supporting initiatives that encourage inter-ethnic, inter-faith gatherings or collaboration (Craig, 2017). While there is a long history of overt racism and racial tensions in the UK, the turn of the century witnessed a peak of inter-ethnic disturbances that raised widespread concerns among policy makers about how amicably different ethnic communities lived together and whether more could be done to overcome apparent segregation (Community Cohesion Panel, 2004). Early definitions of community cohesion emphasised the importance of 'a common vision and sense of belonging' for all communities, 'similar life opportunities', the value of diversity and the development of 'strong and positive relationships ... between people from different backgrounds' (LGA, 2002, p 6). Often this was related to a desire to impose so-called 'national values' or to forge an overarching patriotic identity, such as is embodied in the citizenship education and oaths of allegiance introduced in Britain in 2004. However, research studies around nationality, citizenship and community cohesion have struggled to identify 'common values' and what constitutes 'belonging' (Rattansi, 2002; Modood, 2003; Buonfino with Thomson, 2007; Seabeck et al, 2007; Flint and Robinson, 2008).

Policy initiatives to promote community cohesion have mainly been concerned with issues around fragmentation and the need to build cross-community contact, rather than addressing deep-rooted racial prejudice and grievances based on real or perceived inequality. Xenophobic attitudes and myths of ghettoisation appear as the 'shadow side' of strongly bonded, but defensive, communities (Clarke et al, 2007; Finney and Simpson, 2009), especially in relation to migrants of any sort. Consequently, strategies for promoting community cohesion tend to assert the need for unity based on the integration of different cultures and experiences within society and the creation of place-based 'attachment' campaigns, such as the 'I love Manchester' brand. Achieving this push for inter-cultural respect and a local sense of belonging requires a great deal of thought and effort (Robinson and Reeve, 2006; Zetter et al, 2006; Cantle, 2008, 2012).

Social cohesion is undermined in a twisting spiral of suspicion and competition for what are often scarce resources. In situations where communities feel aggrieved or under attack, they can become polarised and defensive, attempting to stem the tide of fragmentation or to reassert cultural traditions. Community differences are marked by terrain, fashion, jargon and other cultural signifiers. They become embedded in notions of collective identity or belonging. Incompatibilities and rivalries sometimes flare up as intercommunal tensions, sparked off by trivial incidents that are fanned into incendiary significance by rumour and long-standing resentment. For young people, these networks are sometimes erroneously labelled as gangs, rather than being seen as friendship groups organised around estates or ethnicities (Alexander, 2000; Amnesty International, 2018). Terrorist-related atrocities have exacerbated some forms of discrimination, notably Islamophobia, while anti-Semitism seems also to be on the increase. This has led to a growth in inter-faith activities and a rethinking of strategies for engagement, integration and a more informed pluralism (Buckingham, 2018; Muslim Council of Britain, 2018). But when underlying inequalities and tensions are not addressed, or differences are not acknowledged, attempts to artificially generate (or, worse, to impose) a common identity tend to founder. Strategies for managing diversity and promoting cohesion would benefit more than is generally realised from encouraging neighbourliness and facilitating 'bridge building' through intercommunity activities that strengthen and improve informal relationships (Gilchrist, 2004; Harris and Young, 2009; Swales and Tipping, 2018).

Some commentators have argued that modern trends are leading to a fragmentation of society, with individuals increasingly separated into different communities or networks of affiliation, accompanied by growing mutual suspicions and social isolation, for example in relation to faith and ethnicity (Day, 2006). Evidence suggests that diversity is associated with reduced levels of social trust (Putnam, 2007) and is therefore undermining of community cohesion. This need not be about inter-ethnic antipathies, but can be explained in terms of cultural expectations and symbols which people use to interpret the behaviour and intentions of those around them. However, it would be wrong to assume that cohesion is affected only by ethnic or national differences, since other dimensions of inequality clearly shape community dynamics and disconnections, not least class and income differences (Hero, 2007; Flint and Robinson, 2008; Craig, 2016; Swales and Tipping, 2018). We choose or are given multiple affiliations, reflecting our myriad interests and circumstances.

Health and wellbeing

Evidence from a range of qualitative and quantitative studies suggests that personal networks and social relations play a valuable part in maintaining wellbeing (Ruggeri et al, 2016; Bagnall et al, 2018). 'People who have close friends and confidants, friendly neighbours and supportive co-workers are less likely to experience sadness, loneliness, low self-esteem and problems with eating and sleeping […] subjective wellbeing is best predicted by the breadth and depth of one's social connections' (Helliwell and Putnam, 2006). The frequency and quality of everyday interactions with neighbours, colleagues, 'nodding acquaintances' and friends are positively correlated with both health and happiness (Halpern, 2005; Marjoribanks and Darnell Bradley, 2017). The nature and diversity of these community connections offer a useful foundation for non-clinical interventions leading to both protection and recovery from a range of emotional and mental health difficulties.

Relational networks established and nurtured through community or neighbourly activities appear to bring considerable benefits (Searle, 2008) and generally improve people's quality of life (Phillipson et al, 2004; Harris, 2008). Informal and discreet conversations within trusting relationships provide information and advice on various matters. Community networks act as cheap and user-friendly referral systems, supplying informal help at times of crisis, and are often resorted to before professional (and sometimes stigmatised) help is requested from the appropriate agencies, particularly about embarrassing problems (Godfrey et al, 2004). Having knowledgeable people within one's social network is generally useful, assuming of course that such enquiries will be treated in confidence and not form the basis for gossip or disapproval. Social networks supply informal care and surveillance, although evidence suggests that family and friends provide different kinds of support compared to neighbours, a fact that was somewhat overlooked by 'care in the community' strategies (Evans, 2009). In addition to these practical benefits, social networks have an emotional impact. In studies of happiness, social psychologists have concluded that social interaction of almost any kind tends to make people happier, both in the short term and also in terms of their general disposition (Layard, 2005). It appears that it is not only the quantity of social interaction that has this effect, but also the variety. People with diverse networks seem to experience a higher degree of contentment than those with an intensely supportive, but homogeneous, set of relationships (Argyle, 1996; Young and Glasgow, 1998).

This also applies to reported health: individuals with robust and varied networks lead healthier lives than those who are more isolated, lonely or whose networks consist of similar people (Szreter and Woolcock, 2004; Cacioppo and Patrick, 2008). They have stronger immune systems, suffer less from heart disease, recover more quickly from emotional trauma and seem to be more resistant to the debilitating effects of illness, possibly because of a generally more positive disposition or because they maintain a more active life-style (Kawachi et al, 1997; McPherson et al, 2013). Mental health is similarly affected by the quality of people's relationships, especially in terms of their pathways to recovery (McKenzie and Harphan, 2006; Seebohm and Gilchrist, 2008). Furthermore, strong social networks between providers and carers are associated with good mental health programmes, especially where these prioritise self-help and community support (Coker, 2008).

However, poverty and social exclusion also contribute to ill-health and cannot be eradicated simply through the buffering effects of community connections (Cattell, 2001). Effective local campaigns (for example, against harmful conditions, such as pollution or bullying) rely on grassroots networks of activists and their allies. These contribute directly to wellbeing by turning 'private issues' into public concerns and tackling social problems that cause stress, often to the most vulnerable or marginalised people in society (Ledwith, 2019). On a more everyday scale, befriending schemes, targeted activity hubs, such as Men in Sheds (Fildes et al, 2010) or projects that encourage exercising together (see, for example, Saheli.org.uk), often provide vital spaces for people to 'do' and 'make' things in accessible, safe and non-stigmatised environments. Volunteering and neighbourhood activity can be powerful shields against mental ill-health (Thomson et al, 2015). Arts and festivals appear to be particularly effective in promoting informal participation and improving community cohesion across social boundaries (Brownett, 2018).

Collective collaboration and coordination

Weaving through communities are self-organised webs of relationships with layers of semi-formal groupings that emerge as a result of joint activities, regular interactions and conversations. These may be temporary coalitions focused on an immediate problem or shared aspiration, or they may be loosely sustained over years of mutual support and overlapping interests. They operate primarily on the basis of trust and familiarity, but convenience and common benefit are likely to be major factors (Kohn, 2009). Examples might be a babysitting circle, seed sharing at the allotment or a Saturday morning kick-about on the playing fields. Nobody has a formal role in convening or facilitating these, although usually an unsung catalyst may be found among the participants.

Occasionally these loose arrangements morph into something a bit more organised as a response to growing numbers or rising ambitions. Members may be cajoled into taking on formal responsibilities and a method of collective decision making might evolve. Thus roles emerge for community leaders, volunteers and activists which may rotate round the network, or individuals step forward (or are pushed) into accepting particular jobs on behalf of the group.

Grassroots activities such as these occupy the foreground of community life. They enable people to take action and to organise around common interests and identities, perhaps campaigning for improvements in their area or simply to provide social activities, such as trips, parties or entertainment.

Solidarity and resistance

Sivanandan (1990), writing about the struggles of black and minority ethnic communities in Britain, calls these 'communities of resistance' that may take on a political cause. Forming communities of identity or interest can thus be seen as a device for collective empowerment and is a familiar strategy for countering the dimensions of oppression associated with race, class, gender, disability, age and sexual orientation. As Weeks (2000, pp 240–3) writes, 'the strongest sense of community is likely to come from those groups who find the premises of their collective existence threatened and who construct out of this a community of identity'. Ryder (2017) describes a similar situation in GTR communities still struggling to gain acceptance for their life-style and ethnic identity (Clark and Greenfields, 2006).

Bauman (2001) refers to these as 'peg' communities, serving to protect people against fears of isolation or 'otherness'. This political dimension of 'community' articulates a particular perspective or 'consciousness' awakened through processes of reflection and debate. It finds expression in notions of 'pride' (such as Gay Pride parades or the Notting Hill carnival), the self-organisation of Disabled people or through a historical exploration of 'roots' (Ohri, 1998). These actions provide opportunities for people to assert a positive identity in a hostile world by demanding that 'difference not merely be tolerated and accepted, but that it is valued and celebrated' (Oliver, 1996, p 89). The resulting social networks reinforce a sense of belonging and provide a vital foundation for collective action, especially where this is risky or highly demanding, as is often the case when challenging injustice or exploitation. Solidarity in the face of adversity is an important facet of community, but this same 'us' versus 'them' logic can lead to sectarian violence and the stigmatisation of minority groups.

Box 2.2: Sociable soup kitchen: *Laib und Seele*

A network of church-run food banks and soup kitchens has developed under the auspices of Berliner Tafel. Known as *Laib und Seele* (meaning Loaf and Soul), these involve volunteers from the local community to provide a different approach to the usual humiliating and lonely experience for customers. While clients are waiting to be served, they are offered coffee and home-made cake and encouraged to chat with each other, as well as with the volunteers and staff.

This is intended to create ties of neighbourliness and solidarity, breaking down isolation and social barriers, and sometimes connections are kindled across class and ethnic boundaries that make a real difference to local understanding and cohesion. While appearing to be primarily a faith-led charity, the project is proactively building a sense of community, empowering poor or vulnerable people by treating them with dignity and friendship and generally behaving as a 'community that looks beyond its own horizons and stands in for humanity' (Werth, 2018, p 141).

Downsides of community

Communities do not always bring unalloyed benefits. Informal networks can be notoriously private and opaque (Taylor, 2011) and relationships are not universally advantageous, either for the individual or for society as a whole. There are drawbacks to membership, due to uneven or exclusive power relations and sometimes inescapable influences and obligations to 'significant others'. Matthews and Besemer (2015) are ambivalent in their review of the evidence, arguing for a more 'complex and nuanced' understanding of network effects on life chances, while others have suggested that different kinds of connections (equivalent to strong and weak ties, perhaps) may act in opposite directions in relation to crime, poverty, civic health, environmental action and so on.

Peer pressure and exclusion

Communities are sometimes elitist, 'tribal' and oppressive. The dominant norms associated with strong communities may damage the confidence and identity of anyone whose preferences or activities deviate from defined respectable behaviour. Consequently, people who cannot, or do not want to, fit in with what is deemed 'right and proper' may be ostracised so they either pretend to conform or they leave, hoping to find refuge and fulfilment in more tolerant settings. Community-based sanctions are used to uphold shared conventions and perpetuate stereotypes, including malicious rumour, 'sending to Coventry' and, at the extreme, vigilante activity and lynching. Networks are sometimes used to exert these pressures, causing misery as well as bodily harm – a tendency that can be exacerbated by social media.

Community ties sometimes work against wider integration and social inclusion, holding people back from pursuing their ambitions and restricting employment mobility (Hudson et al, 2013; McCabe et al, 2013). Peer pressure can outweigh scientific knowledge and personal belief systems, thwarting long-term benefits and aspirations. We see this in relation to the smoking habits of young people, and patterns of truancy or petty vandalism. Adults are also susceptible, finding themselves influenced by the ideas, choices and behaviour of friends, colleagues and neighbours, sometimes against their own better judgement. Criminal and paedophile rings operate in this way, grooming victims and justifying their activities only by comparison to other network members, rather than against wider social norms. Global trafficking networks underpin modern-day slavery, and so-called 'county lines' recruit vulnerable young people to deliver drugs to provincial areas. Corruption likewise depends on closed networks and misguided loyalties. Communities that are closed to outside influence and scrutiny may become moribund or shunned by the rest of society. Furthermore, networks often contain pockets of power that are difficult to unmask or challenge. Where networks operate against opportunity and equity, a networking approach to community development must be proactive in countering and overcoming barriers set up through personal loyalties, biases and prejudices (Sandel, 2014).

Social media platforms have received a particularly bad press for precisely these effects. With the power of new communication technologies, network connections have become more easily established with like-minded others and more easily maintained remotely. They are also more personalised, for example in the sense of being dependent more on personal choices than on historical affiliations. Further, it can be observed that the social media platforms that facilitate the maintenance of relationships are highly commercialised and embedded in a political ideology that conflicts with the ethos of community development. These issues are explored in more depth in Chapter 10.

Policy dimensions

The call to 'community' can be seen as the hardy perennial of public social policy (Taylor, 2011). The idea of a 'mixed economy of welfare' was initially understood as an acceptance that the state (usually through local council grants, but sometimes channelled directly from central government departments) would share responsibility with charities and voluntary organisations for providing support and services to those in need of help. In the 1990s the government became more explicit about commissioning services from the not-for-profit sector. Competitive tendering was a feature of this system, with private companies competing for business with voluntary bodies that were heavily reliant on volunteer effort to both manage and deliver services at the local level.

Participation and empowerment

Many governments across the world have been strongly influenced by communitarian thinking and a commitment to subsidiarity. This return to ideas of community participation in decision making is to be welcomed, especially where it is based on collective empowerment rather than notions of individualist 'user' or consumer rights. It may seem obvious that the existence of 'community' is a prerequisite for community involvement, and yet few policy officers or regeneration managers realise that key elements of community capacity – networks, interaction, common purpose, collective identity and organisational infrastructure – ideally need to be in place before there can be effective and equal partnership.

Increasingly, the connectedness of social networks is recognised as crucial to the capacity of communities to participate in civil society and deliver policy outcomes (Taylor, 2011; Cabinet Office, 2018), but the explanations for this may be more complex than is first realised (Brannan et al, 2006).

There are four conceptual struts that underpin policy interest in 'community':

- self-help
- social capital
- governance
- service delivery.

Self-help has been a long-standing theme for governments keen to avoid excessive interference in people's welfare (sometimes referred to as the 'nanny state') while limiting public spending. Over many years, programmes have been pursued to mobilise volunteers and neighbours to provide informal care and promote people-powered social action, based on self-help and solidarity, to secure local outcomes such as community safety and environmental improvements through activities such as neighbourhood vigilance or litter picking.

Social capital became a key policy concept under New Labour (1997–2010), seeking to develop greater community engagement and reduce social exclusion. High levels of social capital appear to be correlated with several core policy objectives around improving health, reducing crime, increasing educational attainment and economic regeneration. Given the evidence linking social networks to these policy outcomes, it made sense for the government to support interventions that strengthen networks and build trust (Halpern, 2009).

Governance is about involving community members, service users and other stakeholders in partnerships with oversight and strategic decisions that previously might have been undertaken by elected representatives in local and national governments. Communities have been invited to participate in cross-sectoral advisory and decision-making forums around a number of policy themes or focused on devising area-based interventions or determining local planning priorities.

In terms of service delivery, community groups and voluntary organisations provide significant services through self-organising and community action (Richardson, 2008). The voluntary and community sectors, in particular, have been influential in pioneering welfare services tailored to the needs of specific sections of the population neglected by mainstream agencies. The recruitment and support of volunteers has been a major function of the sector, running local and community activities in addition to providing auxiliary services in public institutions such as hospitals or schools.

As we will see in the following chapter, community networks provide important infrastructure capacity for associational life and civil society. They have a particular relevance to policies and programmes seeking to promote democratic renewal, social cohesion, economic regeneration and public health. Recent political agendas, driven by a commitment to devolution but accompanied by austerity cuts, have been based on a form of 'localism' that decentralises decision making and encourages grassroots responsibilities for running services through town and parish councils, alongside 'ultra-local' social action (Derounian, 2018).

Local community engagement

Under the New Labour government cross-departmental policies championed community engagement, with a range of programmes and policies urging public services and democratic institutions to engage with communities and empower citizens to take on greater responsibilities and civic roles. Across the nation, new posts were created in councils, statutory services and health bodies to roll out community engagement strategies and service the growing number of interdisciplinary and cross-sectoral forums – some strategic, others concerned with delivering services. Community involvement, through representation on local partnership bodies, was critical in making sure that strategies devised to tackle deep-rooted problems of neighbourhood deprivation and decline would reflect the needs and aspirations of residents and harness their knowledge of what might be likely to work in given circumstances. As Milbourne (2013) has noted, there were several contradictory messages in the policy environment during this period, with many voluntary organisations wanting to align with policy opportunities, while struggling to reconcile financial survival and stay true to their founding ideals.

In several respects, austerity policies have raised expectations for how communities and individual citizens might influence local decision making or take responsibility for managing local services and facilities (Aiken, 2014; NCIA, 2015). Current government policies have tilted the balance between state and society towards 'people-powered' social action, associated with the localism, community rights and open public services agendas. The 'community rights' family of programmes, established under the Localism Act 2011, offered grants and supports to communities to encourage them to tackle locally identified problems. This approach, which has been described as '[delivering] differently in neighbourhoods', may include transferring assets such as land and buildings from management by local authorities to community ownership. It has been criticised as not going far enough to empower communities and arguing that this would require a more 'enabling state' (Wallace, 2013; Elvidge, 2014) with major shifts in institutional cultures, enhanced participatory democracy and increased capacity at grassroots level (Commission on the Future of Localism, 2018). The term 'enabling state' needs to be reinterpreted to allow for small community groups to undertake services, perhaps through the auspices of social enterprises and community interest companies (Crowe, 2012). This may mean councils acting more as 'catalysts', creating joint ventures that involve strategic partnerships with the voluntary sector. The 'less formalised structures' of voluntary organisations are seen as advantageous, enabling them to be 'sufficiently flexible and responsive to ensure that services are tailored to meet each user's personal needs' (Crowe, 2012, p 21), with trust and accessibility acknowledged as important features of the voluntary and community sector way of doing things. This orientation towards communities may be a response to growing criticisms of public service hierarchical regimes as being overly bureaucratic and inefficient (Seddon, 2008). The 'cooperative councils' approach similarly aims to reconnect councils with the people they are meant to serve, by 'releasing' the potential value of social capital and encouraging active participation in service design and delivery based on self-help, solidarity, democracy and, of course, mutual cooperation.

Community life can be seen as 'a mechanism that arises to cope with lack of opportunity rather than one that creates opportunities' (Sprigings and Allen, 2005, p 398). Although communitarian thinking prescribes stable and well-integrated communities as a condition for progress and social inclusion, particularly when faced with complex and intractable problems, it is by no means clear how much community participation, as a component of public policy, can be linked to market forms of social justice (see Craig et al, 2008). Indeed, it has been argued that such strategies have exacerbated social exclusion because they have been insufficiently redistributive of either resources or opportunities. This results in 'sink estates', slums and the same neighbourhoods consistently appearing towards the top of successive indices of deprivation. Cynics might claim that community is more about chains than choices.

Populism and polarisation

The aftermath of the Brexit referendum, with rising inequalities and social polarisation along with the worldwide spread of populism (Piketty, 2013; Judis, 2016; Kenny, 2017; Westoby, 2017; Dorling, 2018; Popple, forthcoming), has led to increased fragmentation between communities and mounting levels of resentment and hate crime (Mayo, forthcoming). Widening material inequalities in the distribution of wealth, income and privileges undermine the desired sense of civic togetherness, usually referred to as social cohesion (Dorling, 2015).

Populism is often characterised as reflecting a distrust of elites, such as politicians and experts, along with their associated institutions. Demagogic leaders expound political analyses that place the blame for social ills on scapegoats or previous regimes – messages that get amplified through social media. They claim authority in speaking for 'ordinary people', articulating their grievances and championing a form of 'people power' that, superficially at least, could be seen as aligned with the community development principles of empowerment (Kenny et al, forthcoming). Some right-wing organisations have used local agitators and community organising methods to try to build support for their views, recruiting members via activist networks and mobilising protests around expressed grievances. However, as Kenny and her colleagues assert, there are similarities and tensions between left- and right-wing populism, with their reliance on emotions and sense of disenfranchisement. Community development must not allow itself to be seduced by populist movements, and must appeal instead to a more participatory form of democracy and the politics of hope and justice (Solnit, 2016). The 2016 Brexit referendum and subsequent debates revealed and exacerbated deep divisions within society. This has long been acknowledged as a problem for cohesion, fuelled by far-right propaganda about migrant workers and refugees (Goodwin, 2011). Although economically disadvantaged areas do tend to report lower levels of cohesion (measured on scales of trust or neighbourliness), those communities enjoying super-diversity seem to have high cohesion scores (Laurence and Heath, 2008; DCMS, 2018).

Conclusions

There seems to be broad agreement that 'community' is a universal aspiration and characteristic of most societies, albeit with some dissent and counter-evidence. An emphasis on inter-connecting and constantly changing networks acknowledges that communities reflect diverse cultures and social identities. Indeed, community itself can be usefully conceptualised as a set of 'practices', which people 'perform' to varying degrees through everyday interactions and familiar relationships to develop shared traditions and mutual commitments (Blokland, 2017). We are better off individually and collectively if we are well connected. So how can community be strengthened and sustained through community development? In order to turn the rhetoric of community empowerment and community leadership into a meaningful and sustainable reality, informal and formal networks need to be developed and strengthened so that representatives can be supported and held accountable. This echoes an African maxim: 'If you want to go quickly, go alone. If you want to go far, go together.' Time and effort are needed to build relationships of trust and respect across different sectors and between partner agencies responsible for designing and managing the new plans or strategies.

Compared with law, medicine or even social work, community development is a relatively precarious profession. To some extent, it has become an instrument of state policy, deployed to address perceived problems of what is sometimes called 'social exclusion': poverty, discrimination and an apparent breakdown in public order. Community development supports networks that foster mutual learning and shared commitments so that people can work and live together in relatively coherent and equitable communities. The purpose of community development is to maintain and renew 'community' as a foundation for the emergence of diverse initiatives that are independent of both the public and private sectors. This book aims to persuade policy makers and practitioners alike that networking is a necessary and effective method of boosting bridging and linking social capital, thus enhancing community cohesion and citizen empowerment. It goes on to argue that a core, but often neglected, function of community development work is to establish, facilitate and nurture the crucial, but more challenging, boundary-spanning ties that support collective action and empowerment.

QUESTIONS FOR REFLECTION AND DISCUSSION

✧ Think about the communities and informal networks that are important to you. What do you contribute and what do you gain? Are there any negative consequences for you?

✧ What is your experience of community engagement? How does involving residents or community members in decision making improve their lives? What gets in the way?

3

Community development: principles and practice

> There is no greater service than to help a community to liberate itself.
>
> Nelson Mandela, 2003

If society needs 'community', and community doesn't necessarily just happen, what is needed to help bring it about? How does community work support networks and promote greater connectivity? Chapter 3 provides an overview of community development. It traces the history of community development as a form of funded or external intervention over the past century and up to the present day. The role of community workers in supporting networks is highlighted briefly, in preparation for a more detailed consideration in the following chapters.

This book generally views community development as a professional occupation, a paid role with established values and skills, and associated responsibilities to achieve certain outcomes. I fully acknowledge that many factors contribute to the development of communities, most importantly the time, energy and expertise of local community members themselves, as well as resources, technical expertise and activities offered by partner organisations. Many communities function well without professional inputs, although all can benefit from even small amounts of support, for example advice, facilitation, mediation and reflection.

Community development in the UK has tended to emphasise a generic approach to strengthening community capacity and tackling broader issues around equality and social justice (Gilchrist and Taylor, 2016). Processes and principles are regarded as paramount and this is reflected through an emphasis on working *with*, rather than *for* or *on behalf of*, people. In this book, the term 'community development' is used broadly, encompassing a number of approaches to working with communities, and these different models will be explored further in this chapter.

Definitions of community development

The United Nations referred to community development as 'a process designed to create conditions of economic and social progress for the whole community with its active participation' (United Nations, 1955). This definition captured an approach to working with people that can be used across all countries. It recognised the position of many underdeveloped nations that were on the brink of independence and urgently needed to establish basic infrastructure for transport, health, welfare, water and so on. In the global North the situation is different in that, for most people, these basics are available, even if access to services is not always fair, straightforward or satisfactory.

However, the term, even as used today, generally implies that communities usually selected for such interventions are deemed 'undeveloped' and lacking in capacity. Strategies for building community capacity have been largely promoted by the World Bank in the global South, but have also been used in the so-called developed world. Critics of this approach (for example, Newman, 2016) argue that development is seen as a technical fix rather than a political process, with its emphasis on transmitting skills and knowledge rather than tackling deep-seated power imbalances and inequitable distribution of wealth and resources. Over the years, there has been greater recognition that participation is an essential ingredient to the community development process, so that those with direct experience of a situation are involved in devising solutions and making decisions. Participation is a prerequisite dimension of empowerment – the two principles go hand in hand – and must be underpinned by a proactive commitment to equality and inclusion so that the voices of the most oppressed and marginalised are influential (Adhikari and Taylor, 2016).

In 2016 the International Association for Community Development (IACD) adopted the following definition:

> Community development is a practice-based profession and an academic discipline that promotes participative democracy, sustainable development, rights, economic opportunity, equality and social justice, through the organisation, education and empowerment of people within their communities, whether these be of locality, identity or interest, in urban and rural settings. (IACD, 2018)

Community development is regarded as having a two-pronged approach linking collective action with the provision of technical or other forms of assistance to communities. These combine organisation with education around a set of values expressed as a 'commitment to rights, solidarity, democracy, equality, environmental and social justice' (IACD, 2018, p 13). The IACD definition, which incorporates ideas from standards frameworks across the world, makes it clear that community development practitioners face in several directions – towards communities themselves, but also to influence the policies of the agencies and partners delivering support and services to those communities so that their practices become more empowering and participative.

In the global South and some eastern European countries, development interventions have prioritised improving livelihoods and environmental sustainability. In these contexts, the current preferred term is 'social development', replacing more paternalistic 'extension' programmes which tended to be about transferring technical expertise and modern methods of engineering or agriculture to diverse situations, often without consultation or understanding of the local context or cultures. In western Europe there appears to be more of a focus on social pedagogy, especially with young people, and citizen education to revitalise democratic institutions. The United Nations' Millennium Development Goals and their successors, the seventeen Sustainable Development Goals, agreed by world leaders in 2015, provide a comprehensive framework for interlinked national programmes to eradicate poverty, promote equality and secure progress for everyone on all fronts.

People living in the global North generally enjoy a better standard of living, but the same themes of participation, partnership and power are evident in community-oriented interventions, although more often with a focus on activating civil society, rejuvenating community life and local area planning. Using community development principles should guarantee that people will be involved in decisions about how they are implemented on the ground, and will participate fully in the design and delivery of projects. They ensure that changes are more likely to benefit whole communities and to be sustained over time.

Power is a dominant theme within community development, and in this respect the role is fundamentally about working with people in communities so that they have more influence over decisions that affect them, whether this is about their own lives or about what happens in the world around them. Community development addresses and seeks to change relations of power within communities and society as a whole and it inevitably has a strong political dimension. However, this has become less about confrontation and more about compromise and negotiation, especially since the advent of partnership working.

Three models

Although community development approaches are broadly similar, their theoretical and ideological rationales stem from very different starting points. It may be helpful to think of three models of community development, each related to contrasting political analyses of society and the state (see Table 3.1).

Table 3.1: Models of community development

Model	Political framework	Typical activities
Consensus	Conservative/Communitarian	Social planning Self-help groups Volunteering
Pluralist	Liberal/ Social-democratic	Community engagement Partnership working Lobbying Community capacity building
Conflict	Radical/Socialist	Community organising Campaigning Advocacy work

Consensus model

This assumes that there is broad agreement about social issues, how they can be tackled and how society in general should be organised. Within this model, charitable and state-sponsored community development projects have been devised to:

- encourage local responsibility for organising self-help activities;
- facilitate the delivery of welfare services;
- enhance community liaison and partnership working; and
- support community ('user') participation in consultation processes.

Community workers have been deployed to foster community spirit, for example through cultural activities, and to work with statutory agencies to ensure that the services provided match local needs. The goal for this model of community development is social stability through the provision of a welfare 'safety net' to those most in need, but with pressure to conform to prevalent norms of behaviour. The community is regarded as a partner in the provision of services, a source of local knowledge and volunteers, such that problems would be addressed by involving residents in developing collective solutions.

Community associations and other voluntary organisations are seen as potential managers of projects delivering social care for older people, health education, benefits advice and childcare. This may require some capacity building so that the staff and volunteers involved have the required skills, know-how and confidence to take on these responsibilities, as well as being able to access advice from relevant specialist bodies (Fung, 2016).

Communitarian values of family and social responsibility underpin this approach, especially in relation to volunteering, parenting and active citizenship. These are the embodiment of civil society, expressed through collective self-help and voluntary forms of association (Etzioni, 1993; Blunkett, 2001). Although communitarianism has found advocates within community development, there have also been criticisms of its reliance on moral authoritarianism and a consequent failure to effectively understand and counter structural inequalities and power differentials (Henderson and Salmon, 2001; Henderson, 2005). Community development that is state sponsored or funded by established charities tends to be constrained by top-down agendas, and therefore more inclined to adopt a consensual approach.

Pluralist or liberal model

The pluralist or liberal model draws on an understanding that society consists of different interest groups and that these compete to persuade policy makers and politicians to support their cause. The emphasis in policy is on participation and community engagement in social planning processes. This acknowledges that some sections of the population are disadvantaged and might struggle to gain a fair share of influence and resources. Community development is seen as enhancing public decision making by enabling these views to be heard by:

- supporting members of marginalised groups to identify and articulate their ideas; and
- improving channels of communication to ensure that decision makers listen to and understand these different perspectives.

Historically, many community workers and activists saw this as an opportunity for disenfranchised and oppressed people to find a voice, to articulate their concerns and to have some influence over decisions that affected their lives (for example, Symons, 1981). Community work was defined as having a fundamental role in promoting participation and increasing people's capacity to influence the decisions that affect them (ACW, 1975). At the turn of the century, with the growing emphasis in policy on community involvement and partnership working, community practitioners became responsible for communication across this increasingly blurred boundary between public and voluntary sectors (Banks et al, 2013). They played an important role in facilitating community empowerment in strategic decision making, for example through representation on inter-sectoral partnerships or community planning exercises. Community practitioners might be responsible for outreach strategies, consultation exercises and participation mechanisms such as neighbourhood forums and developing community leadership.

The task of the community worker in this model is to assist communities to organise themselves, to find a collective 'voice' and to put pressure on the policy makers to pay more attention to their needs and aspirations. This liberal approach pushes for reform but is less confrontational than the radical model, preferring to win small gains that improve life for some people rather than taking on the whole world (Twelvetrees, 1982). It is allied with social planning approaches that seek to involve communities and users in developing services that meet their needs or address hitherto intractable issues (Twelvetrees, 2017). Stakeholders work together, often through formal partnership arrangements, to devise ways of meeting local needs and aspirations, but these are often identified by funding agencies or local authorities rather than communities themselves.

Radical model

This version of community development is underpinned by left-leaning political analyses, with a vision of society based on full human rights and equality. It sees community activism as an extension of the class struggle and has been strongly influenced by socialist, feminist, anti-racist and disability equality politics. The more radical version of community development explicitly identifies 'conflicts of interest' within society and aligns itself with the poor and other oppressed groups (see, for example, Mayo, 1979; Ledwith, 2006; 2019; Shaw, 2008). It argues that the causes of poverty and disadvantage are to be found in the economic system and reflect historical patterns of exploitation embedded in social and political institutions. It tackles structural inequalities by:

- addressing issues around discrimination and prejudice;
- raising political consciousness about the distribution of power and wealth; and

- demanding that a fairer share of the 'social wage' should be allocated for community benefit.

Radical community work strives for social justice, seeking to develop powerful forms of collective organising to effect social change through a fundamental redistribution of power and resources. At local levels, for example within communities and organisations, this might involve building campaigns and positive action strategies that enable people (individually and collectively) to combat the roots of their disadvantage and to demand better or fairer treatment.

The more radical workers saw community politics primarily as a means for raising 'class' (and subsequently gender and race) consciousness outside the workplace. Community work was about laying the foundations for a revolutionary grassroots democracy (Tasker, 1975). This involved equipping people with the skills, knowledge, confidence and political 'nous' for challenging the fundamental causes of poverty and discrimination. Some community workers sought to build alliances with the labour movement through Trades Councils and a chain of resource centres, specifically set up to support local campaigning. The radical model favours a more adversarial approach; for example, collective action against some kind of threat or to achieve a positive change in the face of opposition or obstruction by those with the money and power. In this vein, citizen-led action, such as Alinsky's community organising model, purports to challenge existing power structures by asserting fundamental civil and welfare rights. It aims to mobilise residents around issues that have brought them into conflict with economic interests, institutionalised discrimination or state institutions (Alinsky, 1969, 1972; Smock, 2004; Beck and Purcell, 2013; Craig, 2017).

Most current definitions of community development work assert a radical approach, but it can prove more difficult to implement in practice, mainly because workers find themselves in situations where their best intentions are constrained by the expectations of employers and requirements of external funders. Many practitioners lack the consciousness, the confidence and the skills to undertake radical practice and, in reality, might combine these three models, adopting different approaches depending on circumstances and competence.

A historical overview

In the UK, community development has encompassed a range of strategies, including elements of self-help, philanthropy, state-sponsored interventions, engagement and light-touch support. It derives its inspiration and rationale from several traditions, each of which dates back to at least the 19th century. The first of these is informal self-help and solidarity, the reciprocal support and sharing that characterise small-scale forms of social organisation, for example the kind of neighbourly help that is routinely available or that emerges in times of adversity (Crow, 2002; Pilch, 2006). The second strand represents a more organised form of mutual aid, whereby formal associations were established to provide assistance and shared resources across a defined subscriber membership. Collective organisations such as the early craft guilds, friendly societies and trades unions are examples of these, many of which also had a campaigning role. A third approach is based rather more on notions of philanthropy and voluntary service, expressed as a desire to improve the lives and opportunities of others deemed 'less fortunate'.

Some aspects of community development were explicitly remedial, devised to tackle what were seen as 'deficits' in poor communities preventing residents from achieving their potential or participating in opportunities for personal advancement and democratic engagement. The work of the former University Settlements is representative of this approach, combining adult education with 'character building' activities and a somewhat condescending approach to the relief of hardship (Barnett, 1888; Clarke, 1963). Although the pioneers of this movement clearly stated their belief that people living in the Settlements (usually university students on temporary placements) would learn as much from local residents as vice versa, the underlying ethos was patronising and management of the Settlements' resources (buildings, workers and funds) remained in the hands of well-meaning outsiders for many decades.

Community development has also been used as a preventative strategy, intervening in situations to avert potential crises or to address issues before they become conflicts. During the rehousing programmes after the two world wars, whole communities were relocated, causing widespread disruption and alienation. Community workers were employed in the New Towns and on peripheral estates to arrange events that would foster a sense of community and to encourage residents to organise activities for themselves (Goetschius, 1969; Heraud, 1975). These officers were frequently employed by social services or housing departments and saw themselves as 'agents' of the state, acting on behalf of the relevant authority rather than the local residents. Nevertheless, they played an important role in managing the links within and between groups and external bodies to improve social welfare through the establishment of autonomous voluntary groups.

During the 1950s and 1960s community work saw itself mainly as a branch of social work, emphasising both individual growth and collective benefit. The 'community' was seen as offering some protection from the impersonal institutions of the modern welfare state and providing opportunities for social participation. A similar approach placed more emphasis on personal fulfilment, regarding community involvement as a vehicle for self-advancement. Taking part in community activities was seen as:

- therapeutic (staving off mental health problems);
- morally worthy (encouraging mutuality and social responsibility); and
- educational (promoting the acquisition of skills and new understandings).

Adult education classes and cultural societies were seen as 'improving' in themselves, while recreational activities such as amateur dramatics and sports associations were encouraged as a means of diverting people from a life of crime, idleness and social isolation.

A Marxist analysis of the impact of modern capitalism on working-class neighbourhoods became highly influential in Britain in the 1970s, mainly through the fieldwork and research reports of the Community Development Projects (CDP, 1974, 1977). This radical wing saw community work as contributing to the fight for socialism through local, militant community action. There were increasing demands for the democratisation of the 'local state' (Lees and Mayo, 1984) and this led to a belated recognition that the role of the community worker as an agent of change placed them both 'in and against the state' (LEWRG, 1979). The call to pursue provocative, confrontational tactics required an explicit rejection of the idea that the community worker was a neutral agent even when employed by the local council (Cowley, 1977; Loney, 1983).

The removal of economic and political barriers to participation constituted a core, but long-term, goal of community development. During the 1980s and 1990s the basis for community development shifted from state funding of generic posts, such as neighbourhood development workers or community centre wardens, to relatively short-term, project-oriented activities. Earlier, community workers had been able to articulate and respond to local issues as they became evident, helping residents to organise campaigns around, for example, the closure of a nursery, inadequate housing, traffic dangers or unwelcome planning decisions. However, these posts gradually disappeared under a welter of local authority budget cuts, with community and voluntary organisations being particularly hard hit. Between 1979 and 1997, under successive Conservative governments, community development became oriented more towards self-help, voluntary action, training and service provision. The funding regimes of the 1990s meant that many community workers were employed on temporary contracts and had to concentrate their efforts on government priorities (homelessness, drugs, mental health and so on) by running community-based welfare services for specific 'client groups'.

In the voluntary sector generic community development was largely replaced by issue-based work, carrying out government policies, and became tightly constrained by contracts or service agreements containing predetermined performance criteria and mechanistic auditing procedures. At the same time local authority community work became increasingly directive and less concerned with processes of education and empowerment. Instead, job descriptions tended to emphasise responsibility for grants administration, consultation exercises, service delivery, partnership arrangements and bidding procedures for regeneration funding (AMA, 1993). Consequently, work programmes were delivered and evaluated around much more rigid objectives (sometimes imposed by funders), necessitating a greater degree of formal record keeping and accounting. More nebulous activities that promoted community spirit and created community-based assets, but did not lead to measurable outputs, were severely restricted or abandoned altogether. An early casualty was the provision of effective support for communities to develop their own ideas, skills and enthusiasm. The community worker's role in helping to organise community-led collective action all but disappeared, although campaigning itself did not. Instead, the emphasis was on partnership working, with communities encouraged to engage with public agencies to design and deliver services jointly. However, despite the rhetoric, this often only involved a minority of community members in representing local or user views and often amounted to little more than token consultation.

In the 1990s, the radicalism of earlier decades became muted by a turn towards multi-agency, area-based initiatives. New Labour continued this partnership strategy and a new model of working with communities was fashioned, termed 'community practice' (Banks et al, 2007; 2013). Community practice described a relatively new, but rapidly expanding, approach based on community development principles and located usually within an institutional structure. Staff from a range of professional disciplines had a remit for managing the interface between communities and statutory institutions, such as local government, the police or health agencies (Banks and Orton, 2007).

As part of its commitment to neighbourhood renewal and tackling social exclusion, the New Labour government committed substantial funding to addressing what it termed the democratic deficit. During this period a number of programmes aimed to promote active citizenship, community engagement and increased public or user participation in the governance of various services. Considerable funding was made available to employ staff at local levels, fund national and regional community development infrastructure and support civil society organisations. In addition, government began to acknowledge the contribution of professional community workers and in 2006 published *The Community Development Challenge report* (CD Challenge Group, 2006). This called for a more strategic investment in community development resources, enabling interventions to be better coordinated and sustained over the long term. It made a number of recommendations and was widely debated within the field.

However, a change of government in 2010, along with a worldwide economic crisis, precipitated a series of austerity cuts to the voluntary sector and local authorities, with substantial reductions in the numbers of practitioners employed in community development. A national survey of practitioners revealed that most community work continues to be undertaken in geographic areas and is largely generic, supporting local people to organise, to run amenities, to deliver services and to exert influence over devolved and strategic-level decision making. The research investigated the nature and extent of community development in England and found that, despite the cuts and hollowing-out of local government structures, a skilled and resilient workforce still existed and has continued to work within the broad ethos of community development. However, they were operating under a wide range of job titles and in 'diverse arenas of policy' (ESB, 2017). Nonetheless, it is encouraging to think that although specific job roles are more fragmented than previously, the community development field is managing to maintain some kind of coherent practice and professional identity, even though the term itself has gone out of favour or is used synonymously with community organising or community action.

Subsequently, national support bodies collapsed and local authority teams were dismantled or dispersed, considerably weakening their effectiveness. In Scotland, this decline was resisted, aided by the Scottish Government's adoption of a raft of policies that favoured community empowerment and invested in targeting public services to prevent inequalities and address the needs of the most disadvantaged (Christie, 2011; Commission on Strengthening Local Democracy, 2014). Consequently, community development has been reinvigorated. Building on previous work to define and evaluate community development and engagement, Barr (2014) developed a model that locates community development as 'everyone's business', advocating a set of practices within shared values and applied to specific political context and policy streams, such as regeneration, public health and housing.

However, behind this apparent agreement there lie an ambiguity and some inevitable tensions, mostly relating to power and politics. Some might argue that these aspects of community development have been neglected in theory and practice, and that a 'dialectical critique' is needed that highlights inequalities and injustices, acknowledging that the approach harbours both progressive and reactionary or conservative elements (Meade et al, 2016, pp 5–6).

A distinct and emerging profession

Community development is distinguished from social work and allied welfare professions through its commitment to supporting collective organising and partnership working. It is about working *with*, not *for* communities. Community development helps community members to develop a positive long-term vision, identify unmet needs and aspirations and present possible solutions, including arguing for service improvements. If local action and self-help is successful and demand grows, the worker might assist group members to establish the initiative on a more secure footing, sometimes with a formal management committee, constitution, funding arrangements and paid staff. This transformation of a community-run activity into a voluntary organisation will be familiar to most community workers but is not always a straightforward process and may take place over several years. It will involve direct support of individuals as well as help with managing group dynamics and developing appropriate organisational structures.

Community development is primarily concerned with responding to issues raised by community members whose circumstances may have left them poorly provided for, often without adequate services, with limited means to organise and excluded from mainstream opportunities to participate in activities or decision making. Community development seeks to develop collective capacity by providing opportunities for individuals and the community as a whole to enhance their skills, confidence and knowledge. Community development nurtures community infrastructure by supporting informal networks as well as formal organisations.

The UK framework for national occupational standards for community development work gives the following definition:

> Community development enables people to work collectively to bring about positive social change. This long-term process starts from people's own experience and enables communities to work together to:
>
> • Identify their own needs and actions;
> • Take collective action using their strengths and resources;
> • Develop their confidence, skills and knowledge;
> • Challenge unequal power relationships; and
> • Promote social justice, equality and inclusion;
>
> in order to improve the quality of their own lives, the communities in which they live and societies of which they are a part. (ESB, 2015, p 5)

Networking for community development

The use of networks and networking is seen as central to working with communities and building partnerships with statutory bodies. As this chapter has demonstrated, the key principle of community development is to ensure that participation in decision making is democratic and inclusive, enabling people to contribute as equal citizens and to learn through their involvement. Interaction with others is an inevitable and necessary aspect of this. Community workers play an important role in helping people to work together, to communicate effectively and to deal with the inescapable tensions and disagreements that arise from this work. Networks that connect individuals and different sections of the local community, face-to-face or online, are an invaluable resource, functioning as communication systems and organisational mechanisms. The development of 'community' is about strengthening and extending networks between individuals, between groups, between organisations and, just as importantly, between different sectors and agencies. Working to establish and maintain these connections is fundamental to effective community development work.

The idea that the 'essence' of community is to be found among relationships, rather than within the physical environment of 'place', is not new. The early studies of 'community' were very much concerned with describing the patterns of interaction and connection among residents. Almost regardless of ideology or context, community development has been concerned with developing and negotiating relationships. In particular, some early writers on the skills and methods of community work recognised the importance of contact-making, communicating, and convening and coordinating activities (Klein, 1973; Leissner, 1975; Sorter and Simpkinson, 1979), although the term 'networking' appeared only in the early 1980s (Symons, 1981).

From the first stages in the development of community work as a professional activity, writers and trainers have identified the role of helping people and organisations to cooperate and communicate across boundaries as a significant, perhaps unique, aspect of the job. The existence of 'informal, co-operative links' within the community sector has long been recognised, described as 'all kinds of networks whereby members of different groups know each other' (Dharamsi et al, 1979, p 136). Francis et al's survey of the community work occupation concluded that the community workers themselves represented a 'significant network of skills and commitment' (Francis et al, 1984, p 14). In a key early text, Thomas emphasised the linkages between people within neighbourhoods and the need to 'strengthen', 'renew' and 'nurture' existing networks (Thomas, 1983, pp 171–3). These were seen as supporting processes of sharing and dialogue. Fostering informal interpersonal and inter-organisational linkages within communities requires particular expertise and a strategic approach. Milofsky (1988, p 7) wrote that 'community development requires network-building' and Bell refers to networks as 'the crucial steps which take community work on the road to community development'. He emphasised the need for unforced opportunities for people to meet and work together, building mutual recognition and confidence. He also saw community networks as creating 'a new stratum in the power structure which offers the possibility for long-term and important change' (Bell, 1992, p 32). The debates around community work training in the early 1970s identified a role in fostering social cohesion through community activities and inter-organisational work (ACW, 1975). To do this, it was argued, an understanding of local social systems and skills in informal communication and contact making was needed.

In these early accounts, the role of the community worker was described as discovering and utilising existing networks. Networks were regarded as something community workers needed to know about and could work with, but the idea of intervening to change or develop these came later. A more proactive approach was gradually adopted that recognised that the formation and transformation of networks was a legitimate (and desirable) focus for professional interventions. In the second edition of their book on *Skills in Neighbourhood Work*, Henderson and Thomas devote an entire chapter to the skills and strategies of helping people to associate and maintain contact with one another, describing neighbourhood development as:

> about putting people in touch with one another, and ... promoting their membership in groups and networks.... In the act of bringing people together, neighbourhood workers are performing an essential role. (Henderson and Thomas, 1987, p 15)

Since the 1990s, networking has increasingly been acknowledged as an important aspect of community work (Gilchrist, 1995; Henderson and Thomas, 2002) and a necessary aspect of building partnerships generally (Trevillion, 1999). It is now a commonplace term, with time and opportunities built into conferences and events to encourage participants to meet and mingle, often facilitated through ice-breaker exercises or the way seating is arranged. Setting up and servicing networks is a significant aspect of practice and, as the current version of the framework for occupational standards for community development asserts, community development practitioners need to be involved in strategic partnerships (ESB, 2015). The Standards underscore the importance of 'effective relationships between communities and public bodies and other agencies', partnership working, and 'strategically co-ordinat[ing] networks and partnerships' (p 10). The framework asserts the value of informal networks within communities and urges community workers to use these to foster 'dialogue and understanding between and across communities' (p 82). It urges employers to ensure that their community workers are 'resourced and encouraged to attend networking events' (p 116).

Community development may also be deployed by charitable and non-governmental organisations, through funding community-work posts or providing other kinds of support in kind, such as venues, training and technical facilities.

Conclusions

For over a century, communities have experienced the well-meaning intentions of community workers coming from different ideological positions and government programmes. Community development remains a contested intervention, despite some evident continuities in definition and application over the years and around the world (Craig, 2007; DeFilippis, 2008; Mayo, 2008; Craig et al, 2011a). Is it a social movement, a distinct profession or an approach that can be adopted by anyone working on the front line of the state–community interface (Shaw, 2008)? Community development takes many forms. It can be independent and self-organising, mainly pursued through collective action that arises as a result of community members seizing the initiative in response to some common aspiration or grievance.

QUESTIONS FOR REFLECTION AND DISCUSSION

✧ Is it useful to have an agreed definition and standards for community development? How?

✧ How do your own core values and politics align with your practice or what you see your colleagues doing?

✧ Over the past few years, how do you see community development changing?

4

Working with communities: different approaches

> You have to go by instinct and you have to be brave.
> Whitney Otto, *How to Make an American Quilt*, 1990

There are a range of approaches or models of community development practice. While being susceptible to changing political and economic contexts, they are by no means mutually exclusive and all have featured at least for a time in UK practice, as well as being applied in different circumstances internationally.

Common processes, different strands

As much as laying out a set of methods, community development has consistently emphasised its values and principles. Practitioner-led organisations have argued that these commitments are vital aspects of shared definitions and expected standards. In recent years, though, programmes have tended to specify outputs and broader outcomes, only some of which (such as increased confidence and community capacity) might suggest the adoption of community development processes.

The models described in the previous chapter incorporate various processes, skills and outcomes that are involved in community development. In order to distinguish this from community activism or voluntary work, it is useful to think about the role that the paid community worker plays in:

- *enabling* people to become involved by removing practical and political barriers to their participation;
- *encouraging* individuals to contribute to activities and decision making, and to keep going when things get difficult;
- *empowering* others by increasing their confidence and ability to influence decisions and take responsibility for their own actions;
- *engaging* with groups and organisations to increase community involvement in partnerships and other forms of public decision making;

- *equalising* situations so that people have the same access to opportunities, resources and facilities within communities and mainstream services;
- *educating* people by helping them to reflect on their own experience, to learn from others and through discussion; and
- *evaluating* the impact of these interventions.

These seven Es of community development make it clear that the community worker is not concerned with their own interests and needs, but instead supports others (mainly community members and activists) to organise activities, learn together, take up issues and challenge unjust discrimination. The principles of community development have been applied in many ways, but there are some core common functions and parameters that are considered below.

Patch-based local development

Since its emergence as a distinct occupation in the UK in the 1960s and 1970s, resources for community development have often been concentrated in fairly small areas. This was mainly due to the prevailing geographical understanding of communities, with community workers assigned a 'patch' that might comprise an inner-city neighbourhood, an outer estate or a cluster of villages. Community work was concerned with social change and active citizenship, but had a primarily local dimension (Younghusband, 1968; Thomas, 1976). Influential community work 'texts' published around this time focused on the neighbourhood as the most appropriate level for interventions (Henderson and Thomas, 1980; Twelvetrees, 1982).

During this period, community development work was seen as localised and generic, having an overarching purpose of creating integrated and 'harmonious' communities. Staff and volunteers prioritised local activities, such as youth clubs, toddler groups, older people's clubs and community festivals, but would help residents to campaign on local issues. The aims of the community worker were intertwined: on the one hand, to enhance a community's internal governance by assisting local people in developing and managing their own organisations, and, on the other hand, to enable the (preferably consensual) views of the community to be expressed democratically to relevant decision-making bodies through representative leadership or participation in public consultation exercises.

Area-based initiatives and 'zones' designated for specific policy areas (education, health, regeneration) were often the norm for government interventions in the 1990s and early 2000s, with an associated emphasis on partnerships and community participation, or at least representation on local advisory bodies, such as neighbourhood councils or crime safety partnerships. To some extent, this strategy of local development has been phased out of formal arrangements, although the focus on small areas endures through a continuing policy emphasis on localism and devolution. The neighbourhood planning system and national programmes such as Big Local are examples of this approach as we will see below.

Capacity building

A major strand of community development has been about capacity building or strengthening local voluntary and community sector infrastructure, and is predicated on a 'deficit model' of disadvantaged communities. Criticisms of this approach led the United Nations to adopt the term 'capacity development' in recognition that interventions never start from a blank slate (Craig, 2007; UNDP, 2009, cited in Beck and Purcell, 2013). In the past, government funding and training have been made available to support organisations in developing their governance, business competence and information technology strategies. Local authorities and infrastructure bodies have provided advice, grants and practical assistance to the smaller charities and community groups operating in their areas and have also endeavoured to connect these groups through local forums, sometimes around specialist themes such as play or social care. Following the recession of 2008, this support has dwindled and the local voluntary sector appears to be losing much of its ability to respond to community needs.

Government initiatives often focused on the role of individuals in communities, so-called 'active citizens' forming a 'civic core' (Mohan and Bulloch, 2012), with funding schemes to support 'community champions', 'social entrepreneurs', neighbourhood wardens and the like. Capacity development aimed to prepare individuals to take up these roles, but there was little recognition that community leaders needed support so as to understand and negotiate power dynamics and to manage the array of accountabilities associated with partnership working (Gilchrist, 2006a; Skidmore et al, 2006). As well as enhancing skills and confidence, capacity development prioritises experiential learning, training and community-led research.

Knowledge construction: peer education and action research

Learning for community development is different from community education in that it is about tackling structural disadvantage rather than individual deficits (Tett and Fyfe, 2010). It listens to the experiences and amplifies the voices of excluded and oppressed people, for the purpose of mutual understanding and challenging social inequalities. Eversley (2019) likewise sees the co-construction of knowledge as a foundation for emancipatory collective action or putting pressure on authorities to change their services or policies.

The purpose of community-based participatory action research, such as is used in rural appraisals and community consultation strategies, is to provide an evidence base that can demonstrate demand and generate solutions (Kindon et al, 2010; Hacker, 2013). There are various techniques available, including appreciative inquiry, online surveys and photovoice as important aspects of co-designed and co-produced research (Purcell, 2009; Catalani and Minkler, 2010; Whitney and Trosten-Bloom, 2010; Banks et al, 2018). Such research is often based on a collaboration of agencies, community members and groups. Community–university partnerships have become more prevalent, sometimes using communities of practice to share expertise and exchange learning (Hart et al, 2013). Communities of practice work well when there is some kind of occupational connection, 'an aggregate of people who come together around mutual engagement in some common endeavour' that is defined as meaningful to the participants (Eckert and McConnell-Ginet, 1998, p 490). For this approach to be included under the rubric of community development, ideally a defining feature should be that communities themselves suggest the enquiry topics. In addition, community members may be trained up as researchers to gather data and to be involved in interpreting the evidence to identify implications and potential solutions. Thus the investigation should itself involve community members at every stage and ultimately should benefit those who identified that issue in the first place, in terms of problems resolved and increased appetite for further research and development.

Debate and the co-production of knowledge enhance awareness of the conditions that create problems and can be used to work up ideas of how they might be addressed. Imagination is a powerful tool, dreaming of utopian futures (Levitas, 2013; Campbell et al, 2018). It is a means of creating shared visions, challenging dominant discourses, disrupting institutional power and revealing new perspectives on familiar territories that might lead ultimately to innovation and the removal of oppressive political structures. Unrestrained utopianism, however, can lead to unrealistic expectations, disappointment and resentment.

There are further caveats to consider. There may well not be an equal distribution of power, time and resources between community members and researchers, especially if these come from an academic institution. Training, payments and incentives for community researchers may be needed and there are issues to be discussed around the ownership and presentation of the research findings, as these amount to intellectual property that has been co-produced (Facer and Pahl, 2017). There are some important ethical principles that need to be observed, including respect for tacit knowledge and local insights. To avoid some of the pitfalls, it is worth consulting toolkits on community-led action research, including those published by the Scottish Community Development Centre (www.scdc.org.uk/what/community-led-action-planning-toolkit) and the Association for Research in the Voluntary and Community Sector (ARVAC) (http://arvac.org.uk/resources/), which can be used for basic training and guidance for community researchers, community workers and academics alike.

Community learning and reflection: critical dialogue, popular education

Nonetheless, community development has adopted methods to increase skills, knowledge and confidence among community members, such as the 'action learning for active citizenship' (ALAC) project (Mayo and Annette, 2010) and 'training for transformation' approach (Hope and Timmel, 2013).

Informal and experiential social learning has long been an essential thread of community education and one that is especially suited to tackling inequalities (Adhikari and Taylor, 2016). Reflection and 'critical dialogue' underpin several radical models of community development (Ledwith, 2006, 2015; Stephenson, 2007). One method of transformative or emancipatory education, originally advocated by Freire (1972), is to use guided conversations or critical dialogue to examine lived experience and interrogate dominant explanations of why things are as they are. Iterative processes of listening, questioning and reflection are used to examine immediate living conditions and better understand the circumstances that create them in order to take action to challenge the causes of problems (Hope and Timmell, 2013). This is what Freire termed 'conscientisation' and what others have referred to as a 'change of consciousness' leading to 'development from within' (Vidyarthi and Wilson, 2008) or 'below' (Ife, 2009). This process forms the basis for community work practices that seek major social transformation (Purcell, 2005; Popple, 2015). Freire (1972) rejected orthodox ('banking') models of education that bolster social institutions. He advocated critical dialogue to deconstruct prevailing discourses. This found an echo in Illich's call to 'de-school' society in favour of self-directed learning through 'educational webs' (Illich, 1973) and the renunciation of institutional education for a more convivial existence based on 'individual freedom realized in personal interdependence' (Illich, 1975). The purpose of these alternatives was to create what Gramsci (1971) had called 'organic intellectuals' who could develop counter-hegemonic thinking whereby taken-for-granted assumptions, sometimes known as 'received wisdom' or 'common sense', are challenged and replaced by other perspectives.

Public deliberations which deepen and widen democracy through consultation meetings, citizens' juries, debates or informal gatherings are vital to empowerment, but may require facilitation in order to create inclusive spaces for 'new conversational networks'. Community development techniques ensure that indigenous or traditional forms of discussion, which reflect ethnic or local differences, are incorporated into formal participatory processes of citizen-centred governance (Guijt and Shah, 1998; Barnes et al, 2008; Eguren, 2008; Ife, 2013). Participation, especially in developing countries, can too often take the form of communities being 'invited' to take part in consultation exercises used by 'colonial administrators seeking to secure quiescence ... or powerful financial institutions seeking to attain "legitimacy" for their programmes' (Cornwall, 2008, p 281).

Questioning normative beliefs involves unpacking and re-examining previous learning, and this can be uncomfortable, especially when it disturbs long-standing traditions or power relations, for example around class or religion or both (Shahid and Jha, 2016). This peer-led conversational approach has been adapted in more modern times as popular education (Crowther et al, 2005; Beck and Purcell, 2010), life-long action learning (Zuber-Skerritt and Teare, 2013), youth work (Jeffs and Smith, 2005), and to underpin training for active citizenship (Kenny et al, 2015). Story telling offers another possibility for encouraging people to explore their own experiences in positive ways, and this can be used as a form of action research, alongside arts and cultural activities. These methods are specially effective for engaging young people, vulnerable individuals or those less confident in using words and linear arguments (Aldridge, 2016). They could include making comics, rapping, forum theatre, creative writing, felt-making, all of which enable people to express emotion while telling their stories, enabling communities to convey alternative meanings and conjure other imagined futures (Kagan and Duggan, 2011; Bell et al, 2019).

Box 4.1: Geluksdisco, Amsterdam

The Happiness Disco is an almost free (€2 entrance fee) dancing event that takes place every three months and has been running in Amsterdam since 2013. It is open to all, from food bank customers and people with learning disabilities, to professors and celebrities. It is for people of all backgrounds and talents who love to dance but may not be able to afford the more expensive clubs in the city. Former refugees and migrants from countries like Iraq, Iran, Turkey, Surinam and eastern Europe come along, all in search of an inclusive evening among like-minded friends.

It is run entirely by volunteers, mainly local residents, including the DJs. Everyone helps to decorate the room, so that every event feels different. Food and drink are provided by local businesses, including free samosas, snacks from around the world, flavoured water and cheap beer. The founder, Dorèndel Overmars, started it because she wanted to 'get the people walking along the streets, from the bike courier to the unemployed, here together ... These are not the people who come in easily everywhere; that's what you do it for.' Everyone is equal on the dance floor; under the glitter ball, age, ethnic origin, income, education and religion are irrelevant.

The disco is popular and open to everyone. It has created a space for integration where people can socialise and enjoy the music in an atmosphere of fun and creativity. Although the focus is on the immediate neighbourhood, diversity is celebrated with energy and visitors from further afield are welcomed.

See: https://www.facebook.com/Geluksdisco/

Participatory democracy

Participation has been a consistently strong theme for all models of community development and is an important feature of policy programmes designed to reinvigorate democratic cultures and active citizenship. Various programmes have been devised to increase people's influence over decisions affecting them, including participatory budgeting, neighbourhood planning, stakeholder engagement and local forums. However, such exercises tend to 'shape' the space for community voice from the top down and avoid discussion that is not seen to be within their designated scope. Without effective community development support, these spaces tend to attract the most vocal and confident individuals, and are not so accessible to those who have little time or who are struggling to deal with hardship or health conditions. Since many people have other priorities and tactics for coping with long-term disadvantage, non-participation may well be a rational survival strategy (Mathers et al, 2008).

Until relatively recently, there has been a failure to understand that community empowerment requires a longer-term approach that:

- is sensitive to differences within communities;
- understands and works with tensions and conflicts; and
- includes a variety of ways for people to contribute their ideas.

The emphasis on participatory governance has been criticised on political grounds (for example, Cooke and Kothari, 2001), as well as for difficulties around implementation (Andersson et al, 2007; Barnes et al, 2007) without adequate accountability (Richardson and Durose, 2013). In one study, community members who did rise to the challenge became unfairly branded as the 'usual suspects', and the pressures of partnership working often led to them becoming isolated and 'burnt-out', or simply disillusioned by the whole process (Purdue, 2007). 'Programmes were felt to "make" and conversely to "break" "community stars": individuals and groups whose contributions were valued on some occasions and then denigrated on others, depending upon how closely they reflected official agendas' (Anastacio et al, 2000). Disappointment and frustrating experiences of participation can exacerbate feelings of disempowerment, damaging community wellbeing and resulting in personal stress and cynicism (Dinham, 2005, 2007; Kagan, 2006; Popay, 2017).

Communities are not homogeneous, rarely speak with one voice and are often sceptical about the motives of local officials. The requirement for democratic representation is a challenge for even the most well-organised and articulate community (Prendergast, 2008). For civic capability to be sustainable and inclusive, a wider and larger set of people must be recruited and supported to take on governance roles and participate in public decision making. This means increasing the numbers of individuals with sufficient 'resourcefulness, connectedness, confidence and effectiveness' to become local leaders and community representatives (Cox, 2006). Those who have experienced years of deprivation often feel deeply disenfranchised and angry, becoming the 'awkward' rather than active citizen (Bock and Cohen, 2018). A necessary first step is to acknowledge these feelings and to enable people to channel their emotions and experience into constructive and feasible strategies that can transform the quality of life and open up new opportunities. However, participatory strategies are only really effective over the longer term if they acknowledge the political dimensions of these arrangements, actively tackling differentials in power and status (Hickey, 2004; Ledwith and Springett, 2009).

More recent versions of this approach have asserted the transformative nature of democratic participation as a form of radical empowerment (Pitchford, 2008) and the means by which many different forms of oppression and inequality can be overcome (Dominelli, 2006). Shaw and Martin regard actions by people in their communities as the 'essence of democracy' and consider community workers as 'key agents in re-making the vital connections between community, citizenship and democracy' (Shaw and Martin, 2000, p 412). Community workers must continue to create spaces for opposition as well as participation, following Shaw's (2008) reassertion of the importance of political analysis and motivation in critiquing the state's adoption of community development.

User empowerment and outreach 'services'

Service providers and public institutions recognise that their planning and performance are likely to be improved by involving service users and residents in identifying issues, devising solutions and monitoring (Oliver and Pitt, 2013). Individual customer feedback provides only limited guidance regarding potential improvements or efficiencies, and so strategies for community engagement have been developed that range from consultation exercises, partnerships and representation in new governance arrangements to full-scale ownership. Ways of rendering services more accessible and tailored to local conditions and different cultural preferences include supporting groups to run their own activities, occasionally on a commissioned basis, or introducing outreach delivery, such as drop-in advice sessions on community premises.

Community workers are adept at working in many organisational cultures and social environments. This is important for developing cooperation across boundaries and for reaching out to sections of the community that are disaffected or appear difficult to engage for practical reasons. This focus on working with voluntary groups and marginalised communities acknowledges that these groups probably need additional support if they are to operate effectively within organisational environments dominated by powerful private and public sector interests. A key role for community workers is to provide and maintain communication channels between different sectors by linking different agencies and population groups.

Front-line workers in a variety of services are expected to work with communities in ways that are empowering and inclusive. For many this will require changes in their attitudes and professional skills as they learn how to share expertise, deal with differing opinions and involve the least heard groups in society. Community representation is seen as essential to their success, and yet the people responsible for this new approach often struggle with the skills or knowledge required to engage effectively with the relevant communities, especially in the most disadvantaged areas.

Co-production/co-design

Co-production approaches embody another way of thinking about partnership and appreciate that relationships between the public and professionals could be more respectful and more reciprocal (Stephens et al, 2008; Durose and Richardson, 2015). On a collective level, communities can lead initiatives that result in the co-production of services (such as children's play groups) as well as the less tangible outcomes of wellbeing, community spirit and civic engagement (Skidmore and Craig, 2005). Although the term wasn't in vogue at the time, this approach was a feature of community work during much of the 1970s and 1980s and has been resurrected as 'critical community practice', broadly defined as transformatory work with communities (Banks et al, 2007). Practitioners working in this way see themselves as advocates and organisers, helping communities to mobilise effectively around issues they identify for themselves, in order to challenge the poverty and discrimination they experience, and associated attitudes (Zipfel et al, 2015).

Chanan and Miller (2013) have set out to revitalise this multi-agency approach in their model of 'new community practice' or CD2, with the intention of 'developing transformative neighbourhoods'. This emphasises partnership between residents and the 'street level bureaucrats' employed by local service providers, such as schools, clinics, police services and housing departments (Lipsky, 1969). It argues that improvements to the quality of life in areas and the life chances of individuals will be achieved through an active collaboration between sectors, rather than a confrontational relation between community and the state. It moves beyond simple forms of community consultation and engagement to create a 'space of possibilities' (Conn, 2011). These allow workable solutions to neighbourhood challenges to be jointly developed and implemented. Chanan and Miller (p 164) suggest that 'new' community practice varies from traditional community development in taking a more strategic, area-based approach that aims to:

- strengthen the local community sector as a whole;
- improve relations between those involved in public services *and* community initiatives; and
- scope issues using a broad sweep that includes the views of front-line workers as well as residents.

The model advocates that all those who work directly with communities should adopt team thinking and invest in the development of cooperative networks through which all can enhance and contribute their skills and confidence. This is similar to the neighbourhood management model promoted by New Labour in the 2000s, and the comprehensive community development networks emerging in some cities in the United States (as promoted by the Institute for Comprehensive Community Development and the Local Initiatives Support Federation, cited by Beck and Purcell, 2013). It overlaps to some extent with the well-connected community model proposed later in this book.

Community development for health and wellbeing

The concept of co-production has paved the way for more community-oriented approaches to health promotion and community care, in the sense of treatment and support outside of the medical institutions (South et al, 2013; South and Stansfield, 2018). Social models of health and disability tilt power and responsibility towards the individuals needing therapy or assistance, recognising their 'expertise by experience' and using a range of community engagement strategies to reach out to their network of assets to provide necessary support (Foot, 2010; NICE, 2016). Self-help groups and voluntary organisations are seen as potential partners in this strategy, and community development methods offer ways to grow this capacity.

Although for most people in Europe wellbeing appears to be rising, growing inequalities and austerity measures are having a major impact on the mental health of those living at the margins of society (Wilkinson and Pickett, 2010). Social inequalities are associated with higher levels of morbidity and discontent, possibly through reductions in social cohesion and social capital (Kawachi et al, 1997; Marmot, 2015; Dorling, 2018). Stress, social isolation and insecurity (for example, around employment or poverty) can give rise to mental health problems and malnutrition, including obesity (Holt-Lunstad et al, 2015). Subjectively, the notion of wellbeing reflects aspects of our lives such as contentment, health, self-efficacy, sense of belonging and resilience, but it has proved difficult to establish a definitive framework for assessing wellbeing as a collective or social value. Many community-based approaches are focused on connections because the importance of relationships and regular interaction with others is commonly associated with, and statistically correlated with, subjective accounts of recovery and wellbeing (McPherson et al, 2013; Bagnall et al, 2018; Hari, 2018).

Three examples of practice have the potential to unite community development with improved health outcomes. They are:

- social prescribing programmes, which are gaining recognition as part of the repertoire of non-medical treatments available within public health services (Knifton, 2015; Kimberlee, 2016), although they run the risk of outsourcing necessary support to untrained and under-resourced activity leaders or volunteers. Some social prescribing schemes fund 'community connectors' who will liaise with groups and help patients to make that first link;
- the Health Empowerment Leverage Project (HELP), which has been developed to 'empower and transform neighbourhoods with the toughest challenges and the highest health and social spending by strengthening communities and encouraging healthy behaviours' (Chanan and Fisher, 2018; www.healthempowerment.co.uk/);
- the People's Health Trust, which starts from the premise that the level of influence that a person has over their life is associated with their health. Health outcomes are affected by the amount of control that residents have over decisions that affect them collectively. The Trust funds programmes that support local communities to exert greater control over what happens in their neighbourhood as key to creating new and stronger relationships and encouraging a greater sense of belonging.

The People's Health Trust targets neighbourhoods most affected by health inequalities. It is evaluating its programmes to test the theory that an asset-based engagement approach will create confidence, knowledge, influence and social connectedness, which in turn will contribute to health equality. Independent research is being carried out by the National Institute for Health Research through its 'Communities in Control' study. Its findings to date indicate that access to spaces for participation is significant in promoting wellbeing.

Box 4.2: Mendip health connectors

Health Connections Mendip is a patient-led scheme supported by the local NHS. Volunteers are trained to signpost members of the public that they come across (in families, at work or wherever) to find the most suitable health provision, but also direct them to other services such as housing, education and debt advice. They are described as 'providing a bridge between local people and health and wellbeing services' and are said to contribute to wellbeing generally by 'joining up communities'. At the time of writing, hairdressers, taxi drivers, drug and alcohol workers, care workers, CAB team, adult social care workers, primary care staff, sixth-form students, church congregations, peer-support group members have all been recruited as health connectors and are working across local health foundation areas in Somerset.

See: https://healthconnectionsmendip.org/community-connector/

The Royal Society of Arts (RSA) 'connected communities' action research project was designed to boost health and social care in specific areas by encouraging greater interaction. It used social network analysis to demonstrate the value of interpersonal relations for wellbeing. Over a number of years community-led projects invested in and mapped local connections, yielding individual and collective dividends constituting what the research team have termed 'community capital' (Knapp et al, 2013; Parsfield et al, 2015). The growing 'people-powered' social movements for health (del Castillo et al, 2016) similarly emphasise the role that informal networks play in connecting people and professionals to enable them to work together to 'widen circles of participation' and 'building relationships of understanding' (Arnold et al, 2018). All these citizen-centred approaches could be said to have adopted a community development method of operating to improve partnership working between communities and institutions, as well as promoting life-style changes to deliver health outcomes.

Social enterprise and community economic development

Strategies for tackling poverty can be seen as having four broad themes:

- increasing income through access to secure jobs, higher wages, benefit entitlement and take-up, self-employment/entrepreneurship, community enterprise;
- reducing expenditure through debt advice, local markets, energy-saving schemes, digital literacy, semi-formal exchange mechanisms;
- sharing and redistributing resources through community networks and community groups, improvements to local amenities, community finance initiatives, voluntary activity; and
- improving people's quality of life in relation to other factors such as their accommodation, health, access to services and opportunities for community connections.

Communities struggling to survive with few resources may find it difficult to organise and exploit new opportunities. Nonetheless, there are plenty of examples of community initiatives and local economic development that encourage money to 'stick' in an area to counter the 'leaky bucket' effect. Various models have been devised to keep money circulating locally and facilitate peer exchanges. They include housing cooperatives, credit unions, TimeBanks and small-scale community enterprises (Arrandon and Wyler, 2008; Gregory, 2015). Encouraging local spending and local trading through local currencies means that poorer residents are more likely to have access to affordable homes, goods and services as well as support and information about employment and debts. Community businesses are characterised as rooted in, and accountable to, local interests. They trade for community benefit while having a broad social impact – for example, investing profits back into local projects and providing needed services for residents (see: https://www.powertochange.org. uk/what-is-community-business/).

Social finance, community shares and micro-credit have become more prevalent as a means of investing in local initiatives through loans to social businesses or individual entrepreneurs (Yunus, 2010; Murtagh and Goggin, 2015). Social enterprise projects and community cooperatives tailored to suit local needs and add 'social value' provide employment for the most disadvantaged residents, as well as goods and services, such as social care, up-cycled appliances or cafes. Community orientated approaches are also evident in community development finance initiatives, such as cooperative housing schemes, neighbourhood-based job clubs, bulk-buy schemes, credit unions and advice centres (CDFA, 2012). Self-employed people operating insecurely in the micro-economy can be helped to formalise their informal (and occasionally illegal) enterprises to become legitimate businesses that provide sustainable incomes.

Partly as a result of austerity cuts and partly in a bid to make communities and voluntary bodies less reliant on grant aid, there has been a shift towards social enterprise and investment strategies designed to make community-level organisations more business-like (Defourney and Nyssens, 2012). This is to ensure their longer-term sustainability through the transfer and local ownership of assets such as landmark buildings, with communities having a 'right' to express an interest in buying and managing these for local good (Morris et al, 2013). Government and many private foundations have promoted social investment strategies whereby repayable loans, start-up advice, peer-to-peer trading and cooperative businesses have replaced time-limited funding awards, with the expectation that community initiatives, mirroring the experience of public service mutuals, would become self-sufficient and entrepreneurial (Social Enterprise UK, 2018).

Box 4.3: WEvolution micro-loans

WEvolution is a national body that supports a nationwide federation of self-reliant groups that are aiming to build a movement for independent community enterprise. The driving principle of the programme is to encourage small-scale enterprise through small loans to people wanting to set up their own business or realise a long-cherished dream. It operates on a similar basis to micro-finance schemes such as the Grameen Bank. It encourages mutual support using lending circles and low membership subscriptions that are used to fund various start-up projects.

The emphasis is on collaboration rather than competition and for funded projects to be responsive to community-identified needs by designing local and financially sustainable solutions. All the groups are supported from regional hubs using peer networking events, and groups are offered initial training to enable members to participate fully and to pursue their ideas for income generation, either individually or collectively. For many people their involvement in WEvolution has been life changing, empowering people from situations of extreme disadvantage and distress to enable them to fulfil their potential and move away from all kinds of dependencies.

See: www.wevolution.org.uk/

Tackling inequalities

While community development has long espoused its commitment to social justice, the emergence of identity politics towards the end of the last century created additional pressures for change. The concept of social identity is recognised as an important, but fluid, facet of people's sense of their community (or rather, communities), especially when faced with hostility or ignorance (Bhavnani et al, 2006; Modood, 2007; Wetherell et al, 2007). Drawing on the women's and anti-racist movements of earlier decades, community work needed to engage with the debates around institutional discrimination, acknowledging what has become known as 'intersectionality'. Many people, perhaps the majority, experience multiple, intersecting forms of oppression, often the result of unconscious bias and micro-aggressions. The past two decades since 2000 have seen a resurgence of identity and rights-based politics, together with a better understanding of how inequalities intersect around multiple forms of oppression and exploitation (Gilchrist et al, 2010; Hicks and Myeni, 2016). These have spawned multifaceted campaigns for social justice, such as the Black Lives Matter movement or feminist pressure groups that challenge the caste system or gender–based violence (Shahid and Jha, 2016).

Within community development and the more radical parts of the voluntary sector, these strategies of identity-based organising are a legitimate and necessary means of resistance and emancipation, developing services and campaigns that assert specific (and sometimes competing) perspectives on a range of issues (Shukra, 1995; Afridi and Warmington, 2009). Alongside demands for equal rights and equal treatment has developed a recognition that this does not mean treating everybody the same, or expecting people to conform to prevailing cultures or social expectations. The growth of self-organised movements around different forms of discrimination and oppression was a key political development of the late 20th and early 21st centuries, largely supported by community development strategies despite being a source of contention for funders and policy makers. Unfortunately, since 2010, many organisations set up to meet needs in culturally or identity-appropriate ways have folded, due to lack of funding.

Nevertheless, as a consequence of these struggles, a majority view gradually emerged within mainstream community work that anti–oppressive strategies and positive action measures should be incorporated into notions of 'good practice'. While this somewhat 'top-down' approach was contested in some quarters as being heavy handed, 'politically correct' and ineffective, it did ensure that organisations were forced to consider issues around discrimination and access. By the 1990s equality had secured its position as a core value of and a powerful driving force within community development, underpinning its other commitments to participation and empowerment.

Working with communities that have fewer local or conventional attachments, such as asylum seekers (Temple, 2005) or Gypsies, Roma and Travellers, poses different challenges and demands an even more inclusive model of community development. Drawing on his own extensive experience, Ryder (2017) recognises that 'outsider' community workers can play a vital catalytic role, but counsels a two-way process of learning. He advocates a form of 'inclusive community development' that pays close and respectful attention to traditions that should be considered a collective asset for community pride and ethnic identity, rather than a source or cause of exclusion. Ryder argues that, for particularly marginalised communities, cultural practices carry both honour and prestige and can be harnessed as part of processes of change. Time is needed to come alongside the community, understand the full range of social mores and aspirations and so develop relationships with leaders and activists.

Class alliances

Earlier in this chapter we saw how radical community development was characterised by a more explicit analysis of structural inequalities, often informed by class politics or anti-colonialism (Craig, 2016). A number of community workers, notably those employed by the community development projects operating through workshops and resource centres, argued for campaigns to tackle issues by building alliances between communities and the local industrialised workforce. This work continued to an extent into the 1980s and 1990s through, for example, alliances of unemployed people and the unions of benefits office staff, and through unemployed workers' centres, as well as through the pit-closure support groups during the 1984–85 miners' strike in the UK. For a while, joint working across this divide seemed to become dormant, until latent interest in joint working was rekindled to establish community-unionism. Unions use their considerable resources and political know-how to join with activists and community organisations around shared interests and goals (Mayo et al, 2016).

From the unions' perspective, this model of organising aims to reach into sections of the labour force that have not yet been unionised, while simultaneously promoting class-based solidarity and social justice (Wright, 2010). Sometimes these campaigns have been local initiatives, organised in response to immediate threats to employment, services or the environment. Austerity cuts have resulted in campaigns that have sought to link service users with service providers through joint 'struggles' to save public facilities such as hospitals, libraries, care homes and rural railways, or to resist privatisation. These have enjoyed varying success and have encountered obstacles such as the lack of a unified class identity at local level that historically would have been provided by employment at the mill, mine or factory. Communities have become more fragmented and unstable, plagued by divisions and low-class consciousness.

Consequently, unions are also weakened and less understood by new generations of workers. They are being framed by adverse media coverage and so tend to be viewed more sceptically by the general public. Some commentators have criticised the model adopted by the UK's two biggest unions, UNITE and UNISON, as being an outreach exercise to increase their own membership and profile (Tattershall, 2010), but others welcome this renewed form of coalition, pointing to notable achievements such as the London Living Wage campaign (Holgate, 2009), anti-racist work pursued through the Hope Not Hate organisation and smaller-scale successes such as preventing closures of local amenities. An important ingredient seems to be what Wills and Simms (2004) term 'reciprocal community-unionism', highlighting the need for organisers to build trust and relationships between union members and community activists before embarking on campaigns around goals that have been mutually agreed (Wills, 2002).

Modern variations on a theme

Within this broad approach, there are specialisms and particular slants. For example, the strengths-based approach to community development, often promoted as the ABCD model (asset-based community development), acknowledges the benefits that accrue to 'well-connected communities' in terms of their capacity to influence and to organise social action (Kretzmann and McKnight, 1993; McKnight and Block, 2012; Green and Haines, 2015). Relatively new concepts such as resilience and collective efficacy have gained traction and some models acknowledge the contribution of networks to these shared outcomes. Internationally, community development, although in decline in the UK, continues to emphasise the importance of spinning and weaving community threads. The relational processes that foster the 'softer' aspects of human relationships – hope, solidarity, compassion – have regained attention in recent studies of organisation and management. Westoby (2015) has developed what he calls a 'soul perspective' in community work, using 'soul' as a metaphor for how 'animated' and 'connected' energies are needed for meaningful and sustainable social change, calling on us to use empathy and imagination more in our practice and to focus on 'being' as well as 'doing'.

Community development is sometimes deployed to pursue particular policy goals or to work with certain sections of society, such as identity communities, defined by sexual orientation, gender or age, as well as ethnicity. This chapter has already noted community-based strategies for health and wellbeing. There are also numerous examples of community-led projects set up to achieve localised environmental justice and sustainable development, including renewable energy and recycling schemes, as well as the transition town movement (Hopkins, 2008).

Ideally, local community development is about resident-led change, enabling people to come together around shared objectives. The Community Organisers Expansion Programme and Big Local are recent examples of how this ideal is being implemented. The next section provides a brief overview of two contemporary models currently operating in England that incorporate community development principles. Both are medium-term programmes, funded by government and the National Lottery respectively, and both have adopted a relatively 'light touch' approach with an emphasis on resident empowerment and social action.

Community organising: listening and mobilising

There are several forms of community organising, mostly rooted in Alinsky's original model as set out in *Rules for Radicals* (1972). Local leaders are trained to use 'one-to-one' interviews with community members to identify emerging issues. Community organisers undertake a detailed power analysis in order to build alliances for political leverage. Since the turn of the century, community organising has enjoyed a surprising revival in the UK. 'Community organiser' roles are now becoming as commonplace as community workers were in recent decades, and the approach is central to initiatives sponsored by Hope Not Hate, several unions and the Labour Party. Two organisations, Citizens UK and Community Organisers, are wholly dedicated to community organising. They represent two contemporary British models of community organising that have adopted a number of core principles fundamental (and unique) to this approach, notably using local knowledge and contacts to build independent networks of leaders and activists (Imagine, 2015).

Although not new, Citizens UK came to prominence following a successful General Election Assembly with key political parties in 2010. The Citizens UK model of community organising has cast itself as radical and novel, particularly its commitment to campaigning mobilisations (Bolton, 2017) and 'grounded learning' through processes of dialogue and reflection on direct experience (Chambers, 2010). It maps the networks of decision makers to analyse the distribution of power, questions the legitimacy of authority structures and challenges how status and influence are used or abused by identifying 'power holders'. These individuals, usually in key positions (for example Police and Crime Commissioners, council leaders or chief executive officers of large corporations), are targeted for mass mobilisations to exert disciplined and organised pressure. The expectation is that they will hear the validity of evidence and arguments presented, and be persuaded to change course and implement alternative organisational policies or strategies. Assemblies and confrontational demonstrations of popular strength (for example, at annual shareholder meetings), combined with direct actions, are crucial tactics of community organising campaigns. These marshal significant numbers of people and build autonomous, broad-based organisations to create sufficient momentum and 'make change happen'. Notable successes have been the widespread adoption of the Living Wage, the provision of affordable housing within the legacy of the London Olympics site and regeneration schemes as part of preparations for the Commonwealth Games in Birmingham in 2022.

Community Organisers grew from the government's flagship Community Organisers Programme (COP), initially designed to promote the Big Society. A key objective was the recruitment and training of 500 community organisers, hosted by local agencies and supported through Locality, a national federation of community-led organisations (Taylor and Wilson, 2016). In its bid to run COP, Locality presented a theory of change that explicitly argued that traditional community development fostered dependency and 'learned helplessness' among those whom it purported to empower: 'Instead of freeing communities to make changes, government and professionals have often got in the way.' It therefore aimed for a 'real shift in power to communities' so as to build local leadership for community-driven change. The vision was to find 'points of solidarity' amid fragmentation and division (Taylor and Wilson, 2016, p 220) and foster a new social contract between people and power.

Organisers were trained to engage residents through extensive door-knocking campaigns, resulting in thousands of informal conversations or 'listenings'. As common concerns emerged and potential leaders and activists were identified, 'front room' meetings were hosted by residents, often bypassing existing formally organised groups. Community organisers tried to reach beyond the 'usual suspects' to listen to the views of 'ordinary' community members in order to generate community solutions. The idea was to tackle the problems thus identified through collective actions organised by the paid organisers, community leaders and activists, supported by reflection, dialogue and networking. This reflects one of Alinsky's cardinal 'rules' (1972) asserting the importance of finding the connections between people and building trusting relationships with and between local leaders. A crucial aspect of community organising is aligning interests within a community by finding out what matters to people and formulating the resultant messages and campaign goals in terms that will resonate with local feeling and circumstances.

Government funding for community organising has endured through several programme variants and is pledged to continue until at least 2020. The current programme, led by the membership body, Community Organisers (COLtd), provides training and support for community-led change through a network of locally based social action hubs (the National Academy of Community Organising) and other partners. The aims of the current government-sponsored COP are about local change and capacity development. Community Organisers explain their mission as 'the work of bringing people together to take action around common concerns and overcome social injustice … when people are organised, communities get heard and power begins to shift creating real change for good'. This commitment to radical collaboration 'involves the building of networks and relational power (the power of people working together), the facilitation of collective action and the cultivation of a just and caring society' (https://www.corganisers.org.uk/what-is-community-organising/). In this respect they draw on theoretical roots originally set out by Alinsky, but the principles of this modern incarnation appear to have a lot in common with mainstream community development, for example demonstrating respect for diversity, helping people to develop their collective power and the community development staple about 'starting where the community is at'.

The evaluation of the early years (2011–14) of the government's COP was equivocal, with only limited demonstrable impact on expected outcomes (Cameron et al, 2015). However, according to data from the Community Life Survey comparing the patches where community organisers were deployed with matched areas, there were statistically significant improvements in people's reported sense of belonging and increased belief that communities 'pulled together' to improve their areas. The lack of other shifts in collective efficacy or cohesion may be due to inadequate funding, limited training and restrictive time-scales. The government has continued its funding of further tranches of community organisers through COLtd, while some community organisers from early cohorts have set up ACORN branches as community-based 'unions' in several major cities and are campaigning on issues such as decent, affordable accommodation and employment rights (see https://acorntheunion.org.uk/). They use Rathke's original principles, first formulated in 1973 (Rathke, 2018), and are affiliated to an embryonic national federation. Further afield, community organising has found numerous applications through Slum Dwellers International in India, the US Federation of Industrial Area Foundations and Community Development Trusts, ACORN International, and the Sydney Alliance. There has been divergence in the exact methods of these different models but the basic principles of community-led action and empowerment underpin them all (Beck and Purcell, 2013).

Big Local: resident-led change

In 2011 one relatively large programme moved into the austerity-throttled space of the community sector. The Big Lottery Fund created an endowment fund, to be managed by Local Trust, and selected 150 communities which were each to receive £1 million to spend over a 10- to 15-year period. Typically, these were neighbourhoods, villages and small towns that were seen to have low levels of civic engagement and lacked the capacity and infrastructure to apply successfully for Big Lottery and other funding.

Big Local was designed as an innovative and experimental approach to community development, one that was qualitatively different to previous initiatives and 'in stark contrast with previous neighbourhood change and regeneration programmes in that areas are not driven by top down targets, annual spend and externally imposed goals and outcomes' (McCabe et al, 2017). Initially, the programme was informed by learning drawn from a small-scale Joseph Rowntree Foundation neighbourhood-based empowerment initiative (Taylor et al, 2007) and scaled up in terms of financial support, 'light touch' facilitation and longevity. It aimed to be a 'hands off' programme; communities were expected to set their own priorities and to organise themselves in ways appropriate to their area. In the National Council for Voluntary Organisations (NCVO) evaluation report of Big Local's early years, the core elements of this light-touch approach are described as minimal rules and regulations, support and guidance provided in an enabling way through simple systems and processes, and a learning culture (James et al, 2014). There were very few prescribed targets, and outcomes were deliberately broad, focusing on communities identifying local needs, designing appropriate responses and consequently making a difference to where they lived.

Big Local still has a way to go; it runs until 2026. The overall strengths-based approach hasn't wavered. It continues to be 'underpinned by the concept that resident-led action is a catalyst for change as well as a mechanism for managing that change' (McCabe et al, 2017). Inevitably, the type of support offered has been modified in the light of learning about what is of most use to communities as they have moved from creating a vision for their area to partnership development, to managing an area-based strategy and, in some cases, delivering that strategy themselves. Every one of the 150 areas has a partnership comprising a majority of residents and a unique delivery plan which is regularly reviewed. Funding to implement the plans is usually handled by one or more Locally Trusted Organisation (LTO) – local accountable bodies appointed by the partnership to carry out its bookkeeping and, in some instances, to employ Big Local staff. The LTO model aims to free partnerships from internal bureaucracy and help residents to concentrate on achieving their vision. Each partnership can access a package of flexible support, primarily through a Big Local 'Rep' appointed by Local Trust, as well as additional specialist support as is necessary. In addition, there are a range of peer learning opportunities provided through regional and national networks and thematic workshops.

From the perspective of a funder, Big Local is a big risk, and for communities it is a big 'ask'. It is an ambitious programme with little inherent central control. It has also evolved in a context of austerity, a gradual withdrawal of the local state and huge cutbacks in pre-existing community infrastructure. As such, there have been unexpected twists and turns. For example, in 2011 it was perfectly reasonable to assert that Big Local monies should not be used to backfill statutory services or be hijacked by public agencies, but reductions in youth services have led a large proportion of Big Locals to support activities for young people financially, not because of pressure from external agencies but because residents felt these were needed. In the same vein, many of the areas have prioritised the setting up of community hubs, partly in response to disappearing or unaffordable community venues. Partnerships view community hubs as vital for connection and interaction, but they also present challenges with regard to financial viability.

Local Trust has embraced the risk element as an opportunity for learning, for itself and for the Big Local partnerships. A significant, though unsurprising, insight for experienced community workers is that the 10- to 15-year timeline for Big Locals is helpful in enabling communities to work at a pace which suits them, and to achieve something that is durable and lasting (Local Trust, 2017). Community groups tend to ebb and flow as people depart and new people join, tensions arise and are resolved, local energies soar and wane. The Big Local time-scale allows for this up and down cycle. It has provided 'the opportunity to develop new skills and knowledge in the community, to strengthen existing networks' (Sheffield, 2018) and has allowed the time it takes to build trust 'across communities and between communities and their partners' (Baker et al, 2013). 'Resident-led' change is complex and there are a range of understandings as to what it looks like on the ground. The programme's multimedia longitudinal evaluation, 'Our Bigger Story', has found that Big Local areas approach their community leadership role differently: some are aiming to support community groups to build their fund-raising skills; some provide services; some have very local aspirations to bring people together through networks and promote 'neighbourliness'; some have ambitious strategies to influence, and benefit from, large-scale (re)development in their area; some are more concerned with making sure residents have a voice and opportunities to be heard by those with influence and power. What they all have in common is a desire for maximum engagement of the wider community and a legacy of increased community activism (McCabe et al, 2019.)

Discussion

Perhaps less well appreciated is the more difficult and subtle work of assisting people to make connections and sustain relationships where there are cultural differences, practical obstacles or political opposition. This requires political awareness, emotional sensitivity and advanced interpersonal skills (Hastings, 1993, p 76). Community workers operate within complex multi-organisational environments, so they need to be strategic in making links and building relationships among a huge variety of potential and actual collaborators, including people from all sections of the community. In particular, community development often works best by identifying and supporting the 'linkers' (Fraser et al, 2003) or 'moving spirits' (Gibson, 1996): those individuals who are not community leaders as such but who work, often invisibly, at the grassroots level to connect people with institutions, bringing about change in very subtle ways.

Community workers are expected to be in touch with a sometimes bewildering range of individuals and organisations. Their role in facilitating communication and cooperation within communities is alluded to in much of the early community work literature, in the guise of, for example, community newsletters, liaison meetings, festivals, resource centres, social gatherings and forums that were often serviced, managed or entirely run by community workers. Nowadays we must add a dizzying range of online and instant communication channels to this list, such as Twitter feeds, Facebook pages, texts, e-mails and community-run websites. These can all be powerful vehicles for networking, enabling people to meet to share ideas and to gain experience in working together. As we shall see in later chapters, community workers often find themselves in key positions within formal and informal networks, coordinating organisational arrangements as well as managing a complex array of interpersonal relationships.

Community workers are themselves a resource or a tool in this process, but do not usually have a 'stake' in what happens as a result of those connections. They act as stewards or custodians of the networks, rather than using them to promote their own interests. Responsibility for network development and management is increasingly recognised as a job in its own right. Recent reviews of civil society, the third or social sector and localism (Civil Society Futures, 2018; Commission on the Future of Localism, 2018) worry about the fracturing of society. Both reports recognise 'connectedness' as a feature of strong communities, and therefore the legitimate focus for funding and community development support. Community organisations need networking capacity in order to build a wide base of participation, sustain partnerships and create coalitions for action. This helps them to connect members of different communities, to access resources and power in external institutions and to manage tensions with other stakeholders.

Conclusions

In the main, community development is well defined and understood by those familiar with its practices. However, the range of approaches described in this chapter indicates its contested nature and the variety of applications. There are also ongoing debates within the field regarding, for example, the interplay between formal and informal procedures when working with communities (Gilchrist, 2016); the balance between top-down versus bottom-up agendas; and perennial deliberations about how an emphasis on processes should be countered with a desire to achieve community-defined goals. Finally, the discussion about the relationship between professionals, community leaders, volunteer activists and residents continues unabated. These roles frequently overlap and comprise strong networks, with overlapping or competing interests, personal affinities and antipathies, even conflicts. Due to their status as paid officials, community workers may find themselves in positions of unwarranted or unearned influence. This gives them legitimate responsibilities to guide communities in self-determined development while at the same time treading a fine line along the spectrum of encouragement, persuasion and coercion.

Nonetheless, most practitioners can agree on a set of core themes and common values, namely that community development is about working together for social change and collective benefit. Its intended outcomes are universal: justice, greater equality, resilience, shared capabilities, a sense of belonging and collective empowerment. In order to achieve effective and sustainable cooperation the nature and extent of connections and interactions matter. Where it has been successful, community development has sought to strengthen relationships between individuals, groups, agencies and sectors so that the needs and aspirations of communities can be met effectively through collective action and improved services. The work involved in establishing and maintaining these boundary-spanning linkages has come to be known as networking but has often been hidden from public view. The following chapters aim to make the skills and strategies that underpin networking more explicit and, hopefully, better recognised by managers and funders.

Networking practices for community development are primarily about facilitating and fostering networks. What is it about networks that makes them figure so prominently within the community and voluntary sectors? This question will be considered in the next chapter, which explores specific features of networks as a form of organisation and their relationship with wider social environments, particularly looking at informal voluntary activity. Studies of the community sector and the emergence of community activities over time suggest that community groups, forums and semi-formal networks provide the seedbed for the growth of more formal voluntary associations and campaigns (see Milofsky, 1987). The networking approach to community development described in this book recognises the significance of informal networks in gathering the energy, motivation and resources needed to organise collective activities and address crucial issues around equality and social justice.

QUESTIONS FOR REFLECTION AND DISCUSSION

✧ Think about your own recent experience of working with communities. How has it changed? What has stayed the same?

✧ Do you tend to prioritise particular aspects of community development in your own practice? If so, what factors and preferences affect your choices?

5

Networks: form and features

> How do you hold a hundred tons of water in the air with no visible means of support? You build a cloud.
>
> K.C. Cole, *Sympathetic vibrations*, 1984, p 38

In recent years the concept of networks as a form of organisation has gained in currency both as a metaphor and as an explanatory tool for a range of natural phenomena (Barabási, 2014; Newman, 2010). The term 'network' seems to have been available in the 19th century, although it was first used in academic literature by Radcliffe-Brown in 1940 and early sociologists recognised its significance as an aspect of social living (Warner and Lunt, 1942). It offers a useful model for examining the interactions of daily life and thinking about community dynamics. As the previous chapter showed, within community development, networks are seen as the means for coordinating collective action, supporting the activities of practitioners and providing important means of communication through various technologies, increasingly using online platforms and social media, as well as face-to-face interaction.

This chapter provides an introduction to network theory, specifically examining form and function. It reviews analytical models developed from group and organisational studies and identifies key features often associated with effective networking. Networks are presented as an effective mode of organising in complex and turbulent environments. They play an important role in the development of successful coalitions and partnerships. Networks can either be described as 'organic' – sustained as a natural result of the interactions between members – or they can be seen as 'engineered' – devised and established by an external agency for a specific purpose. Networks can be closed or open, depending on how membership is defined or how porous boundaries are, operating as opaque cliques or dynamic adaptive systems (Kastelle and Steen, 2014).

Form and function

Networks support networking: they enable people to share ideas, consolidate relationships, exchange goods and services, and cooperate.

Networks generally operate on the basis of shared values and informal connections that are maintained by a continuing and reciprocal commitment. They differ from formal organisations in being less dependent on rules and structure and tend to function through personal interaction between people who know (or know of) each other. For community development purposes, networks are important because they:

- provide resilient and dispersed communication channels;
- facilitate collective action and alliances;
- underpin multi-agency partnerships;
- support citizen engagement;
- promote community cohesion and integration; and
- create opportunities for reflection and learning.

Networks operate as vehicles for initiating and sustaining collective action in communities and social movements. Loosely coordinated networks of direct action (such as deployed by modern social movements) have become important campaigning vehicles for discussion and mobilisations, made more accessible and perhaps more powerful through social media technologies (Castells, 2012; Chomsky, 2012). A networking approach to empowerment is developed using a 'circuits of power' model that emphasises the value of boundary-spanning work in promoting cohesion and managing diversity.

Key features and characteristics

Essential characteristics of networks are a web of lateral connections and avoidance of formal bureaucratic structures. Of course, a web is only a metaphor, and social networks are by no means uniform in their configuration of contacts and relationships. The filaments that connect people vary in strength, directionality and density; and change over time. As shown in Figure 5.1, a network comprises fundamentally:

- a set of nodes (where connections are made either through individuals or organisational units); and
- the linkages between them, sometimes referred to as 'edges'.

The pattern of connections for any given network shows clusters (where many nodes are connected), gaps and boundary-spanners, described by Burt (1992) in the technical literature as structural holes.

Figure 5.1: Diagrammatic representation of a network

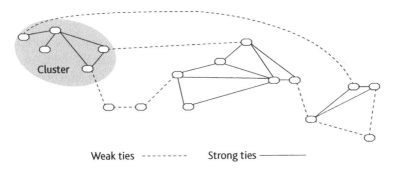

Weak ties ---------   Strong ties ————————

Networks often have outliers that are only sparsely connected and may also contain disrupters that block or divert potential connections.

Networks are not always the organisational panacea that many envisage, often failing to fulfil their intended function, and may not be as value-free as was once imagined. This insight has been echoed by the dearth of debate over the value-base of social media platforms until very recently in 2019, following outrage over their abuse by terrorist organisations and covertly political campaign groups – an issue that is reviewed in Chapter 10. Networks contain patterns of prejudice, preference and power, reflecting personal choices that are both 'tactical and strategic' (Chambers, 1983, p 216). Networks have limited ability to reach and carry out consensual decisions, making it difficult to deal with internal disputes and resulting in hidden elites and cliques which are hard to challenge. As Freeman noted in her book about the 'tyranny of structurelessness' within the women's liberation movement, informality can become a 'smokescreen for the strong or the lucky to establish unquestioned hegemony over others' (Freeman, 1973, p 1). Power disparities and rivalries between network members can undermine the reciprocity that is needed to sustain relationships and may provide a systematic advantage for a specific faction. This is both unjust and inefficient because it fails to harness or fairly reward ability.

Nonetheless, networks have retained their popularity, perhaps because the voluntary and community sector can itself be characterised as a complex and dynamic environment, inhabited by interacting organisations that often compete for resources (members, funding, status) while advocating cooperation and partnership. Informal relationships based on trust and shared values enable voluntary and community organisations to cooperate around matters of principle. At local levels, these interpersonal connections can form a network of like-minded and dedicated individuals who serve on each other's committees. This enables them to work together to coordinate activities and develop new organisations.

The sector thus achieves both coherence and creativity without sacrificing the autonomy of separate organisations, or its ability to act in concert where necessary. However, many of the arrangements which support collaboration within the community and voluntary sector become disadvantageous when these positive links and affiliations prevent organisations from dealing with difficult situations, such as fraud, incompetence or discrimination. Improprieties and conflicts of interest may be deliberately hidden, or simply underplayed, in order to avoid explicit disagreements. This collusion is damaging and, if unchecked, can seriously erode the credibility of the whole sector.

Network structures

The significant attribute of network ties is that they enable the nodes to influence one another. Some nodes are more significant than others to the overall functioning of the network, depending on their current state and specific pattern of linkage. Pressure placed on these 'soft spots' can have a profound effect on the whole system, and community workers do well to seek out these especially sensitive or influential people within communities and organisations. A persuasive nudge through encouragement or information sharing can result in far-reaching changes in collective understanding or commitment. Decentralised multi-tier, open-lattice arrangements of nodes and edges exhibit maximum resilience. They optimise network effects and function better in some situations than a network model consisting of centralised hub and spokes, or a densely connected, equipotent mesh (Ogden, 2018).

In so far as networks have structure, they can be represented as having polycentric and dynamic patterns of interaction, which are neither random nor explicitly ordered. Networks operate on the basis of informal relationships rather than formal roles, with membership tending to be voluntary and participative. The existence and vitality of the linkages are determined by personal choices, convenience, circumstance or occasionally sheer coincidence. Cooperation between members relies on persuasion and reciprocity rather than coercion or contracts. There are often no clear affiliation mechanisms or boundaries, and membership itself is a fuzzy category with constantly shifting criteria and allegiances. The tenuous nature of network connections makes it awkward to refer to network membership as if this were a defined category. Perhaps 'participant' is a more appropriate term, conveying the idea that networks are actively constructed and maintained, even though 'affiliation' may sometimes be unplanned or unwitting. The most important and useful aspect of a network is the configuration of its connections, which normally reflect an underlying value base, a shared interest or simply the geography of overlapping lives. Goligoski's (2018) distinction between membership and subscription is useful for understanding how networks mobilise people for action. Members tend to be active joiners, who choose to participate (thus maintaining their connection) because they believe that by being involved they can contribute to the shared goal and gain benefits such as status, opportunity or congenial company. Subscribers, on the other hand, sign up (and usually pay dues to help service the organisation) in order to access a product or benefit. They do not necessarily interact with other subscribers and simply carry out transactions via a central hub.

Network analysis

Nowadays the word 'network' is often used to describe multi-affiliate organisations, such as a partnership, federation or association. These have a disparate membership but more or less formal structure. This use of the term is confusing, as the essence of networks is to be found in their flexibility, the relative 'flatness' and informality in their array of linkages and the diversity of ways in which individuals or bodies are connected, allowing them to contribute and participate differently at different times and for different purposes. Networks are neither groups nor organisations, although they create the conditions for these to emerge and evolve. Networks enable members to form clusters that undertake specific activities that are focused on a common purpose or function and coordinated on a semi-autonomous basis. This mode of organising is termed 'flexible specialisation' and is a feature of many complex systems, especially where innovation and creativity are at a premium.

Early attempts to investigate the structure and function of networks originated in the *Gestalt* or holistic approach to human psychology, which recognised that in order to understand individual behaviour it was necessary to study the 'whole' context, including interactions with others in the social landscape (Scott, 2000). *Gestalt* methods were applied to 'real life' situations and produced results that had the appearance of scientific rigour reinforced by an intuitive familiarity. Early studies of community relations carried out by the Chicago and

Manchester schools of network sociology (for example, Park, 1925, 1929; Warner and Lunt, 1942; Mitchell, 1969) used both observation and interviews. The researchers noted patterns of interaction and also asked people about their personal affiliations. Rather than studying just individual actions, social network analysis (SNA, as it became known) was concerned with mapping arrays of informal relationships as a means of understanding the organisation or community as a whole. For example, SNA was used to examine the ties between people to discern patterns of communication, transaction and allegiance in order to investigate decision making and alliances (Laumann and Pappi, 1976; Burnage, 2010).

Network analysis reveals how different positions and the frequency of interactions may have 'real world' significance. It has allowed researchers to identify key roles such as leaders, connectors, influencers and intermediaries, thereby generating a number of useful theoretical developments in the social sciences. These include ideas around leadership, trust, coalitions and innovation, all of which are relevant to community development. The social psychologist Milgram used the idea of interpersonal connections to explain the global reach of social networks in what has become known as the 'small-world effect', also popularised as the notion of 'six degrees of separation' (Milgram, 1967). Experimental studies to replicate and explain this phenomenon have consistently demonstrated that people are able to use tenuous connections and informed guesses to reach a total stranger on the other side of the world within just a few steps (Buchanan, 2003; Watts, 2003, 2004).

Of particular relevance is Granovetter's research on the strength of 'weak' ties. Granovetter investigated how people use personal connections to obtain information and share ideas. He identified the importance of the 'weak ties' between acquaintances in 'bridging' the gaps between different social clusters and maintaining social cohesion in modern urban life (Granovetter, 1973, 1978, 1985). This was a useful counterbalance to earlier community studies that had focused on networks based on the 'thick ties' of kinship and friendship operating within neighbourhoods and villages (Bott, 1957; Young and Willmott, 1957). Several of the studies using SNA generated interesting observations regarding the operation of power in society (Hunter, 1953; Knoke, 1990a, 1990b) and the importance of informal interactions within organisations (Emery and Trist, 1965). The methods of investigation, however, were fairly crude compared with the inherent complexities of most real networks and, unsurprisingly, network analysts tended to gather evidence in situations that were relatively stable, bounded and integrated. They largely failed to capture the intricacies and dynamics of personal relationships, especially where these involved tensions and negative attitudes.

Since the end of the last century, network analysis has developed more sophisticated techniques of mathematical modelling using graph theory such as the Erdős–Rényi model for random graph analysis. This uses vertices (nodes) and edges (links) to understand the shape and dynamics of a network (Bollobás, 2001). Computer programmes were developed to calculate statistical algorithms and display them in diagrammatic or matrix form (for example, Stephenson, 1999; Freeman, 2000). Software packages such as UCINET, SIENA, Gephi and Netdraw have made it considerably easier to statistically analyse and visualise the pattern of connections between interacting agents (Scott, 2000; Borgatti et al, 2002; Huisman and van Duijn, 2005). They have the capacity to monitor changes over time – an important potential application for measuring the impact of this networking approach to community development, as well as other interventions.

Network analysis has found practical applications within organisation development and some welfare professions (Baker, 1994). Many theorists, notably Burt (2000), Cook et al (2001) and Lin (2002), argue that network structures are fundamental to understanding social capital, and this is broadly the approach taken here. It is the nature and configuration of the 'weaker' connections or what Burt describes as the 'bridges' across 'structural holes' that are especially valuable. Although in its preliminary stages, there have been moves to evaluate the effectiveness of community development by tracking changes in the connectivity between people and organisations. Network analysis offers a potentially fruitful avenue for community action research and participatory appraisal methods which explores the interactions and perceptions within whole systems, such as communities and the partnerships that serve them (Burns, 2007).

Network or organisation?

The word 'network' can be applied to a whole variety of multi-agency configurations, but it is useful to begin by thinking about what are the distinguishing features of networks. Networks have been variously described as a new, intermediary or hybrid form of organisation. Since the 1990s, network has become a familiar term and has risen in popularity as a way of describing a loose collection of actors that are connected but not bureaucratically structured or formally regulated. Some organisation theorists considered networks to be an entirely novel form of organisation, different from either markets or hierarchies and suited to postmodern conditions (Ouchi, 1980). Others see networks as characteristic of all kinds of organisation, weaving a complex web of informal relationships in and around the formal structures (Frances et al, 1991).

True networks have no central organising or control mechanism. Function and authority are distributed across the nodes and linkages, such that decision making and implementation are conducted through informal and temporary mobilisations of actors and resources. Within networks, influence operates predominantly through informal processes and connections based on trust, loyalty, reciprocity, civility and sociability (Misztal, 2000). Network enthusiasts tend to assume that network members enjoy a nominal equality, ignoring issues around elitism and exclusivity. In reality, networks also include relationships based on fear, jealousy, animosity and suspicion.

Some have argued that the network concept is valid only in the context of formal modes of organising, suggesting that the metaphor of a 'circle' is more appropriate to describe the pattern of informal connections operating within communities (Giarchi, 2001). However, this distinction does not allow for the inherent complexities and blurring that typify many situations where formal organisations and informal webs of relationships coexist (Gilchrist, 2016).

Organisations, on the other hand, exercise control over jointly owned or managed resources through formal procedures and explicit decisions. They function through roles and regulations that exist independently of who might be occupying or implementing them. In contrast, networks operate through connections between specific individuals whose attitudes and actions shape interpersonal interactions and incorporate local conventions. Organisations use rules and protocols to coordinate activity. Networks use relationships that are active and are acknowledged to influence behaviour and change minds. They are more malleable, less hierarchical and therefore more responsive to unexpected shifts in the environment. Networks live within and around organisations, breaking through 'silo mentalities' by linking people in different departments and external bodies (Tett, 2015). Their informality may well improve an organisation's performance, providing a hidden resilience and flexibility, but they can also sabotage its democratic structure and mission, undermining authority, lowering standards and circumventing official procedures (Gilchrist, 2016).

These distinctions are summarised in Table 5.1, but are not always clear cut. They provide a rough guide as to whether a network or an

Table 5.1: Key differences between networks and organisations

Characteristic	Network	Organisation
Nature of connections	Interpersonal relationships	Formal procedures and lines of accountability
Membership	Fuzzy category, depends on ongoing participation and interaction	Clearly defined by affiliation, subscription, employment
Nodes	Individuals/organisational unit	Roles/posts/units/teams
Type of structure	Non-centralised web of connections	Usually bureaucratic arrangement, with central control from the top
Boundaries	Unclear, permeable; many boundary-spanning links	Defined and maintained, often through constitution or written protocols
Mode of interaction	Based on custom, personal history and mutual affinity	Rules and regulations
Basis of exchange	Trust and favours	Contracts and directives
Common bond	Shared values and interests	Agreed aims and objectives

organisation is the most appropriate term to describe an assemblage of people working together. This is not just a semantic issue, as we shall see later. Expectations are different for networks, and for many purposes they may not be the most suitable mode of organising. Yet people often choose to set up loose networks when a more formal structure would do the job better and more democratically. Sometimes both types are needed and what starts life as a network may deliberately be transformed or evolve into a formal organisation as its functions and environment change. Community development is often concerned with developing organisations and working to challenge the policies of institutions.

It has been suggested that network configurations reduce transaction costs (Williamson, 1975), primarily through bonds of trust that are said to minimise risk and enhance mutual commitment (Perrow, 1992; Boeck et al, 2006; Allen et al, 2014). But there are indeed costs associated with networks, usually absorbed within informal social and quasi-professional activities. These costs accumulate outside the organisation's normal accounting procedures through invisible and unaudited trading of resources, ideas and favours. Community workers, as individuals, often bear the hidden costs of networking through personal, 'out of hours' investment of time and emotion in relationships which benefit their paid work. In a network-type organisation, members are generally loosely connected through a variety of formal and informal linkages that enable them to share information or trade with one another.

Networks may themselves become organisations, through formalising constitutions, or they may spawn new organisations, creating structures for specific purposes while leaving the networking function intact. The transition to more formal structures is neither always universally desired nor even always feasible. It is vital to stay focused on the group's own goals and style, so organisation development is better understood as a process of evolution rather than controlled engineering or construction. Organisations do not have to be formal in order to be effective, although it helps if they are adequately funded (Gilchrist, 2016). Difficulties often arise where there is resistance or lack of clarity as to why a network needs to encumber itself with the constitutional trappings and formal accountabilities of a 'proper' organisation. Confusion over function can sometimes lead to networks being set up by external agents rather than emerging organically from participants' interests and interactions. Research into the benefits and limitations of non-governmental networks in the field of international development found that these worked best when donors were prepared to fund the processes of networking, rather than insisting that the network followed a normal project cycle. Those networks that evolved endogenously were more effective and more sustainable than those that had been instigated from outside or engineered from above (Liebler and Ferri, 2004).

For several years from the 1980s onwards within the voluntary and community sector the network form of organisation became the favoured alternative to hierarchy and competition, encapsulating (it was thought) egalitarian and democratic values often associated with the feminist and anarchist Left (Ward, 1973; Ferguson, 1984). Somewhat paradoxically, and despite acknowledged examples of elitism and secrecy, many working on the radical wing of community development embraced the network model wholeheartedly. During the 1980s a host of 'network-like' organisations appeared to displace (in name at least) the federations, councils, associations and similar multi-agency consortia that had previously brought together diverse groups. Networks were assumed to operate according to principles of collective decision making and mutual accountability rather than bureaucratic control. However, as Miller (2004, p 14) has observed:

> accountability is often messy in networks, not easily corresponding to conventional ideas of due process and

democracy. The qualification for inclusion in a network is enthusiasm and a willingness to work with others, but this can develop to a point where the people who are the most enthusiastic and most connected ... can dominate.

Patterns of power

Within both formal and informal arrangements it is impossible to ignore questions of relative power (Mayo and Taylor, 2001). In the early studies of organisation and decision making, the issue of power was seen as relevant only in conflict situations where there are competing interests. The zero-sum model, as it came to be known, tended to assume that there exists a fixed amount of power and that this is distributed across actors (individuals or organisations) who exercise influence or authority over others in order to secure an intended outcome or promote a particular interest (Weber, 1947). Lukes (1974) extended the debate around power by introducing a pernicious 'third dimension' which infiltrates the hearts and minds of 'ordinary' people to induce attitudes and practices that reinforce opinions and protect the interests of the elite or governing class.

Empowerment and participation combine cognitive and emotional processes to discover or define a shared problem and develop a collective solution (Damasio, 2006). Personal feelings and attitudes affect how people interact, and their willingness to work together (Hustedde and King, 2002; Hoggett, 2006, 2009). This can generate dilemmas for community workers who may find their professional accountabilities (in the shape of expectations from line managers and funders) at odds with their personal motivations or politics (Clarke et al, 2006; Hoggett et al, 2008).

Community representatives are similarly driven by a range of feelings, including idealism, loyalty, pleasure, vengeance and anger (Purdue, 2007). The emotions that flow through community networks are an important dimension of organising and empowerment (Flam and King, 2005), so community workers need to pay attention to the affective or emotional practices of community members as well as managing their own in order to alleviate the stresses and strains that accompany community leadership and participation in policy making (Wetherell, 2011; Anderson, 2013). Individuals use personal networks to raise their esteem, awareness and aspirations. Feelings of compassion, loyalty, admiration, love even, are often the driving force for many community and voluntary activities, but so too are the less positive emotions of pity, resentment, anger and fear, observed in the 'moral panics' that give rise to vigilante groups or campaigns against supposed local threats, for example in relation to suspected paedophiles, asylum seekers and migrant workers (Lewis, 2005; Hudson et al, 2007).

Several theories of power draw attention to its concealed aspects, such as Gaventa's power cube with its visible, hidden and invisible sides (Gaventa, 2006). Authority and power are usually associated with formal structures and styles. Indeed the adoption of formal constitutions and positions is often accompanied by grabs for power and legitimacy. They tend to favour those who already occupy or are accustomed to formal roles, and there have been numerous attempts over the years to dismantle or discredit formal systems in order to empower those who are excluded or marginalised by these. Communities that have experienced long-term systematic discrimination often need assistance in setting up their own organisations, as well as positive action strategies to challenge existing power blocs. If power is distributed across shifting systems of relationships and stakeholders, rather than embedded in the political or legal establishment, then strategies for the empowerment of disadvantaged groups require more fluid and decentralised forms of organisation. By acknowledging the diversity of constituent elements, networks channel information and energy to where they can influence decisions or affect the course of events, making things happen and exerting pressure towards (or against) different interests. Some such attempts are based on alternative ways of 'doing politics' through 'empowered spaces' for 'everyday talk' and more formalised deliberative democracy (see Parkinson and Mansbridge, 2012; Burrell, 2015). They include 'network-like' models for deliberation such as people's assemblies (Feldman, 2009), citizens' conventions and mini-publics that are designed for 'strategies that innovatively disrupt entrenched forms of bureaucratic governmental institutions'. There are also a plethora of online platforms for debate such as OpenDemocracy and Netivist that aim to galvanise individual action as well as mass mobilisations and petitions.

Power has elastic, effervescent qualities (Maffesoli, 1996). It may be facilitative and generative: a vital force for achieving cooperation and mutual benefit rather than dominance and exploitation. But networks can be selective and superior, enrolling members through bizarre systems of preferment and ritual, such as experienced by novice freemasons and frat clubs. The 'old boy' (and occasionally girl) networks, based on public schools and Oxbridge colleges, are said to exert a strong and enduring influence on opinion formers within British politics. Similarly, a ground-breaking study in Bangladesh using participatory research carried out a rudimentary form of network analysis to reveal a 'net' of powerful men and their followers who were systematically exploiting and abusing landless villagers, intercepting aid intended for the poorest families and subverting democratic and legal processes (BRAC, 1980). This network of the elite had not been visible previously to outside donors and government agents. It could be dismantled only by the combined efforts of villagers, aid workers and civil servants, 'lancing … a long-festering abscess' (Chambers, 1983, p 70).

Social networks channel power for collective ends by maintaining solidarity and allowing risk to be shared (Allen et al, 2014). Wheatley (2006) regards power as the 'capacity generated by relationships', which she sees as energy flowing through organisations, facilitated rather than controlled by those in positions of leadership. Women theorists in particular have asserted the positive aspects of power as a productive and enabling resource (for example, Elworthy, 1996). They have stressed the importance of building facilitative connections in order to initiate and manage organisational change (Kanter, 1983; Helgesen, 1990). As Florence, a rural health trainer in South Africa, recognised:

> I have learned not to under-estimate the strength of each woman, organisation and community…. Every woman is born with that power, it is not created by the [Western Cape] Network, but the Network enables women to use their power. (Womankind Worldwide, 2000, p 6)

Postmodernists have likewise emphasised the dispersed and dynamic nature of power (Foucault, 1977; Bauman, 2000). They focus on the micro-practices governing relations between people, and between people and institutions, arguing that power differentials within systems direct the flow of influence towards and against decisions. Foucault and other postmodernists join with Gramsci in examining the nature of dominant discourses, arguing that the prevailing ideologies that permeate society and mould 'common sense' are mediated through cultural as well as political ideas, permeating 'capillaries' of influence and dictating the parameters within which options are considered. This has profound implications for how communities are supported and challenged to question, learn and articulate their own thinking and interests (Ledwith, 2019). Postmodernism regards power as fluid, inherently ambiguous and multifaceted (Hindess, 1996). It affects the patterns of interaction in everyday life, influencing behaviour and thinking without recourse to explicit force or actual punishment.

Power relations are embedded in organisational cultures and personal behaviour to the extent that different dimensions of oppression become internalised in our personal and collective identities. Alternatively, the flow of information and commitment through networks generates synergy and can be seen as empowering, especially for those who have been deprived of opportunities to participate in decision making or collective activity. Deliberate and innovative methods are needed to connect these 'yet to be reached' or 'seldom heard' sections into mainstream opportunities for empowerment.

This articulation of power as flowing through a network of relationships has been further developed by Clegg (1989) in his 'circuits of power' metaphor. A networking approach to empowerment adopts a similar model of power, recognising that it can be positive, contextual and relational. Agency, the capacity to make things happen, is achieved by making connections so that power can flow to where it is most effective. Online technologies have taken this to new heights, extending reach and simplifying messages to develop what has been dubbed 'new power', harnessing the wisdom, energy and passions of crowds to create effective campaigns that thrive on participation, transparency and collaboration (Timms and Heimans, 2018). Examples include the #MeToo movement against sexual harassment and Wikipedia (Benkler, 2006).

Community development appears to have adopted, perhaps unwittingly, this postmodern approach to empowerment that reiterates a long-standing emphasis on processes of collective empowerment rather than formal institutions. Although community workers must avoid abusing the power of their professional role, they will inevitably apply their knowledge and skills to influence the opinions and behaviour of community members, and use their status and connections to change the policies and practices of institutions. As Shuftan explains, 'empowerment is not an outcome of a single event; it is a continuous process that enables people to understand, upgrade and use their capacity to better control and gain power over their own lives' (Shuftan, 1996, p 260). At one level, it could be said that it is factors in the social environment that empower (and oppress). Processes of empowerment might include increasing, improving and incorporating useful and positive connections into the routine interactions and habits of people's everyday lives. Networking practices within empowerment strategies can be used to enhance community credibility and influence within decision-making arenas. Empowerment is about self-help and collective organising. For the individual, networking is self-empowering because it reduces isolation, provides supportive mentoring and offers opportunities for personal learning and advancement. Almost by definition, empowerment is anti-oppressive and will often be resisted by those holding power because it involves challenging discrimination, prejudice and marginalisation. This was recognised by the anti-slavery campaigner Frederick Douglass, who declared that 'If there is no struggle, there is no progress ... power concedes nothing without a demand. It never did and it never will' (Douglass, 1857).

Conclusions

This point, echoing down the years, of persistent inequalities in how power is distributed and exercised, has important implications for how community workers promote and maintain community networks, making sure that the power of leaders and representatives is both earned and accountable. The 'circuits of power' metaphor helps us to see empowerment as altering the flow of power through connected series of events and decisions, operating through networks of relationships (see, for example, Gilchrist and Taylor, 1997). These reconnect people and power, thereby providing an important part of a community's capacity to implement viable and sustainable change strategies. By opening up experiences of oppression, exploitation and injustice to shared scrutiny, community networks encourage mutual responsibility and solidarity based on compassion and interdependence. The complex nature of power – its association with protecting elites as much as with promoting solidarity – presents networking strategies for community development with a dilemma that will be explored in following chapters.

QUESTIONS FOR REFLECTION AND DISCUSSION

◇ Has being involved in formal or informal networks supported your work or improved the capacity of communities you know to get things done?

◇ Map out a network that you are familiar with, paying close attention to any power dynamics and the positions of key actors.

6

Network functions

> The reason we form networks is because the benefits of a
> connected life outweigh the costs.
> Nicholas Christakis, Interview in *Wired: Business*, 2010

As we saw in earlier chapters, participation in community life holds
a number of advantages (as well as some drawbacks). This chapter
sets out how networks specifically perform useful functions that are
aligned with the purposes and principles of community development,
especially their ability to carry ideas, information and resources across
boundaries and to build meaningful relationships enabling people to
cooperate in addressing shared challenges.

Information procession and knowledge management

In some respects, networks can be regarded as informal knowledge
creation and management systems. They are usually non-hierarchical,
with a range of access points and a multitude of transmission routes.
This means that information can be obtained and transferred between
any number of different nodes without being monitored or censored.
This multiplexity is a major factor in the resilience of networks to
structural flaws, disruption or attempts to control the through-flow
of information.

Network-type structures are particularly useful in situations when
information is ambiguous or risky, since contradictions can be clarified
by turning to alternative sources for comparison and checking.
Dialogue and debate within networks transform information so that
it becomes intelligence (about the current situation) and knowledge
(about the wider context). This is vital for solving immediate problems
and for adapting to a changing world. Community connections are
like the neural networks made of axons and dendrites in the brain,
processing, integrating and transmitting information across linguistic
and cultural boundaries like some kind of supercomputer constantly
revising a shared but dispersed model of the world (Dunbar, 1996).

Conversation and peer learning

A huge amount of information and 'common sense' is communicated via informal networks, whether face-to-face or online, one to one or in open or closed groups. Conversations among friends, acquaintances, colleagues and neighbours convey rumour, opinion, local knowledge and news, allowing constant revisions to our understanding of the immediate and changing world in which we live (DiFonzo, 2008). The networks themselves become a repository of local intimate knowledge and 'gossip'. As Smith recognised:

> Experienced community development workers develop the art of 'jizz' over time and find it invaluable.... Gossip is among the most precious information in community work. (Smith, 1999, p 13)

Maintaining connections with different sources within and beyond the community allows a form of intelligence gathering, enabling people to gain access to advice, services and resources that they might not otherwise know about or be able to influence. Conversation is also a way of learning from different experiences, generating new ideas and insights. Networks can be used to suppress views that question prevailing assumptions and customs, but they are also the mechanisms by which subversive ideas circulate, gather momentum and finally surface to challenge the status quo (Laguerre, 1994). People use their informal networks to develop controversial or critical opinions, often initially through muted debates among known allies or conversations with strangers that allow them to reveal risky thoughts and rehearse arguments. The 'off-stage' nature of these discussions allows alternative versions of the world to be constructed and for a new consciousness to emerge.

As Alinsky noted, 'happenings become experiences when they are digested, when they are reflected upon, related to general patterns and synthesised' (Alinsky, 1972, p 69). The fact that much of this occurs in settings where formal accountability and scrutiny are minimal or non-existent allows such opportunities to explore ambiguity, contradictions and dissent. Knowledge dispersed through networks does not become 'thinner' but, rather, provides a collective wisdom that is empowering because it creates a 'people's praxis' based on direct experience and empathy (Rahman, 1993, p 80). Local knowledge emerges through processes of collective interpretation, iteration and induction and is the result of the learning generated by connected conversations and feedback within communities and organisations (MacLean and MacIntosh, 2003; Adams and Hess, 2006).

Community development work has tended to prioritise setting up formal organisations and groups, helping them to grow, evolve and occasionally dissolve. These often emerge from and are sustained by networks of volunteers, activists and professionals that are constantly changing. Community workers, therefore, need to understand how networks operate, what functions they perform for individuals and communities, and how they can be maintained. By talking together, comparing ideas, discussing common experiences and perhaps undertaking some kind of joint activity, people usually come to understand and trust one another. This lays the foundation for collective action. 'Dialogue becomes a horizontal relationship of mutual trust. Trust is established by dialogue; it cannot exist unless the words of both parties coincide with their actions' (Freire, 1972, p 64). Dialogue is often taken to mean a conversation between two parties, but this is a misinterpretation of the word's Greek origins, since 'dia' means 'through' (not two), and so a more authentic (and, in this context, appropriate) application is to see dialogue as a means to achieve understanding through words.

Informal networks are essential to processes of social change, especially those which open up access to new ideas or encourage incompatible views to be exposed (Humphries and Martin, 2000). This form of collective reflection encourages experimentation and the creation of new paradigms. Networks allow for a construction of 'reality', which, although subjective, is grounded in experience and able to stimulate new insights and transformative action (Ledwith, 1997).

A notion of the 'common good' emerges, based on a deeper wisdom derived from listening to, interpreting, comparing, reviewing and evaluating views from divergent sources (Robinson, 2004). As Bayley (1997, p 18) asserts:

> the most fundamental tenet of the community development approach is that the worker takes time to develop a real understanding of how things look from the standpoint of those with whom she is working, that is to understand the culture, the assumptions and the priorities of those she is seeking to help.

An important function of social networks is to convey meaning, which is filtered and refined through a series of 'nuanced asynchronous and asymmetric exchanges' between mutually interested parties (Stephenson, 2004, p 39). Informal and collective learning represents a potentially important route to empowerment because, as Schön (1990) and others have observed, learning often involves 'unlearning' the older, perhaps more dominant, ways of thinking.

Many forms of social and adult education acknowledge the importance of people learning from one another, and this is viewed as a core process of community integration and citizen empowerment (for example, Woodward, 2005; Mayo and Rooke, 2006). In their study of voluntary and community organisations, Elsdon et al (1995) highlight the learning that takes place within inter-organisational networks, often through chance conversations, involving personal interaction. They stress the importance of warm, caring, mutually supportive relationships that enable people to overcome barriers to learning and build their self-confidence. For many marginalised communities this is a necessary step along the road to collective action. Networks enable people to identify shared concerns for themselves, and to articulate the issues that they want to pursue either through participation in a broad partnership arrangement or through self-organisation and campaigning.

Cross-sectoral working

A primary function of networks is to facilitate boundary-spanning cooperation, coordination and communication. Using digital and online technologies, they can also operate outside some of the constraints of place and time. The value of lateral connections within and between organisations has been noted for some time. Decentralised networks, founded on norms and trust (rather than administrative edicts) have a particular advantage over formal organisations in what Emery and Trist (1965) termed 'turbulent environments'. By this they meant situations where there is rapid change and unpredictability. Benson (1975) took this one step further by introducing the idea of the 'inter-organisational network' needed to cope with changing conditions by being more responsive, more connected and more creative. Informal patterns of interdependency among organisations have been identified as an important source of stability and coherence within complex fields (Gilchrist, 2016).

Cross-cutting area-based forums provide opportunities to build bridging and linking social capital, creating relationships between people from different backgrounds and with different remits. However, inequalities in power and access must be addressed if such opportunities are not simply to become occasions for further disempowerment of community members, especially those from already marginalised groups. Partnerships represent an intermediate joint working arrangement, in which expectations are more likely to be formalised but also incorporate networking processes that need to be adequately resourced. Co-production can be seen as a way of renewing local or 'everyday' democracy by involving players from outside the public sector system in new forms of networked governance and 'community rights' that sit alongside traditional forms of social action and representative democracy (Barnes et al, 2004; Bentley, 2005; Davies and Spicer, 2015). While community–state partnerships enable coherent and efficient delivery of policy and services, they may also provide a 'creative response to austerity' (Bovaird et al, 2015).

Networked governance

Community development makes use of similar, but more open, methods of coalition building to challenge vested interests and empower communities by creating new forms of governance and communication channels based on 'social networks of trust' (Riley and Wakely, 2005). The bottom-up connections enable a 'capillary approach' that draws influence up from community levels to local partnerships and policy networks (Considine, 2003; Adamson and Bromiley, 2008). Skidmore et al (2006, p 50) assert that 'participants in governance will find it much easier to mobilise others and plug into their networks if the formal structures they inhabit are places where real power lies'.

More participative or 'network' forms of governance are being created that rely on multi-agency partnerships in which communities are strongly represented as stakeholders and local 'experts' (Stewart, 2000; Somerville, 2005; Kim, 2006). In Britain, this trend was typified by New Labour legislation and initiatives to promote active citizenship and community empowerment. Since 2010 subsequent administrations have similarly embraced themes of localism, social action and self-help, originally bundled together under the ill-fated Big Society wrapper (Scott, 2011; Ishkanian and Szreter, 2012), with added emphasis on volunteering and collective responsibility to sustain public services and local assets, while leaving neoliberal capitalism largely unscathed (De Angelis, 2012).

Partnerships formalise arrangements for joint ventures through the sharing of resources and responsibility between multiple stakeholders. Issues around public participation, power, trust and accountability are key to understanding and improving partnership working. Human relationships are critical to the effectiveness of partnerships, emerging from 'a complex reciprocal process' of working and learning together. Networks are often the precursors to these arrangements, and continue to be important in maintaining commitment, dealing with tensions and ensuring proper representation. Inclusive networks enable information and resources to be shared across group and organisational boundaries. They provide the means to compare, challenge and contradict different versions of the world, and in doing so to discover new ideas (Agranoff and McGuire, 2001).

Newman (2012) takes a more engaged stance, recognising that mostly people working at or across such interfaces have their own social and political goals, and reiterating the feminist argument that the 'personal is political'. Through a series of interviews with women involved in campaigning work, she explores how they operate as 'intermediaries' to negotiate the 'perverse alignments' flowing through 'spaces of power' to unlock opportunities that will enable cross-sectoral partnerships. Her analysis of their practice emphasises the relational nature of such alliances and the importance of shared values. She argues that 'sociability and identity are produced through networks, ideas and things, rather than membership of the shared space of belonging' (Newman, 2012, p 40), echoing Cresswell's (2010) notions of constellations of mobility and representation. Intermediaries have much in common with 'meta-networkers' (as developed in Chapter 8), using their position in these fluid governance arrangements to broker and translate between sometimes unlikely partners.

People in these roles often use their intuition and existing contracts, while seizing serendipitous or convivial moments to make connections that may result in unexpected but fortuitous coalitions between policy makers, activists and professional service providers. Newman calls this border or edge work, suggesting that it is both generative and gendered (Newman, 2012, p 130), while also acknowledging power relations structured by social and institutional forces. The women in her study were neither inside nor outside, but tended to straddle across organisational boundaries using their accumulated knowledge and reputation to assemble new associations and cultivate alternative practices and policies. Working in these ambiguous, sometimes liminal spaces involves juggling multiple identities and allegiances. It can create an ambivalent strain and discomfort for the individual worker in managing contradictions and antagonisms between various positions in the networks and complex affective practices (cf Hoggett, 2000; Wetherell, 2011).

Trust is a key ingredient of such arrangements, although it can be an ephemeral and disarming virtue, evoked and revoked to suit the continuing power of professionals. In their study of community leadership, Purdue et al (2000) observed that feelings of trust and empowerment are linked, but that the power dynamics of the partnerships often oblige community representatives to trust the authorities because they have no sanctions and relatively limited access to independent technical expertise. The legitimacy of community representatives is sometimes questioned when they challenge prevailing assumptions and aims. This can lead to resentment and withdrawal of cooperation from some partners.

Inclusive and accountable processes

Communities affected by proposals have a right to be influential, not merely involved, and this means making empowerment a practical as well as political reality, engaging with those who are most alienated or angry, as well as the 'active citizens' who have sufficient time, confidence and skills to become community representatives (Fraser, 2005; Shaw, 2008). Networking, using proactive and explicit targeting of the most disaffected and marginalised, enables shrouded, often dissenting, views to emerge and allows for new knowledge, drawn from lived experience, to inform the dialogue (Adams and Hess, 2006). For communities to feel genuinely represented and empowered in these situations, they need to be able to trust their representatives and to know that these in turn are trusted within the partnership structure (Lowndes and Sullivan, 2004). Networking contributes to this by building mutual commitment, generating trust and enabling accountability (Gilchrist, 2006a). Without community networks actively supporting local leadership and governance, state and market forces become much more significant in regulating social behaviour because the voices of users, residents or other potential partners/ beneficiaries are distorted or suppressed altogether.

Face-to-face interactions are vital. Networking within and across the sectors provides an effective means of building new forms of trust and accountability. Accountability issues arise whenever people are engaged in joint endeavours and permitted to act with discretion within a broad framework of agreed aims. This takes three forms:

- giving an account of what was done and why;
- taking into account the interests of different stakeholders; and
- accounting for the use of resources, especially finances.

In formal terms, accountability operates through systems of contracts, audits, scrutiny exercises and complaints procedures in ways that are usually transparent and quantifiable. Face-to-face interactions tend to increase 'felt' accountability, with a consequent partiality towards familiar (and presumably liked) stakeholders. In this respect, informal networks constitute covert and irregular policy communities, searching out opportunities to influence or subvert formal decisions (Laguerre, 1994). Voluntary organisations are particularly prone to these influences, tending to be accountable to several constituencies, including a range of funders and users. Without strong community networks holding leaders to account and providing them with support, there is a high risk of power tarnishing individual motives and integrity. Arrangements are needed that place a 'premium on transparency and communication' in order to manage the multiplicity and diversity of expectations (Taylor, 1996, p 62).

An understanding of how networks operate within and between organisations is essential when it comes to helping communities to develop their own ideas and infrastructure. Many voluntary organisations and community groups evolve to meet a perceived need within communities. Networks provide the conditions from which these initiatives spring. 'Well-connected' communities (characterised as a rich web of relationships between established voluntary associations, community groups, forums, links to external bodies and robust informal networking opportunities) are well placed and well equipped to make a major contribution to multi-agency developments around many issues and at all levels. This is repeatedly recognised in the British government's reviews and strategies for strengthening of civil society, which acknowledge 'connectivity' as an important aspect of community and civic strength (Office of the Third Sector, 2007; Cabinet Office, 2018).

Discussion is a very important aspect of 'joined-up' working, where organisations with quite different cultures and traditions are expected to collaborate around a set of objectives, often externally set. This takes time. Multi-agency organisations need common aims and priorities if they are to achieve their purposes. Informal networks often provide the spaces for 'behind the scenes' interaction that can ease tensions, enhance understanding and consolidate mutual commitment. The informality of these unrecorded conversations allows people to express their reservations, explore 'wild' suggestions and admit that they might be having problems with the 'bigger picture'.

Collective organising

Marwell and Oliver (1993) suggest that in the initial stages of developing collective activities, organisers should use their social ties to contact people who are most likely to participate, ensuring that a threshold for collective action is achieved as speedily as possible. Organisers with many 'weak ties' in their networks are able to target, canvass and recruit potential contributors across many organisations and social groups. These boundary-spanning links are relatively cheap forms of communication, but highly effective in contacting sympathetic allies and mobilising resources. Knowledge about the interdependencies and connections among the network members is vital in making good use of the network as a communications system, otherwise the flow of information might be disrupted by channels that have deteriorated or become dysfunctional because people have fallen out or lost touch with one another.

Effective organising requires a balance between the costs of maintaining networks (time, effort, money or other resources) and the expected gains (Gray, 2003). Each individual makes their own micro-calculations about how they can contribute, but this is influenced by the perceived decisions and behaviour of those around them. Networking is an example of optimising behaviour such that the least amount of effort is expended for the most gain (Zipf, 1965). Marwell and Oliver (1993) emphasise the role of 'entrepreneurs', who may come from outside the community of interest and disproportionately absorb the costs of organising, perhaps for political or moral reasons. These individuals often have useful assets and talents to offer and can act as brokers or catalysts to get things started. They tend to be well connected with other resourceful or influential people.

In this respect, it would appear that extensive and diverse networks are more advantageous than overlapping, close-knit sets of similar people bound by strong ties and shared outlooks. Individuals who are linked, but slightly peripheral, to several distinct networks are more likely to provide the 'bridging mechanisms' that allow for cross-fertilisation of ideas and create the conditions for creative thinking. This is often the role played by community workers or community leaders, and it can prove problematic for those individuals in situations where there are many tensions and differences.

Developing community action

Networks can be used for empowerment by mobilising a 'critical mass' of allies for achieving change, often using collective action strategies. It is well known within community development that people tend to become involved in community activities or to join a local organisation if they already know someone involved or are persuaded through face-to-face contact or a personal invitation. It takes a lot of courage or sheer desperation for someone to come along to an event without a prior introduction or conversation. A poster announcement or leaflet invitation is rarely sufficient, while information provided via websites is usually too remote and impersonal to support sustained participation. However, social media announcements seem to carry greater weight, as illustrated by participants in recent research (quoted in Harris and McCabe, 2017b, p 29):

> 'The presence of some information on Facebook seems to make something more real and definite to people, more than just a poster or newsletter – a kind of authenticity.'

> 'It's an endorsement of something as real – if it's on Facebook it's happening. People would be less inclined to engage with something if it didn't exist on Facebook.'

Generally, people enter into collective arrangements because they are already linked in some way with others involved. A connection exists which persuades them that the benefits of participation are likely to outweigh the costs. Credit unions and micro-loan schemes operate in this way, although they require meticulous administration as well. The element of risk can be countered or mitigated through judicious networking to identify reliable allies and reach a modicum of consensus. Despite the risks of unreciprocated contributions, loss of independence and expenditure of time and effort in meetings or social events, involvement in networks generally helps to reduce isolation and increase credibility. The networking approach to community development helps people to develop useful relationships and find common cause. In addition to psychological factors, local norms and conventions play an important role in creating the conditions for effective collective action (Chanan, 1992).

Social networks act as informal communication channels, engender a sense of shared purpose and are used to recruit for community-based organisations (Milofsky, 1987). They offer cost-effective means of achieving a 'critical mass' of support, which encourages wider participation. Four key factors appear to influence people's readiness to contribute to a collective initiative:

- the motivation of potential participants;
- the availability of resources;
- ease of communication; and
- social processes of interaction.

Collective empowerment

Empowerment is achieved through learning and collective organising. It has been defined as enhancing people's capacity to influence the decisions that affect their lives and is a central principle of community development. In this context, community development is primarily concerned with improving the skills, knowledge, confidence and organisational capacity within communities so that they can engage more effectively with decision-making bodies, such as public authorities and strategic partnerships. Empowerment processes require a redistribution of power, and therefore involve changes in the culture of mainstream institutions so that these become more transparent, more responsive and less preoccupied with maintaining control. Challenging the sometimes oppressive power of institutions is a crucial aspect of community development, as is changing the flow of power through organisations and communities themselves. Collective action is empowering in its own right because it enables people without much influence to assert their interests in decision making. Networks contribute to empowerment on a psychological level by enabling people to compare their experiences, learn from each other's successes and develop greater awareness of the wider politics of inequality.

As we saw in Chapter 3, radical community workers have long been aware of the dispersed nature of power and have seen their central task as shifting the balance of power within society by helping people to make connections with others who share their oppression or predicament. Empowerment is not an 'all-or-nothing' strategy involving opposition and conflict. It can be considered as a continuous process of increasing capacity to influence decision making, of connecting people with power. The community organising model takes this approach, undertaking a power analysis in order to identify the power holders and devise a strategy for contesting the legitimacy of existing power dynamics (Beck and Purcell, 2013; Craig, 2017).

A networking approach to community development seeks to increase influence primarily through processes of connection, negotiation and persuasion. It strives to manoeuvre stakeholders into a position of saying 'yes' as a group, even if they start as adversaries (Goldstein et al, 2008). Strategies using 'incremental commitment' gradually build relationships through increasing levels of emotional and other forms of investment (Cialdini, 1993). In this model, empowerment occurs by reconfiguring relationships and patterns of influence, rather than 'seizing power' (Hothi et al, 2008).

Box 6.1: FEMNET: African women networking for empowerment

FEMNET is a women's rights network, set up in 1988 and formally titled the African Women's Development and Communication Network. It is based in Nairobi and connects a membership of 'pan-African' feminists stretching across five regions of Africa. It aims to tackle all forms of gender-based injustices, taking up issues around violence against women and girls, and sexual and reproductive health. It uses multiple communication channels to share information and advocate for women's leadership and empowerment.

FEMNET is growing a women's movement, with capacity-building projects supported through funding by international non-governmental organisations such as Womankind Worldwide. Currently it claims 500 member organisations and is building a powerful collective foundation to challenge patriarchal traditions, such as female genital mutilation. In addition, FEMNET coordinates strategic efforts, such as the gaining of African state signatories to the Convention on the Elimination of All Forms of Discrimination against Women and Girls and convening continent-wide conferences.

See: https://femnet.org/about-us/

Organisation development is an important strand of community development, and community workers frequently find themselves assisting in the creation, management and occasionally the demise of formal structures, including partnerships. What has been less recognised is the role played by community workers in supporting and managing informal networks that are capable of promoting both autonomy and solidarity.

Alliances and social movements

Networks provide the foundation and 'life-blood' for a variety of multi-agency organisations, ranging from formal consortia with specific remits set out in a constitution or memorandum, through open forums, to the most flexible of informal alliances. All of these are important vehicles for developing collaborative action and are usually based more on faith and trust than on explicit rules. At a collective level, networks help people to find allies and build organisations to promote their views within and outside the decision-making arena. This can be used to develop internal problem-solving strategies or to assert a particular viewpoint. Networks often underpin techniques for self-organisation among populations which are scattered, isolated or oppressed (Fujimoto, 1992). Terrorists and insurgents organise as networks of cells, and may have widespread links into other networks fighting different causes (Gunaratne, 2005; Riedel, 2008; Atran, 2011). Political activists will be familiar with the use of caucusing to influence and mobilise others to support a particular position or faction. Communities are the 'incubators' of collective activity, with social networks acting as 'mobilising devices' (Tarrow, 2011). It is useful to cultivate links beyond the immediate community, building alliances with individuals and organisations that have greater access to power and resources.

Coalitions and social movements

Social movement theories have recognised the crucial role of informal networks in developing and sustaining involvement in mass political activity (Klandermans, 1997; Tarrow, 2005). Research on social movements reveals that networks are informally maintained and continue to exert influence even when they appear to be dormant (Melucci, 1996). There is a growing recognition of the micro-social processes of political and collective action: the interactions, the dialogue and the emotional ties between participants (Ray et al, 2003). The alliances that emerge need to be flexible and robust so that they can accommodate the diversity of experience and values that motivate people, even on an international scale (Bunch with Antrobus et al, 2001; Miller, 2004). This breadth of spirit and the colourful 'rainbow' image of such coalitions provide a model for collective organising that values diversity, promotes solidarity and supports challenging interactions.

Coalitions represent temporary, tactical arrangements through which disparate actors combine forces in order to achieve a goal that benefits each of them or fends off an external threat. They are generally semi-formal, ad hoc arrangements whereby separate agencies coordinate their activities in order to share resources and operate better in an uncertain environment (Scott, 1992). As Boissevain (1974) asserted, coalitions tend to emerge from networks of 'friends of friends', including the tangle of loose associations that characterise neighbourhoods or interest communities. A coalition might be built in response to events, forming a pragmatic and informal 'action-set', or it might be the basis for a full-blown national campaign (Mogus and Liacas, 2016). Its aims will generally be focused on achieving a limited goal, such as winning a policy decision, organising an event, defending or obtaining a common asset. Once the coalition has achieved its purpose it may either dissolve or transform itself into a more structured organisation that could take on the management of a service, a building or another more permanent project.

Relational organising

In the US, Kris Rondeau has developed an alternative model for trade union activity and negotiation that uses this approach, known as relational organising. She describes her methods as 'building a community of workers' and has been remarkably successful in negotiating advantageous deals for union members (Hoerr, 1993; Cobble, 2004). Relational organising is based on the principle of 'conversation leading to action' and is used extensively by the broad-based organising movement. Formal organisations are important, but they are not the only means of collective empowerment. The 'new' political movements have consistently stressed their fluid, diverse and organic nature. In contrast to more traditional social movements (such as the trades unions or early tenants' organisations) they might be described as networks of networks, in that they are more flexible, avoid central control mechanisms and seem content to operate with high levels of autonomy and low formal accountability. Campaigners 'do their own thing' within a broad set of political goals, with activities loosely but effectively coordinated, often via the internet, establishing what Tayebi (2013, p 89) has termed a form of non-localised 'communihood', which he refers to as 'the context for human and social life in the twenty-first century that provides opportunities for active citizenship and local activists to improve the quality of life'.

Since the beginning of this century, protest movements have increasingly used online apps and information technology, such as WhatsApp, Short Message Service (SMS) and Facebook, to build alliances and mobilise for demonstrations and direct actions, apparently without the need for formal leaders or organising committees. The use of social media has changed political organising significantly, enabling actions to be arranged more efficiently, whether at global (Castells, 2001; Edwards and Gaventa, 2001; Mayo, 2005; Tarrow, 2005) or local levels (Hampton, 2003, 2007), or both at once, a phenomenon that has been termed 'glocalisation' (Wellman, 2002). E-petitions and websites such as 38 Degrees and Avaaz are used to mobilise opinion on a worldwide basis, galvanising thousands, possibly millions, of people to express their views on a huge variety of issues.

Managing differences

Networks within communities, among people carrying out their normal, everyday activities, are also a vital source of bridging social capital and community cohesion. Working within and between diverse communities in ways that simultaneously honour different cultures and challenge inequalities can be a complicated process. The concept of community should be able to encompass and express both variety and unity, but in reality communal identities often underpin a tendency to segregate and promote narrow, rather inward-facing loyalties. Inter-faith organisations in Britain have been effective in bringing together people of different religions for joint activities, events and forums that have increased social capital as well as providing important opportunities for sharing ideas and resources (Furbey et al, 2006; Dinham et al, 2009; Dinham, 2012).

Networks are generally better able to accommodate divergence and dissent, rather than attempting to impose either unity in action or a spurious (and often fragile) consensus. Networks are particularly adept at managing contradiction and are useful organisational tools for promoting the kind of meaningful interaction that seeds genuine understanding and integration. This is true for organisations as well as individuals. Diversity challenges dogma and orthodoxy by generating alternatives, but it can also create fault-lines within society that erode social capital (Briggs, 1997; Putnam, 2007).

Cross-community networks offer a means of stabilising 'turbulent' environments and dealing with intercommunal or sectarian antagonisms. Conflicts often arise because people want to use communal space for apparently incompatible purposes. Informal networks can be used to foster a 'democratic and permissive culture' in communities and organisations, creating 'the capacity to contain conflicts without being exploded apart by them' (Jeffers et al, 1996, p 123). Community workers frequently operate in situations characterised by simmering tensions, especially when they are helping communities to challenge poverty and discrimination. The 'outsider' can contribute by coordinating and facilitating such interactions, acting as a 'weak tie', helping people to communicate directly and interpreting when things get awkward (Ryder, 2017).

Box 6.2: Places of welcome

There is an expanding network of designated 'places of welcome' across the UK, run by local community groups who want to encourage neighbourliness and a sense of belonging, especially for people who feel isolated or newly arrived in their areas. Each is unique, but they share a commitment to inviting people into a friendly space for a chat and free cup of tea. They take place in accessible buildings such as libraries, churches, mosques, temples and community centres.

Activities are available that encourage people to share interests and skills, but the main point is to listen, and to provide information and help for people to navigate the community and build relationships.

See: www.near-neighbours.org.uk/places-of-welcome

The networks of refugees and asylum seekers are crucial to ensuring their successful settlement (Temple, 2005; Ager and Strang, 2008; Phillimore et al, 2010; Strang and Quinn, 2014). Bridging connections and 'spaces of encounter' are useful for encouraging integration, as well as enabling them to access the advice and support they need from mainstream services (Navarro, 2006; Kindler et al, 2015). Gilchrist (2004, p 7) developed a model of cohesion which referred to 'a collective ability to manage the shifting array of tensions and disagreements among diverse communities'. An infrastructure of informal networks based on 'meaningful interaction' and tolerant understanding, underpinned by an equitable distribution of opportunities, material resources and residential stability, helps to create this capacity and should result eventually in mutual respect and cooperative solidarity (Hudson et al, 2007; Somerville, 2009). Research by Harris and Young indicates that 'bridge-building activities' between different ethnic and religious communities at the grassroots level are often facilitated by remarkable individuals, working through community organisations to organise social, educational, sports and cultural initiatives (Harris and Young, 2009). Community development can both support these individuals and link them with others to establish a more strategic approach that nurtures mutual respect and finds ways of valuing a dynamic mixture of multifaceted and hyper-connected social identities (Fanshawe and Sriskandarajah, 2010; Cantle, 2012; Foresight Future Identities, 2013).

Networks can help to anticipate and defuse tensions before they become full-blown conflicts. Amin suggests that in multi-ethnic societies intercommunity relations would benefit from 'the habit of interaction' in places where people relate on a day-to-day basis, such as clubs, schools and workplaces (Amin, 2002, p 11). The inevitable 'prosaic negotiations' in these supposedly neutral spaces, if sensitively handled, might serve to tackle ignorance, dogma and prejudice, thus establishing a foundation of understanding and empathy for acknowledging and adjusting to differences (Lownsbrough and Beunderman, 2007). This could involve managing or engineering live, dynamic interactions through 'banal encounters' in everyday life (Lowndes et al, 2006). The relative informality of networks enables contrasting cultures and perspectives to be explored without them necessarily becoming confrontational, and where there is opposition, positive experiences of working together, and of finding consensus in the past, make it more likely that solutions or compromises can be negotiated (Gilchrist, 1998a).

Discussion

Community development values and methods are important in managing the overall web of connections to promote empowerment and support participation. The primary function of the professional community worker is to establish and nurture the cross-boundary connections to be found among the 'weak ties' and linking capital of community and inter-organisational networks. Networks tend to be organic and complex. Unlike organisations, they cannot be established, controlled or moulded for a particular purpose. The connections grow and wither away according to their usefulness, rather like routes across a natural landscape (Finnegan, 1989). In this sense, community workers operate as social engineers, using relationships and inter-organisational links to carve out new channels, construct pathways, cut away the undergrowth, erect bridges and occasionally tunnel into the depths of seemingly impenetrable institutions. Working to alter the flow of influence and information through these networks opens up access to resources and contributes to a redistribution of power.

In many ways, networks are strange and problematic vehicles for mobilising resources for collective action. Network features, notably their flexibility and informality, are an advantage when working in uncertain conditions with multiple actors. But inevitably they reflect people's proximity, power and personal preferences. Uneven and homophilic patterns of connectivity are held together through blurred boundaries and a ragged mutuality. This inevitably leads to divisions and inequalities. Networks can be exclusive, and this poses challenges for anyone working with community development values trying to champion participative democracy and inclusive processes. Community work posts are often located at the margins of organisations and have a special concern with edges and barriers (Williams, 2002). Vital and difficult work takes place across interfaces, between partners and between different sections of the community. Community workers support and facilitate networks that connect people who might otherwise find neither reason nor means to interact. The patterns of power within networks naturally reflect the social and economic environment, so community workers have a key responsibility in making sure that the flow of resources and influence through networks is as egalitarian and democratic as possible.

Conclusions

The evidence presented in this chapter has indicated just how important networks are in our daily lives and in regulating society as a whole. They seem such a natural part of life that it would be easy to imagine that networks just happen without any particular effort or thought. However, a few minutes' reflection on how we sustain and shape our own networks reveals that time and attention are needed to keep certain links intact. We probably invest most in those connections that are useful or bring pleasure, especially when social media can make routine network maintenance an easy habit. Life events, such as births, marriages and deaths, are important occasions for reinforcing family ties and expressing our commitment to friends. Cultural or religious celebrations present opportunities for initiating and maintaining friendly relations with colleagues, neighbours and members of our community through the exchange of greetings and gifts, often accompanied by updates on personal news. Studies of organisations found that the high-performing individuals were notable not for their individual expertise but for their extensive and diverse personal networks used to channel resources and influence, thereby generating 'hidden power' for those well-connected people (Cross and Parker, 2004). It is through such informal interactions that these mutual loyalties and reciprocal exchanges develop. This can benefit some, while disadvantaging others who have equal merit and potential. So, what do people do that makes them 'well connected' and therefore highly effective within and beyond their communities? The activities that are used to do this can be grouped under the generic term of networking, which will be the focus of the next two chapters.

QUESTIONS FOR REFLECTION AND DISCUSSION

✧ What is the pattern of your connections and how might you change this to become more effective?

✧ Think about your own involvement in community activities and identify how networks have 'added value'.

✧ How have networks helped in organising events or joint actions?

✧ Review the last three months of your work or life to identify the contacts and connections that you have actively maintained. Which networks have been most important to you?

7

Networking principles and practices

> To understand is, as ever, to put choice in place of chance.
> Charles Handy, *Understanding voluntary organisations*,
> 1988, p 113

Networking involves the creation, maintenance and use of links and relationships between individuals and/or organisations. Networking itself is a neutral tool: it can be used for a variety of purposes – selfish, political, altruistic – or simply to get things done. Networking for community development is obviously influenced by key values around equality, empowerment and participation. It may also seem a popular, albeit mildly manipulative, means of gaining personal and political advancement.

The evidence used in this and the following chapters was mainly gathered from my doctoral research, which included a case study of the coordination of the Bristol Festival Against Racism (Gilchrist, 1994) and a Panel Study involving 11 community workers. Over a two-year period in the later 1990s they were asked about their involvement in networks and encouraged to reflect on their own experience. In particular, the enquiry aimed to unpack the principles and processes of networking to examine how this contributed to their work and what made them 'good' networkers. The initials after each quote refer to the panellists, all of whom were happy to have their identity revealed in the acknowledgements. (For details of research methodology, see Gilchrist, 2001.) This evidence is supplemented in this edition with observations and insights from my own practice and more recent research in this field, notably projects investigating the habits, profiles and practices of 'change-makers' (Social Change Project, 2018) and smart urban intermediaries (Durose et al, 2016; www.smart-urban-intermediaries.com).

Networking is something that most people do in their everyday lives, mostly without consciously thinking about their behaviour or motives. It encompasses the processes of developing and nurturing links with a selection of people through work, volunteering and in the course of neighbourly, social or leisure activities. Since this book is about community development, it is not primarily concerned with the relationships that constitute our family and friendship networks, although of course there is some overlap. The focus, rather, is on connections with colleagues, neighbours and the people we know through a variety of activities and whom we regard as members of our different communities. Some of these may be no more than 'familiar strangers' or nodding acquaintances (Milgram, 1977; Morgan, 2009). Others may be people we chat to while 'out and about', or at a club, but whom we would not necessarily invite into our homes. Others again we may know because of their role in an organisation that is significant in our lives.

Relationships constitute more than mere contacts or connections. They have an emotional content, sustaining people in their jobs and enabling them to undertake specific tasks by providing access to vital resources, knowledge and influence, which might not otherwise be available. To be effective, these relationships must be authentic and reliable. For community development, interpersonal relationships within communities and between organisations need to be established and maintained in ways that contribute to the overall work programme of individual workers or agencies. The networking approach advocated here requires that community workers have a good understanding of how networks function and how they can be sustained. Community workers facilitate these processes by finding links, creating opportunities for shared activities and encouraging dialogue across apparent boundaries so that even the most disenfranchised community members can be included (Stephenson, 2007).

Key aspects of networking that are relevant to relationship formation include modes of communication, building trust and managing diversity. This chapter and the next consider how we use connections to:

- give and receive support;
- obtain and share resources;
- influence the behaviour and attitudes of those around us; and
- anticipate and deal with conflicts.

What makes a good networker?

A major theme of this book is the skilled and strategic nature of networking. Like other aspects of community development it may involve planning, implementation and evaluation. Preliminary research and preparation might be undertaken even before the initial contact, for example, making a conscious decision about whether to attend particular events on the basis of the likely participants. The community workers on the research panel reported that they scanned attendance lists for conferences to identify useful contacts and used their knowledge to decide where to sit or which workshops to attend so that opportunities for informal conversations might arise. They would consider how to present themselves (protocol, dress codes, use of jargon) and generally how to manage that crucial first impression. Clearly this needs sensitive judgements about other people's expectations or about what circumstances dictate as 'appropriate' behaviour.

Non-verbal communication provides important clues about other people's intentions and emotions. For example, an unknown colleague at a conference might be approached because they 'looked interesting', held a certain position or reacted in a particular way that caught the attention, such as laughing at something that had been said or making eye contact. The ensuing interaction fulfils at least three simultaneous functions: to establish rapport, to gain information about the other and to impart information about oneself. The conversation can be fairly casual, tends to be 'off the record' and often takes place in an informal or 'off-stage' setting, such as during a refreshment break or while travelling. Networking often exploits opportunities that are incidental but a necessary adjunct to the 'main event'. Such interactions can be used to seek out common connections and may involve a far-ranging series of conversational leads, including disclosure of personal matters:

> 'What I tend to do is try and ask about the person, try and find out a bit about them and ask about their work or find something to talk about which perhaps isn't related to work, find some sort of common point that we could talk about.' (TD)

The panellists felt that they generally adopted an informal style, without being or appearing casual. They engaged people in conversations around their likely interests, pitching and moderating their language accordingly, and used humour to put people at ease or when expressing a slightly ambivalent or unorthodox position. There was a strong sense that networking needed to involve convivial experiences, since most such interactions would be voluntary.

Panellists identified interpersonal skills as important and considered themselves as highly proficient in one-to-one interactions, where they referred to counselling-type techniques such as listening and clarifying, as well as in group situations. Good networking involves sophisticated interpretations of individual conduct and group dynamics. It sometimes means intervening in situations to shape or open up interactions that are being distorted or blocked for one reason or another. Some of the relationships maintained might not be selected consciously, but develop anyway through reciprocal attention and care. Panellists made sure that they stayed in touch with certain colleagues at a personal level, even where the connection was predominantly work related. This included 'catch-up' phone calls, making time in conversations to share personal news and views, marking significant life events and generally arranging social time together:

> 'I would offer help and support, would sort of make some space to have a bit of a personal chat as well as a kind of work chat, so like "How are you? How's life? How's bla bla bla?" and then "Oh well then so what's this about?", or at the end of the conversation after we dealt with the business, you sort of say "Well, how are things going for you then?"' (FB)

Networking requires an ability to operate appropriately in different organisational and cultural settings, using the agility and adaptive capacities of a chameleon (Trevillion, 1999). Good networkers need to be able to interpret and transmit information across boundaries, directing it in appropriate formats to where it might be useful. Flexibility and informality appear to be significant qualities – an important point for people accustomed to working in bureaucratic environments (Gilchrist, 2016). What seemed to characterise people's aptitude for networking was not so much specific tactics but the versatility with which people were able to use them to develop their connections with a wide range of people. Good networkers are able to communicate effectively in a variety of modes, using a broad repertoire of communication styles ranging from formal report writing right through to the subtleties of cross-cultural body language.

Through networking, the community worker finds out about local concerns and initiatives, hears about developments through informal chats and is able to pass this information on to others. People's willingness to engage in conversation is affected by a number of factors, not least whether they like and trust the other person. Networking allows people to shift between roles while maintaining a clear identity and sound ideological base. The panellists were convinced that their ability to form relationships was about being 'straightforward', neither having nor colluding with 'hidden agendas'. They felt that others saw them as honest, trustworthy, reliable and sincere. They found that people confided in them readily and seemed to respect their advice. They described themselves as approachable, using words like 'popular', 'charming', 'sociable', 'extrovert' and 'comfortable'. The community workers in the Panel Study were able to identify personal qualities that they felt enhanced their networking. These attributes can be clustered according to Table 7.1.

Personality traits seem to have a significant impact on networking ability. This includes a commitment to perceive and value the whole person, showing interest, empathy and attention. Remembering personal details about individuals and their families, and making genuine efforts to understand different points of view, helps to build respect within a relationship. Good networkers make a positive contribution at a psychological as well as a practical level. Being optimistic and reliable helps to maintain morale, while following through on offers and commitments is vital to sustaining relationships because it demonstrates trustworthiness. A good networker is oriented towards other individuals, seeks affiliations but values autonomy, is non-deferential and tends to be less tolerant of formal organisational constraints.

In community development, effective networkers exhibit many of the attributes that predict transformational leadership: self-esteem, consideration for others and intuitive thinking. They provide leadership and show entrepreneurial flair, but without (apparently) the drive for personal ambition or profit. Networkers need to be able and willing to defy conventions, break bureaucratic rules, operate effectively in unfamiliar (social) territory and establish personal connections swiftly and smoothly. Informal networking usually takes place 'behind the scenes', making contacts and giving subtle encouragement in order to manoeuvre others into the limelight or into positions of influence. It is unusual to claim credit for such interventions and, consequently, the value of this work has often been overlooked.

Table 7.1: Networking qualities

Affability	Warmth, compassion, empathy, humanity, gregariousness, responsiveness, attentiveness
Integrity	Self-awareness, trustworthiness, reliability, realism, honesty, openness in dealings with others, respect for confidentiality
Audacity	Relishing of change and innovation, preparedness to challenge authority, take risks and break rules
Adaptability	Tolerance of differences, enjoying cultural diversity, flexibility, non-judgement, openness to criticism
Tenacity	Patience, persistence, being comfortable with uncertainty and stress

Establishing contact and forming relationships

Not everyone is capable of managing large social networks and not everyone wants to. There are costs to offset against the benefits and some people are more adroit at maintaining this balance. Relationships are sustained through opportunity, common interests and social skills. The range and nature of social interactions are affected by a number of factors, including class, gender, life roles and ethnicity. Non-family relationships progress through various stages, passing from initial acquaintance through to any number of potential endings. People adopt different strategies to express and consolidate affinity and acquire the life skills involved in managing social interaction. In extensive studies of relationship formation, Duck (2007) demonstrated the importance of communication in regulating the social processes of adaptation and exchange. The transition from acquaintanceship to friendship involves strategic use of self-disclosure, sharing information about oneself and testing out likely alignments (Fehr, 1996). The significance of 'everyday chit-chat' lies in the processes of mutual discovery and bonding, through which credibility is established, attitudes are explored and uncertainties about the 'other' are reduced until those involved feel that they know each other and have a certain sense of obligation.

Generally relationships move through different phases while remaining balanced for reciprocity. Different abilities are needed to manage relationships at various points. People recognise and take advantage of opportunities to form relationships and use strategies for encouraging likeable or useful people into their personal ambit. They also deploy social skills to maintain and repair relationships during periods of conflict or adversity. Good networking requires self-awareness, strategies for self-presentation and skills in establishing rapport in a range of situations.

While networking techniques are usually conscious (identifying useful connections, responding to gaps in the web and so on), the actual processes of building relationships should ideally be emotionally authentic, otherwise the links are perceived as ingratiating and worthless. Non-verbal cues are crucial, especially in the initial stages. Face-to-face interaction allows communication of emotional signals through body language, such as grins, tones of voice, shrugs and posture. Good networkers will pay close attention to the paralinguistic dynamics of meetings and group interactions:

'Why is it I can go into some situations and the vibes tell me to be cautious? Nobody's really said anything, nobody's done anything to make me think that, but there's just a look, an action … and you just think be steady in this situation.' (LM)

Although they are more time consuming, face-to-face meetings featured strongly in panellists' descriptions of networking. These seemed to accelerate and enhance the development of personal relationships and commitments. Direct encounters often demand one's full attention and this usually makes the connection more memorable:

'I think that all those things happen at the first meeting. It's almost inevitable that we'll have made a relationship and sometimes that's far more important than the actual business.' (KT)

Non-verbal communication was regarded as important in consolidating relationships and interpreting responses:

'You're talking about whether or not people have eye contact through conversations, simple things like that or whether or not you're making judgements on the basis of personal behaviour, whether a person smiles, whether a person looks confused, whether a person looks happy, or whatever, there are a whole range of judgements there, about our personal effectiveness.' (CT)

In the course of routine work arrangements, panellists recounted how they would go out of their way to make occasional face-to-face contact, even where this was not necessarily the most convenient or 'efficient' mode of communication. Several expressed a preference for this form of communication and sometimes made an effort to visit someone in person, rather than communicate by e-mail, social media, phone or post:

'Last week I decided to consciously hand deliver to somebody a piece of paper that I could easily have put in the internal mail … I thought, no I'll walk across to that particular office with it because I'll be able to say "Hello" to whoever's in that office and just pick up on the gossip and news. That's quite a pleasant thing to do, but it also just nurtures in their minds the existence of the work that I do.' (MW)

Others made a habit of 'popping into' or 'hanging around' places where there was a high probability of meeting people with whom they needed to maintain links. One panellist described how she would occasionally drive home through a particular area in the hope of "catching a wave" (LM) with residents there, and possibly even stopping for a chat. Others described how they deliberately structured their work so as to be 'out and about':

> 'I'm not office based, I don't sit behind a desk every day, I make phone calls, I'm proactive, I go out of my way to go and see people regularly, whether it's sitting having a cup of tea in someone's home ... whether it's making a prior appointment to go and do that, or it's because somebody has made a particular point of contact and I've responded by saying "Yes, I'll meet you".' (CT)

Panellists described how they made themselves 'ubiquitous', 'accessible', 'welcoming' and 'friendly' and were extremely flexible in how they did this. Living locally was an advantage, but other strategies mentioned were 'having lunch in different places', walking between appointments where possible and generally using the same amenities (shops, pubs, public transport and so on) as the community members they wanted to network with. This approach creates possibilities of meeting people in ways that are neither intrusive nor overly formal. It is about being in the right place at approximately the right time, and then making good use of whatever happens. This is clearly strategic in that it involves knowledge about local customs and habits. It may involve deliberate planning, but also responding opportunistically to unexpected encounters.

Making contact sometimes requires some audacity, for example 'buttonholing' a comparative stranger from the crowd of potential contacts and then rendering the connection memorable and pleasant, so that the other person has an incentive to continue with it. Studies of effective management and leadership identify important personal qualities, such as vigilance in processing information about the social environment and sensitivity to the feelings of others. Experience suggests that face-to-face encounters and social gatherings are crucial to establishing a valid connection between people, probably because they allow a more accurate understanding of what people really think and feel.

Networking demands both analytical and intuitive thinking. It involves an awareness of how people are relating to each other, and identifying potential areas of compatibility or friction. This sensitivity is sometimes referred to as intuition and seems to be an important quality for community development. In an early exploration of the community work role, Williams (1973, p 3) advocates the use of an 'imaginative sixth sense' when 'playing the networks'. Many of the panellists felt that their ability to form appropriate links and relationships was based on 'hunches' about what was going on in a meeting or social situations. It has been suggested that intuitive judgements are one of the characteristics of expert performance that use learning from previous similar experiences but unfortunately are largely inaccessible to technical analysis (Dreyfus and Dreyfus, 1986). At the heart of professional practice lies an 'ineffable knack' that defies measurement and description (Heron, 1996, p 112). The ability to perceive and activate potential connections is one of the 'knacks' of networking, so expert networkers are able to make rapid and sophisticated appraisals of complex and dynamic processes from their observations of personal interactions. These abilities and insights are not developed overnight, but through experience and reflection.

Maintaining and using connections

A crucial but sometimes neglected aspect of networking is the need to maintain mutuality in relationships. This does not necessarily mean that within each and every transaction there has to be an equal balance of give and take, as this is not always possible. Rather, it is more about maintaining an overall perception (within the network) that nobody is in charge and that nobody is freeloading. Voluntary relationships tend to be sustained if they are based on fair and equivalent levels of exchange. For individuals, the cost of maintaining the connection has to be more or less offset by the benefits and there should be a rough reciprocity among those involved. Relationships that lack this balance eventually dissipate or are deliberately terminated.

Although not every contact might prove immediately or obviously useful, nevertheless information about it should be retained somehow. When a link can be established and appears fruitful, it needs to be nurtured. This should not be left to chance. Business cards and leaflets can be exchanged and definite arrangements made to meet again. Alternatively, a way would be devised to consolidate the encounter with some kind of follow-up, for example with a relatively immediate e-mail or Facebook posting. This might appear fortuitous, such as noticing and sending a magazine article or hyperlink that would be of interest to the other party:

'[I] ask them questions and listen to find out what their interests are, what are their needs, to note them internally and sometimes on paper. I then find that I can follow those up. Whatever people tell you, there's some kind of reverse Sod's Law. If they are interested in matchboxes there'll be an article on matchboxes in your tray or newspaper in no time at all, and so I'm able to follow that up with something concrete.' (KT)

Others talked about finding ways of demonstrating a genuine commitment to the other person's wellbeing or work. Equally they might arrange to be somewhere where they were likely to 'bump into' that person:

'And if it's something about grassroots level within the community, then ... I would go out of my way to be in a place where that person was if I wanted to continue those links. It may be just something simple like a coffee morning I know they always attend, or [that] they always go round to the shops at a certain time. If I needed to see that person and I wanted to build up the links with them to be the secretary of a particular group or something like that, I would go round it that way, sort of plan my actions but it appears casual.' (LM)

Building trust, taking risks

Relationships do not just happen and often involve elements of risk. Learning to trust another person entails being prepared to rely on their judgement and actions. This is hard to establish in virtual environments, but combinations of face-to-face and social media seem to allow for positive reinforcement. An expectation develops that their behaviour and motivations will be more or less consistent and reciprocal. Gifts and favours express mutual attraction and/or obligation, and provide the vital interchange for voluntary relationships (Fischer, 1982; Werbner, 1990). A balance between the parties involved is usually maintained informally, but not necessarily, through material transactions. Conviviality (pleasure, humour, fun) and empathy are valued in themselves, and form the basis for a generalised social relationship whose key components are 'trust, reciprocity, altruism, commitment, sacrifice, tolerance, understanding, concern, solidarity and inter-dependence' (Twine, 1994, p 32). Even apparently superficial courtesy represents an acknowledgement that our lives are connected, that our actions have an impact and that the feelings and behaviour of other people are likely to be influenced by what we do or say.

This is illustrated by an initiative in Melbourne (Australia) which found that deliberately increasing levels of smiling on the street enhanced people's sense of wellbeing and reduced their fear of crime, engendering a sense of civil connectedness (Singer, 2007). Similarly, an experiment that gave people a trivial lucky experience (such as finding a coin) found that this improved the likelihood that they would assist a stranger in the next few minutes (Isen and Levin, 1972). Generating a good mood appears to predispose more altruistic behaviour and a more communal orientation, even when based on only fleeting encounters. In the Big Local programme (see Chapter 4) some of the areas have included in their vision and ideas for long-term legacy that people make eye contact with one another and to smile more, as a way of illustrating that the funding has been invested to develop a better sense of 'community'. Sometimes community participation requires a more proactive approach so as to overcome shyness, unfamiliarity or prejudices, encouraging people to get to know one another rather than simply pass on the streets.

Relationships are initially fairly risky in that they involve both hazard (being let down or betrayed) and uncertainty. Relations of trust are important in mediating risk and are a necessary precondition to the exercise of collective power. Trust is usually developed incrementally, over time and through demonstrated honesty and reliability, rather than as a spontaneous leap of faith (Brownlie, 2014). It is renewed rather than eroded through use and cultivated in civil society through active, reliable and mutually beneficial cooperation. Between individuals this creates the basis for friendship and neighbourliness. At the community level it translates into shared conventions or social norms that regulate interaction and promote cooperation for the common good (Kohn, 2009).

These unwritten mini-contracts are created and maintained mainly through social interactions. They allow us to make decisions about whether or not to engage in collective action when it is possible neither to control the outcome nor even to predict what it might be. Trustworthiness was a theme that emerged strongly in my research. The Bristol Festival Against Racism was made possible because the key protagonists had built up good reputations within the relevant networks and could be trusted to deliver what they were promising. Stakeholders were willing to contribute to the initiative because they believed their money, energy and effort would be used to good effect.

They were prepared to commit organisational resources and their own credibility to what at the time was a fairly risky venture, both politically and in terms of its sustainability. For the panellists, trust had a number of interlocking components. It involved fulfilling commitments and being frank about one's own role and motives:

> 'I think the openness is important because the process of networking is carried by people building up trust and relationships between each other ... I think you build up trust with people if you're straight with them about what's possible, what you think, what you disagree with, not promising things that you can't deliver.' (MW)

Benefits and limitations

Networking allows people to cut across organisational boundaries and gain access to resources, expertise and advice. This enables problems to be solved quickly and without going through official procedures. Informal and reliable contacts save time and effort because they can be used to request or negotiate support, especially funding, more easily, and to link individuals into relevant groups. Personal contacts also provide access to external professional guidance for specific pieces of work, for example in relation to legislation and grant applications. Reciprocal working relationships develop through regular participation in relevant events and activities; using contacts to build up interdependence by "giving as much as I receive", as one person (KT) put it. This includes offering knowledge and advice, as well as simply sharing information and skills. There were many forms and levels of cooperation referred to in the interviews. People are able to avoid formal procedures by calling in favours:

> 'trading in kind rather than having to account for them [gives] flexibility ... anything that doesn't have to go through the accountants.' (GrS)

This seems to be especially necessary for workers in the voluntary and community (or 'third') sector, and may represent a covert redistribution of resources between statutory or intermediary agencies and smaller community groups.

It is the personal aspects of relationships that ease the processes of multi-agency working. These allow people to move through and beyond the formal bureaucratic procedures to establish genuine mutuality, rather than 'paper' partnerships. People use their networks to cross organisational boundaries in order to solve short-term problems and to develop a collective response to common issues. Cooperation need not always imply direct collaboration. It may simply be about making sure that activities augment or complement each other. Networking with other organisations is useful for ascertaining the current 'state of play' and adjusting one's plans accordingly, for example to avoid competition for funding:

> 'We contacted other people doing a similar sort of bid; not to pinch what they were doing, but to find out what their experience was and what their particular need was. We wanted to ensure that we weren't all making the same competitive bid, which could penalise all of us.' (JM)

Helpful connections can be nurtured, avoiding unnecessary (and wasteful) rivalries. Multi-agency partnerships and intermediary bodies are important in providing opportunities for this kind of coordination. The erosion of infrastructure support and decline of partnership working, along with constraints placed on community-oriented staff, have inevitably affected this and, to a growing extent, small organisations have had to fend for themselves, with many going under (NAVCA, 2015). The erosion of the intermediary layer of support, due to the loss of such posts in Councils for Voluntary Service and the like, has removed important hub nodes from local third sector systems, disrupting connectivity as well as reducing the quality and availability of community development support in many areas (ESB, 2017).

Conclusion

As we saw in Chapter 1, networking is a natural and ancient process that has made humans successful cooperators. Like any aspect of behaviour, it gets better through practice and can be used for personal or collective benefit. Within the context of community development, networking underpins all forms of community activity and should be seen within the framework of values set out in Chapter 3. However, networking can also be a self-promoting, manipulative and superficial way of getting ahead in life through the use (and abuse) of contacts by 'schmoozing' and 'name-dropping' for personal advancement. Community workers need to be alert to these tendencies and adopt strategies to counter them. Networks in themselves do not guarantee improved decision making or better access to information. Their informal nature and lack of mechanisms for resolving conflict or ensuring a balanced representation means that their activities are frequently unaccountable and exclusive. If left to their own devices, recruitment and communication within networks may become biased towards those 'in the know' or whose 'face fits', while those who might bring a different perspective may be surreptitiously, but systematically, bypassed. Networking usually relies on casual or serendipitous processes and personal perceptions. When these are based on local conventions, they inevitably reflect the convenience and comfort of those already involved. Networks can reinforce prejudices and elitist practices when they operate predominantly on the basis of cliques and rumour-mongering. A proactive and strategic approach is needed for community workers, using what Newman and Geddes (2001) call 'positive networking' to ensure social inclusion within partnerships. It is here that community development, with its core values of equality and participation, can play a role in creating and maintaining accessible and diverse networks.

This chapter has indicated the key traits and tactics for successful and sustainable networking. It has emphasised the importance of interpersonal relationships and face-to-face interaction, arguing that the work involved in networking should be properly appreciated as contributing to the development of community capacity and effective partnerships. The next chapter examines the specific contribution that community workers can make to these processes through assisting people to make connections that might otherwise prove difficult or fragile.

QUESTIONS FOR REFLECTION AND DISCUSSION

✧ Think about your own networking. Can you identify particular skills and strategies that you use effectively?

✧ Are there aspects of networking that you could improve?

✧ How might you go about doing this?

8

Networking for community development

In life, the issue is not control, but dynamic inter-connectedness.

Erich Jantsch, *The self-organizing universe*, 1980, p 196

Interpersonal relationships within communities and between organisations need to be given greater significance to ensure that they are developed and maintained in ways that contribute to overarching outcomes such as collective resilience, social justice, cohesion and sustainability. Networking clearly involves both common courtesy and good communication. It is about maintaining a web of relationships that can support a useful and empowering flow of information and influence. This chapter will examine how community workers facilitate the networking of others, whether colleagues, partners, policy makers or members of the communities they work with. It looks at what community workers actually do to establish and maintain connections that are useful to themselves and others, what aptitudes are required and what strategies are deployed in a networking approach to community development and how these might be improved. There will be particular emphasis on the creation and use of links that span organisational and community boundaries in order to promote partnership working, release social capital and foster community cohesion. The idea of meta-networking is introduced, looking at the role of community workers in devising opportunities for people to meet and work together.

Community development often feels somewhat nebulous, fostering collective capacity and stimulating social action from unpromising beginnings. Good networking practice requires both planning and proficiency; it can fairly be described as work. It supports community organising and sustains mutual cooperation, especially during periods of dispute and demoralisation. Many of the difficulties and frustrations faced by community workers derive from their position on the edges of organisations. They are 'everywhere and nowhere': marginalised, misunderstood and yet expected to act as mediators between different agencies or groups. They 'network the networks', forming boundary-spanning links across which information and resources flow to where they can best be used. Good community workers act not as gatekeepers but as signposts and springboards, helping people through barriers, mitigating risk and navigating 'safe' routes over unfamiliar or difficult terrain. Some of this will require disrupting familiar patterns of relationships or sets of assumptions to prompt fresh links and coordinated assemblages that generate innovative solutions to hitherto intractable problems (Obstfeld, 2017).

Networking as core practice

The use of 'network' as a verb has quickly become widely popularised to describe all sorts of social encounters. It has inevitably produced its own parody in the question: 'Is it networking, or not working?' Since this book was first published there has been a sea-change in the use of the term, with networking increasingly recognised as a vital component of community development practice. Job descriptions and person specifications frequently include 'networking skills' as a requirement, and posts exist specifically to develop, coordinate and manage networks, indicating the value attached to this way of working, especially within the voluntary sector.

The Community Organisers Programme explicitly trains its Member Organisers in how to connect people and support networks. The rationale is that these member networks will form the basis of listening initiatives and lead to local, regional and national initiatives that stimulate collective action and create change. Local community organising networks have defined their purpose as creating groups of people who enable others 'to work together to grow happy communities and neighbourly spirit'; and 'Bringing diverse people together to effect change in society through collective power and action'. The member networks have developed differently, some meeting to share concerns and design strategies for action, while others focus on building personal awareness and organising skills.

In the Panel Study described in the previous chapter, interviews with the community workers revealed the vitality and richness of networking, with comments such as "absolutely central", "the start of everything", "the life and breath", the "sap" of community development, and "pretty vital to all of it". Networking was seen as a core process of community development, and also a key purpose:

> 'Community development happens through networking ...
> the process of community development work is [about]
> developing relationships with people and encouraging

people to build relationships with each other which are for the purpose of getting things done... and how they can best relate to sources of resources and power.... It's essential. You couldn't do it without networking.' (MW)

The community workers in this study deliberately allocated time and effort to developing and maintaining their networks:

'I consciously, in my own mental work plan, say that I must spend a certain proportion of my time networking and proactively setting up networks of different sorts.' (GrS)

They were often tactical about whom they formed links with, careful in their approaches to different people and conscientious in monitoring and maintaining connections. People acted with design and deliberation:

'I'm strategic ... in the sense of almost making a list and saying "Who do I need to pay attention to next?"; "What network do I need to invest some of my time and energy into next?"' (MW)

Community workers in the Panel Study took risks and were proactive in making contact with others. But they were also pragmatic and opportunistic in their use of happenstance encounters and conversations. Networking was both serendipitous and strategic, in the sense that the workers deliberately created or sought out occasions where they were likely to make useful connections. Panel members were skilful in their networking and versatile in applying different techniques in different situations. Responses to my interview questions often began with the phrase "it depends ...", followed by a sophisticated appraisal of the context and purpose of interactions, including explanations of why one approach would be more appropriate and effective than another. Nevertheless, there was considerable agreement that effective networking involved certain core organisational skills, loosely clustered around communication, interpersonal relations and knowledge management.

Recruitment and participation

Assisting people to 'self-organise' on the basis of a shared interest or oppression can be regarded as a legitimate form of consciousness raising and empowerment. Networking is used to identify and to recruit individuals likely to contribute to collective ventures. 'Rising stars' are nurtured, volunteers are invited to take on more responsibilities and community members are cajoled into new roles as representatives or committee members. This is particularly necessary in the early phases of developing a project or setting up a new organisation:

> 'We set up discussion meetings to which we invited people who we thought would be interested in the idea. Before and after those meetings we chatted people up ... and sold the idea to them, sometimes meeting people over coffee.' (MW)

At community level, informal conversations support a constant process of matching interests, needs and enthusiasm. One-to-one work with individuals might be followed up with suggestions that they join a particular group:

> 'If I think it would be really good for them to be involved in that, I'd say to them, "Oh, you should know about this, this is the person to contact to invite you to the next meeting", and then I ring the person who I suggested they contact and say "Oh I met so and so the other day and I've suggested they phone you, I think they would be really good to invite along to this next meeting".' (FB)

The 'grapevine' offers an efficient and far-reaching means of gathering participants for community activities. Interpersonal networks appear to be more effective than posters, leaflets and newsletters in mobilising people for collective action because of individual motivations, social solidarity and a sense of shared risk. However, it is important to use public forms of communication, especially social media, as well as to ensure that information is openly available to everyone whom you might want to attract.

Box 8.1: Sunny Govan

Sunny Govan is a community radio station based on Glasgow, Scotland, but it does far more than simply broadcast news and music to a local audience. A core objective is to 'stimulate community development and capacity building' by empowering local people to be active in the community. The project sees itself as an inclusive learning and support hub, providing live forums for current political debates and hosted hustings during the local elections. Its website includes a directory of useful contacts and the channel carries adverts for small local businesses. It promotes community festival and city-wide campaigns, for example around homelessness and illegal evictions of asylum seekers and refugees. In addition, it lists lost and found property and posts requests for equipment such as musical instruments, as well as running sessions to support budding performers and training in music technology.

Sunny Govan is a not-for-profit organisation, mainly run by volunteers; its income comes from its work as an approved training provider, donations and sponsorship from local businesses. All are welcome to participate in Sunny Govan's activities and the project's commitment to diversity is captured in this inspiring statement: 'Every single person has capabilities, abilities and gifts. Living a good life depends on whether these capabilities can be used, abilities expressed and gifts given. If they are, the person will be valued, feel powerful and well-connected to the people around them, and the community around the person will be more powerful because of the contribution the person is making.'

See: http://sunnyg.com/

Influencing decisions

Networking can be used to lobby decision makers around specific concerns and as a means of building people's capacity to influence decisions. Panellists admitted to using personal connections with policy makers to promote particular points of view, but they also saw their role as enabling other people to develop their own links with powerful bodies:

> 'So when you're networking ... the particular outcomes that I'm aiming for are things that I think will strengthen the ability of the local community to represent itself and to get resources for itself and to develop a relationship with big-power agencies like the local state.' (MW)

Informal community networking is a means of developing a collective, but not necessarily unanimous, stance from which different views and interests can be channelled. A more formal kind of networking is to create community forums that can be used as part of public consultation processes, although constant work is needed to make sure that these remain genuinely representative, transparent and accessible. Strategies for enhancing community engagement should include support for networks that create space for dialogue and dissent, not just for selecting and supporting community representatives. Genuine empowerment must be developed through support for communities to become better connected by tapping into the informal networks that are the forerunners of civil society organisations, especially for newly arriving communities (Beirens et al, 2007; Theodore and Martin, 2007). This poses particular challenges in areas of super-diversity or population fluidity, where community development support can additionally be used to set up links between incoming communities and those in the public, private and third sectors who have power, resources and technical expertise (Blake et al, 2008).

Meta-networking

In community development, good networking is about developing and managing a diverse array of contacts and relationships. Workers make judgements about how best to initiate and support useful links between themselves and others, and, more importantly, use these to help community members to make and maintain connections with each other and outside bodies. This latter function I have termed meta-networking to indicate that it is about the work involved in supporting and transforming other people's networks. It represents an essential contribution to the development of the well-connected community. The concept of meta-networking will be explored further in the concluding chapter, but for now the key components of effective meta-networking can be identified as:

- mapping the social and organisational landscape;
- initiating and maintaining interpersonal connections through referrals and introductions;
- creating spaces and opportunities for interaction and conversation;
- managing and monitoring relevant networks;
- anticipating and dealing with tensions within and rifts between networks;
- encouraging and supporting participation in networks where there are obstacles or resistance; and
- assisting in the development of relatively informal structures and procedures that will ensure that networks are inclusive and sustainable.

Meta-networking is especially important if the social environment seems alien and fragmented or if people lack the confidence or skills to initiate contact for themselves. This might be due to cultural differences, impairments, prejudices, power imbalances or perceived conflicts of interest. Community workers can facilitate these processes by finding connections, challenging preconceptions, creating opportunities for shared activities and encouraging dialogue across apparent boundaries. Many communities already have such meta-networkers, the 'fiery spirits' that people in villages and neighbourhoods look to for information and encouragement. They are often women and usually operating below the public radar, so may easily be overlooked by outside agencies (Fraser et al, 2003, pp 53–4; Soteri-Proctor, 2011). Community workers need to identify and work with these connectors, rather than relying just on prominent leaders who may be self-appointed or represent only one set of interests within a community. Because meta-networking is about assisting the networking of others, it requires a working knowledge of shifting power dynamics and allegiances. Given current levels of discrimination and inequality, meta-networking should include the use of positive action measures to overcome practical obstacles, unconscious bias or oppressive attitudes (Gilchrist, 2007). The worker's own networks provide an 'intangible resource' that can be used to build 'bridges to participation' (Rees, 1991) and this means that they must take care to ensure that these are as inclusive and diverse as possible.

One community worker felt that it would be difficult to initiate effective collaboration

> 'if there isn't the infrastructure of networking, if you don't know who is around and could usefully be involved in partnerships. Again I suppose it's the information and knowledge in the first place, then the personal contact.' (GrS)

Knowing how networks operate and having a mental map of the relations and attitudes of individual members makes it possible to channel information in order to influence decisions and enhance the likelihood of particular outcomes. It helps to know who in an organisation is likely to respond favourably to an invitation, so that sympathetic individuals can be targeted within a larger bureaucracy in the hope that they would either contribute themselves or find a suitable alternative from among their own contacts:

> 'I've got to try to be quite strategic, suggesting specific people who would be useful to invite from specific organisations ... Because if you just send a blank letter up

to the agency, the chance of anybody picking it up is kind
of minimal really.' (FB)

Networking involves forethought, sensitivity and a thorough
knowledge of the context, including knowing how to engage
someone's attention. Community workers are often points of entry
to other networks or more formal systems. A personal referral makes
it easier for people to access the specialist help they need:

'It's much better if you can say, "Well I'll phone my mate
Fred and say that you're here and while I'm on the phone
you can make an appointment to go and see him", or
whatever, and in some cases with particular sorts of people
it's actually better to go along with them.' (GrS)

Networking the networks

As well as maintaining their own links and relationships and helping
others to forge connections, panellists described an additional role of
'networking the networks':

'I think my networks work ... they are actually very diverse.
There is some overlap with them but there isn't a very core
tight-knit group. I'm sort of very conscious I'm the hub of
lots of networks.' (GrS)

Community workers deliberately and strategically maintain their
involvement in a number of networks, adjusting the level of their
participation to ensure that the range of connections reflects current
and potential work priorities:

'Networking the networks has become very much my
job, initially by default – it had to be done like that ...
linking past, present and future, these things are always very
important to me but implicit rather than explicit ... I think
I'm always bringing a broad overview.' (KT)

Community workers often played a vital role in setting up and
coordinating umbrella bodies that bring together people and projects
operating across a variety of settings and issues. Several panellists
were active in convening and chairing such forums. They performed
a 'behind the scenes' function: servicing meetings, maintaining

membership lists, sending out mailings and providing a point of contact. Multi-agency networks facilitate exchange and discussion across organisational or geographic boundaries. Forums and federations and, to some extent, local associations (such as neighbourhood or parish councils) aim to represent different sections of a community and to articulate particular perspectives.

In Britain community workers play crucial roles in supporting interface connections between communities and local government offices and politicians, thereby enhancing democracy and civic participation. This aspect of community development, strengthening the links between communities and external resources, is an essential component for both empowerment and engagement (Kubisch et al, 2002). Informal networks create opportunities for people to link up with others who may have different interests and various identities and yet share some kind of common values or purpose (Brah, 2007). Their ability to function effectively is determined by the quantity and quality of both internal and external connections.

Networking as information processing

Community workers are important channels or relays in networks because they are in touch with many different groups. This is especially valuable around complex or disputed areas of knowledge because access to a range of perspectives brings additional intelligence, insights and a broader understanding. Panellists were conscientious in using networks to convey information to where it could be useful, thinking about

> 'how to use what knowledge I've got and pass it back, because I really do believe this thing about information is power and that's part of networking'. (SM)

They noticed and passed on items of news, not always immediately but saving it for the right opportunity or person. Receiving and retrieving information is an important area of competence, notably asking questions and really listening to the answers so as to notice (and remember) potential connections:

> 'Sometimes it's just storing that little bit of information away in my brain, and it might not be apparently of use to me at that time, but I am aware that sometime in the future it might be of use to me or someone else.' (FB)

This aspect of networking practice ranges from simply transmitting information, through to convening and servicing network-type organisations. Community workers are a resource that others use to obtain information. One community worker referred to their role as a conduit through which information flowed, as well as acting as a databank for other groups and the media. They become a kind of human encyclopaedia of local knowledge, "a walk-in file index" as one person (FB) described herself, but one which functions actively as a key node in a vast communication system. Good administration is a neglected aspect of effective networking – using old-fashioned methods such as notebooks, filing systems, card index boxes, diaries and address books as well as various apps and platforms such as Dropbox and LinkedIn to keep contact details and share records.

Obviously there are limits to the amount of information one person can be responsible for, so talking to colleagues and members of various umbrella organisations is vital for staying up to date with the latest issues and news. Making time to read relevant minutes, newsletters and periodicals is also important, although being on dozens of mailing lists can result in information overload, particularly in these days of instant online communication when every other e-mail or posting seems to offer yet another set of facts, requests and invitations to be assimilated or declined. Information can sometimes seem too much of a good thing.

Widening horizons

Informal networks are a source of inspiration and challenge, supporting a continuous flow of ideas and opinions. They enable people to gain an overview of situations and debates, gather useful insights, establish the bigger picture and compare experiences. Networking is a way of monitoring reputations and appraising the links between groups. This is helpful at an individual level and contributes to the construction of a communal model of the world that can be used to determine collective strategies for change. Networking enables community workers to intervene directly in political or social processes, and to advise others on how these can be influenced:

'You've kind of got a sense of where people fit on the map of networks and you have a sense of where you fit ... you gradually build it up and you hear different and contradictory things from different people and you form your own judgements. So it's a gradual process of becoming part of that landscape of relationships, networks and power dynamics.' (MW)

For community members, networking extends horizons and broadens perspectives, enabling people to gain an overview of the (policy) context and develop a broader understanding of issues. Networking enables people to stay in touch with changes in the organisational field, as well as the dynamics of community politics. It is especially useful for obtaining unofficial views to match against public pronouncements.

Networking events, such as exchange visits between similar organisations, encourage the transfer of ideas and learning from one community to another, so that they do not need to start from scratch in setting up a project. This means that groups are

> 'not inventing the wheel all the time. Somebody has done something, they can learn from that, they can learn from other people's mistakes so they don't make the same mistakes, they can go one step further.' (PH)

Groups discover that local difficulties may be part of a broader problem that neighbouring communities are also facing:

> 'I try and keep in mind that we've got to learn from other people's experience, locally and wider. Keeping ideas coming; and of course that's key and crucial to networking anyway. It's one of the purposes of getting as broad a spectrum of experience together as possible so that you can compare, contrast and learn.' (KT)

Drawing in new perspectives seems to be particularly crucial in this respect. Community workers used connections outside the immediate arena of their work to inject fresh, sometimes challenging, ideas. One community youth worker on the Panel justified her decision to become involved in projects beyond the actual remit of her job thus:

> 'There is no doubt that [this experience] benefited the community of young people because they then got input that they would never have got if I'd stayed as a peripheral suburban youth worker, not networked into inner-city projects and current political thinking and stuff like that.... If networking brings something new then it has to be a good thing, even if it's a different perspective and ... that

is a product of having bothered to go out of your usual circle.' (SM)

Another panellist contrasted the outlooks of two clubs for older people, only one of which was prepared to make links beyond its immediate membership. Its members

> 'are prepared to listen to others, to learn from others, to contribute themselves, so it's a two-way thing which makes this communication important.... This need to want to listen to others, to improve not just the thing you're involved in but your knowledge of things generally and have a wider look. Is networking really just a wider look on things?' (LM)

As a result of their links with other bodies, such groups become more adaptable and improve their chances of survival in an unpredictable funding climate, especially where there is increasingly an expectation that organisations will work in partnerships and mergers are actively encouraged (Harrow and Bogdanova, 2006).

Valuing diversity and inclusivity

Cultural and other forms of diversity may bring complications and challenges due to different understandings of what kinds of interaction are 'normal' or 'acceptable'. Such differences provide dynamic opportunities for comparison and debate, promoting greater levels of satisfaction for those involved and benefits for collective problem-solving. A major role for the community worker involves convening and servicing groups which bring together individuals across organisational and identity boundaries to develop 'critical alliances' (Ledwith and Asgill, 2000). Such coalitions recognise and respect differences but nonetheless are able to find sufficient temporary alignment to tackle a common grievance or achieve a shared goal. This may involve some ingenuity and a certain amount of risk in bringing together experiences that could be mutually challenging, even confrontational.

Building bridges across perceived community or organisational boundaries is a first step in generating a dialogue which might eventually break down barriers of fear, prejudice and antipathy. Diversity also creates the possibility of innovative combinations and adaptations:

'Collective, collaborative action [is] a means to solve problems, to make changes. It's just being open to finding the new. This is what's exciting about having a mixed community. It sets problems when new people come in and there's a mix but one of the good things is that you might come up with new solutions because of that.' (KT)

A major aspect of community development practice involves supporting communication and cooperation across psychological or cultural edges and organisational boundaries, while bearing in mind that individuals and communities are often in transition. Networking creates occasions and spaces where people can learn from one another to develop greater tolerance and understanding (Chauhan, 2009). Judicious appraisals may be needed about when and how to bring people together in situations that match their level of comprehension and commitment. This may include direct introductions at prearranged meetings or visits. It might involve accompanying people to events and assisting them to make contact with those who might be useful to them by

'trying to break the ice between people … making connections between people and convinc[ing] them that talking to a particular person is a good idea…. I'll encourage people to come to a meeting perhaps because I know that somebody else is going to be at that meeting that they could make use of so it's generally not just a "spur of the moment" thing.' (PH)

Community workers also need to assess when to withdraw from hands-on involvement so that people can manage their own interactions.

Networking inevitably reflects personal interests and prevailing power dynamics, so networks easily become exclusive and cliquey. Community workers should use anti-oppressive practice to reduce practical barriers and political biases, and to support the contributions of people who are less confident or articulate. One panellist described how she would accompany people from the community on their first attendance at a formal gathering:

'They would ask to come along with me … just to give them a bit of confidence really. I mean when I'm there, I don't hold hands with somebody all day. I mean I would deliberately not do that. I would find an excuse to move out the way, and give the people their own space.' (LM)

Disabled people continue to face challenges around being accepted and finding accessible ways to participate in community activities and networks. Bigby (2008) found that the social networks of people with learning difficulties who had moved into the 'community' were, five years later, still predominantly confined to family members and friends from within the system, relationships that predated the move to so-called independent living. Clearly, informal networking processes have not enabled them to integrate in ways that might reasonably have been anticipated and person-centred strategies are needed to enable isolated or more vulnerable people to contribute to community life (Poll et al, 2009). Black and minority groups in rural areas are especially isolated and dependent on informal networks to maintain a sense of community, build capacity, influence policies and obtain help, but they are often marginalised from conventional voluntary and community sector activities (Ware, 2015). Young people operate informally to create their own social milieu, sometimes in semi-formal gangs but more often in peer friendship networks (Bragman et al, 2017). They also maintain informal links to the broader comparative stability of community and these are important hooks (Bauman, 2001; Measor, 2006).

Networking is not simply about cross-validation and corroboration, as seems to be the case sometimes with the 'bubble' or echo-chamber effects of social media (Hampton et al, 2017). Panellists actively sought out views that would challenge their own interpretations by meeting with people in other organisations or from different backgrounds. If connections with like-minded people are important elements in the network, so also are those that bring difference and dissent. As John Stuart Mill remarked over a century and a half ago, 'It is hardly possible to over-rate the value of bringing human beings together with people dissimilar to themselves ... it is one of the primary sources of progress' (Mill, 1848, p 581). These links require more effort, more diplomacy and more imagination. This is where the work of meta-networking takes place: setting up and maintaining the links between different (and sometimes antagonistic) sections of society. Some individuals and groups may need additional or alternative strategies in order to connect them into existing networks, and this may mean challenging or circumnavigating dominant interests and cultures. One panellist explained, for example:

> 'Sometimes it is noting in a network that I'm in that they're not there. Sometimes it is so that the network can get them in but sometimes it is just reminding ourselves that we need

to do something else. We need to go out and talk to these people ... because it's not always possible to get them into a network.' (KT)

Good meta-networking involves a capacity to communicate across a range of different cultures and perspectives:

'The fact that I've got a multidisciplinary background helps me in a practical sense of being able to anticipate, but I think more important is the theory that not everybody understands the same thing from the same set of words or concepts and having that in mind is really helpful when it comes to mediating. It leaves me open. I don't make a judgement.' (KT)

Getting people who have different cultures, interests and social status to work together can be fraught with difficulties and tensions. Networks can be used to manage that plurality in very positive ways by building links and mediating between factions to resolve personality clashes, confront dogma and overcome intransigence. It helps to demonstrate interest in other people and curiosity about different lives and cultures. Good networking values diversity and deliberately seeks out experiences that will educate and challenge. Networking is used to translate jargon and interpret between people and agencies that are not in direct or clear communication with one another.

Managing conflict

Community workers are frequently invited to act as intermediaries between opposing parties, using their role to find common ground. If their relationships are robust and authentic, then disagreements may be dealt with amicably and effectively. Conflict can be anticipated and averted or handled informally. Disputes often erupt in communal facilities where people want to use the same space for different purposes. Tensions run high, and this seems to be particularly the case when young people are involved. One panellist described how she was able to contain the anti-social behaviour of local young people by relating to them personally. It was a

'huge advantage because I know them [the teenagers] by their names ... especially if they're the kids that also cause quite a lot of trouble.... The fact that they're not anonymous actually makes an enormous difference, and also working with the detached youth workers makes a lot of difference.... [The kids] know that their behaviour is what we do not like, it is not them.' (FB)

Informal discussions are often useful in addressing controversies before they become confrontational or require that one party retreats from their chosen position:

'If there is another point of view which they have not taken account of ... You have to talk to people about that as well. So in that networking ... it's the place where differences of agendas, differences of opinion ... get had out.' (MW)

In order to cooperate, organisations must acknowledge competing interests or divergent ideologies. There may be differentials in power and perceived ownership that the community workers should be aware of and seek to minimise.

Where disputes continue, it is vital to create a 'safe space' for discussing contentious issues and for members to have the opportunity to get to know one another personally. Strained relations within and between communities are inevitable, but they can generate an important impetus for learning and transformation:

'I really genuinely believe that conflict is a really healthy thing ... I abide by that statement that says "From conflict breeds consciousness", but also because in my experience if you constantly live your life with people of the same values and shared vision then you never tighten up your arguments.' (SM)

In community development it is often necessary to challenge existing practices and assumptions. Networkers can use their informal connections to 'grasp the nettle', by asking awkward questions or giving constructive criticism. Personal networks are an effective, but occasionally risky, way of circumventing bureaucratic procedures and undermining the rigidity of corporate culture.

Facilitative leadership

The authority and trust required for community leadership is earned through a multitude of micro-interactions. It relies on good networking skills, ensuring that individuals are able to communicate well across the community and maintain their own profile and reputation. Without these it would be impossible to mobilise people to participate in social actions or to engage with consultation or planning exercises. 'They are grassroots leaders, who emerge as leaders because they have strong links within the community: they are likely to have a strong network of connections and meaningful relationships' (Terry, 2018, p 6). Their role is to empower rather than direct.

A new paradigm for leadership has appeared that seems more suited to the network age. It is based on convening, curating and weaving together people along with resources for nimble and transparent peer-to-peer cooperation (Holley, 2012; Ogden, 2018). Bateson (2016) writes: 'Leadership for this era is not a role or a set of traits; it is a zone of inter-relational process', a means of 'holding the whole' network across large and complex systems of actors, organisations and resources so that collaborative actions can be catalysed and facilitated. Also called system or 'bridging' leaders and network entrepreneurs, these individuals have developed a distributive form of leadership in which they are important free-roving nodes working inside a 'constellation' at different points in the 'node community' (Baker, 2014; Wei-Skillern et al, 2015). They do not act as hubs; nor do they try to control events or decisions. Rather, their role is to connect multiple stakeholders (and sometimes reconfigure the patterns of power among them) in order to provoke new thinking and create some kind of goal-oriented problem-solving coalition that will build synergy for strategic cooperation and large-scale social transformation (Brown, 2015).

Identifying allies and building coalitions around a common vision involves working across a range of different experiences and perspectives to find (or construct) a working consensus. This requires imagination and diplomacy. It is rarely a straightforward matter of aggregating the separate parts:

> 'It's really difficult but ... often those people with completely opposite values can actually develop a relationship because there might be some other common issue that they share and eventually the fact that they're a different colour or different sexuality doesn't matter.' (TD)

Community and inter-agency networks can and should be vehicles for empowerment, affording greater access to decision makers and facilitating the emergence of community leadership (Sullivan et al, 2006). It has been argued that the role of the leader in the 21st century is not to organise directly but, rather, to inspire and connect people so that they gravitate towards exciting projects that solve problems through collaboration, rather than competition (Gratton, 2008). For communities, leadership appears in many different ways, and is not always expressed overtly through obvious, charismatic or traditionally hierarchical roles. Community leadership may evolve through the strengthening of interpersonal relationships and the nature of the interactions across networks at a micro-level, creating an informal power base exercised through networks of influence. As Onyx and Leonard (2011) assert, 'The task of the leaders is to nurture and enable, not to command or control'. In this regard, leadership development has been described as 'rhizomic', emerging from hidden roots to create equilibrium at system level (Kenny et al, 2015, ch 10). Leadership responsibilities may be distributed across a number of activists, none of whom would see themselves as 'heroic' but, rather, as servants of the wider community. They use relational skills to enable 'followers' to achieve their potential contribution to the wider mission (Wilson et al, 2013; Coetzer et al, 2017; Gandolfi et al, 2017).

Hierarchical models of decision making and accountability, exercised through bureaucracy and/or representative forms of democracy, seem dependent on conventional notions of 'top-down' leadership. However, in this age of active citizenship and community empowerment, governance models are developing that embrace notions of collective, distributed and emergent leadership (Wheatley, 2006; Davies, 2011; Skinner, 2019).

Importance of informality

Networking requires a range of abilities, not least an understanding of how formal and informal modes complement each other and knowing how to operate using both genres (Gilchrist, 2016). Misztal talks of the 'dialectic' nature of the relationship between formal and informal, referring to the ways in which they are intertwined and complementary, while seeking to achieve an optimal balance (Misztal, 2000, p 53). Everyday settings, habits and connections shape people's priorities and how they interact with one another. Informal community relations and customs form the backdrop (and behind-the-scenes action) to government interventions and local strategies for community engagement. They therefore affect how and when people choose to participate or contribute (Jupp, 2013). The networking approach to community development challenges the view that 'formal' is the optimal or default mode for third sector organising, arguing that informal interactions are crucial for encouraging inclusive participation, networking and flexible organisational development. Gilchrist (2016) identified a 'praxis' based on knowing how to blend, braid and balance the informal with formal modes of operating, using the skills, knowledge and values that characterise experienced facilitators and community workers.

Networks operate through informal interactions and this is key to their effectiveness. Formal events can be useful for networking, not always because of the items on the agenda, but in order to obtain contacts and advice. The discussions 'around the edge' of the meetings are often more productive than the main business and are a way of exploring how people stand on different issues. Equally, meetings are occasions for fostering links in one's professional network and maintaining a reputable profile. Even in these formal situations, humour and informal remarks are used to reveal paradoxes, ambiguities or potential resistance. Network gatherings are usually characterised by an informality that allows people to talk directly across organisational and status boundaries on a seemingly more equal basis. The absence of formal structures and procedures allows people to be candid. This was identified as a major advantage of one network's meetings:

> 'People have been able to say what they would not [otherwise] be able to say ... because they're not seen as representing their organisation really, so they can say things about their own department that they wouldn't say in a formal situation perhaps.' (PH)

The development of more personal relationships provides the durability and flexibility of many community-based organisations:

> 'I think it's at the informal level that you build up trust and real relationships ... It's not just people, ideas and resources ... the informal networking is absolutely crucial, not only because you need it in a practical sense but, I think, because it actually reflects community.' (KT)

The Bristol Festival Against Racism illustrated how informality made it possible for participants and partner organisations to contribute on their own terms. This is important for community development, which relies on the voluntary efforts of community members. Informality encourages spontaneity and commitment, while paradoxically creating a sense of security. People use their informal networks to check things out and then are able to make a more informed decision. The situation feels less risky, reducing the sense of trepidation, and is experienced as empowering. One Festival event organiser described it thus:

'If the approach is informal, the person being approached can measure their involvement, whereas if it's some kind of formal invitation you either make a commitment or you don't, whereas if it's informal you can bargain around how much commitment there is. It doesn't feel difficult in an informal setting.' (LC)

In organising the Bristol Festival Against Racism a lack of bureaucracy released people's initiative and imagination:

'People were not being regimented into any kind of structure I suppose ... I think that therefore people were able to be a lot more creative.... They could feel free and I think people tend to be a lot more responsive that way.... [They] didn't feel pressured. They felt trusted to come up with the right thing.' (RS)

Informal methods of organising require less explicit commitment and provide easy escape routes. Such encounters allow people to explain, to elaborate and to explore what might have happened in a formal setting. Informal interactions are used to clarify ambiguous or contrary interpretations of events:

'People stay behind and talk to you and check out: "How do you think that went?", "What went on?", "Who said what?", "How do you think ...?" I'm checking out, reviewing and evaluating what's going on, making sure I've been to the same meeting as everybody else. Checking out what's happening.' (GaS)

Conversations held at intersections and exits, where people have easy routes and excuses to depart, can often be the most interesting, probably because people feel they can take risks with opinions they venture and what they reveal. Such exchanges may take place at the corners of streets or at the end of shared journeys, when the pending 'escape' encourages the sharing of confidences or heretical ideas. I call these 'threshold' or 'crossroad' conversations because that is where they often take place in a physical sense. They can often lead to shifts in people's thinking, activities and relationships. A good networker will make use of these opportunities, as they can be rich in significance and trust.

Seemingly casual comments or encounters are usually neither observed nor recorded, evading surveillance by the authorities. Consequently, these conversations appear to be more sincere, revealing what others really think as opposed to the official 'line'. Subversive or downright bizarre views can be voiced, usually resulting in further contentious or creative discussion. Informal chats are where news is exchanged about personnel changes, the results of funding applications or a chance to 'float' projects that are still only sketches on the mental drawing board. News of proposed policy changes travels through the 'grapevine', allowing them sometimes to be 'reformed' even before they are officially formulated.

Discussion

This chapter has illustrated the skilled and strategic nature of networking for community development with evidence and examples. Effective meta-networking can be conceptualised as linking clusters or spanning boundaries by creating a connecting node to fill the gap and then building the connection so that it is free standing. Position in a network is important (Kastelle and Steen, 2014), but so are the processes of introducing people or organisations to one another. It may be necessary to maintain the 'bridge', but without 'gatekeeping', until your support is no longer needed.

Outsiders can play a useful role in mediating and brokering across sectoral boundaries, weaving connections between informal networks and formal organisations (Holley, 2012; Morgan-Trimmer, 2014). People who take on these intermediary roles exhibit particular competences in networking, negotiating and diplomacy, operating at the interface between citizen and state services as 'special agents' (Williams, 2013) or navigators, bringing outreach, advice and advocacy services to communities (Turning Point, 2010; Knapp et al, 2013).

Collaborative behaviour, whether in formal organisations or through informal collective action, is driven most effectively by common purpose rather than rules and commands. And yet such arrangements can be highly charged with a range of competing interests, raising strong emotions that need expressing (or at least acknowledging) through informal outlets if they are not to spill over into the formal discussions. The feelings, tensions and expectations that swirl around community networks may undermine or tarnish local relations and may need managing. The 'emotional labour' that this entails can be hard for lone workers or community leaders, especially if the role assigned them is to remain neutral and to facilitate debate with the aim of ultimately reaching consensus and collaboration. Community-level ways of getting things done primarily incorporate elements of sociability: the human inclination to seek companionship, to help one another and to cooperate. Working with communities must value and enhance trust, mutuality and friendship (Wheatley and Frieze, 2011). In community development, as in life itself, the formal and the informal are inextricably and symbiotically enmeshed.

This is not so easy in an environment of short-term contracts, competition for project finances and low pay, because people are forced to change jobs frequently and often cannot continue working with a community for long enough to build up their local networks properly. The retreat of community development in many areas of the UK, mostly due to the withdrawal of government funding to national infrastructure bodies and austerity cuts in local government budgets, has resulted in the steady dismantling of the professional field, with many hard-pressed neighbourhoods and rural villages losing their access to a reliable community-work presence. Increasing numbers of people who are paid to work with communities (for example as Big Local representatives or community organisers) are employed on short-term projects, sometimes as interns or contracted as freelancers, expected to operate with only 'light touch' support. This exacerbates issues around the continuity of contact and support, posing a considerable challenge to the networking model of place-based community development.

The COLtd model of community organising is described as 'the work of building relationships and networks in communities to activate people and create social and political change through collective action'. A specific aim is to 'strengthen networks and drive social action'. To this end, member organisations in the Community Organisers Expansion Programme are supported to improve their network awareness and networking skills. In the Community Organisers latest framework (COC, 2018), the first three of the eight strands for building people power are reach, listen and connect, using informal meetings and story telling. 'When people start to connect in this way they begin to come up with their own ideas for change. We don't just work with small groups though. We start to link up the groups and to bring them together, breaking down barriers and building bridges' (COC, 2018). Big Local places a similar emphasis on meta-networking, with resources allocated for local, regional and national networking events that bring residents together. These are well attended and much appreciated by residents (Local Trust, 2017).

Conclusions

Much of the literature on communities, organisations, volunteering and networking highlights the importance of personal relationships, developed at the micro-level of interpersonal interactions or at the macro-level of structure and agency (Rochester, 2013). Informality, trust and empathy are vital ingredients for these. Less has been written about the meso-level (or middle layer) of collective activity: establishing and managing effective networks that can be used for a variety of purposes, including collective problem solving, resource mobilisation, organisation development and social change. Traditionally, community development has emphasised the role of the professional in establishing groups and organisations with specific aims and activities. The idea of meta-networking as a core function turns the spotlight away from formal arrangements to focus on informal practices. It is another way of looking at the well-rehearsed arguments about the balance between 'goal' and 'process'.

Meta-networking creates and maintains linkages within complex and dynamic situations that enable new organisational arrangements to emerge, through processes of adaptation and evolution, in response to changing circumstances. These ideas of emergence and complexity will become important themes in the next chapter, which sets out a model of community development as helping communities to operate as complex systems of interactions poised at the 'edge of chaos'. The final chapters explore the implications of this for policy and practice.

QUESTIONS FOR REFLECTION AND DISCUSSION

✧ What examples from your recent practice could be described as meta-networking – helping others to make links or to find potential allies and collaborators?

✧ How do you use informal processes and spaces to develop the connections that contribute to community-level outcomes?

9

Complexity and
the well-connected community

One must have chaos inside oneself in order to give birth
to a dancing star.
Friedrich Nietzsche, *Thus spake Zarathustra*, 1878, p 9

Networking can be used to develop the well-connected community,
but why are networks such a ubiquitous and useful aspect of community
life? We have seen that networks are especially effective modes of
organisation in managing change in complex situations. Community
networks are based on relationships, not simply connections, which
are sustained through interactions and reciprocal exchanges between
individuals. The personal, emotional dimensions are important. So are
flexibility and informality. Networking is a holistic process, involving
a strategic interweaving of knowledge, skills and values. It is a vital
aspect of community development, as well as supporting multi–agency
partnerships and alliances. This chapter uses complexity theory to
present a model of interactive networks creating the conditions for the
evolution of new and adaptive forms of organisation.

Networks serve an important function in society, as we saw in
Chapter 1, and patterns of interaction and connection are strongly
related to what is generally understood by the term 'community'.
Thriving communities are characterised by informal interactions
across many-tiered and multifaceted connections in a mobile, often
delicate lattice of diverse relationships and serendipitous encounters.
This has important implications for community development as an
intervention for managing social complexity and strengthening the
web of interpersonal connections. The idea of 'community' continues
to reflect core values associated with a socially just and sustainable
civil society, namely respect, equality, mutuality, diversity and, more
recently, cohesion. Why does the desire for 'community' persist and
seem so prevalent across all societies (Somerville, 2016)? How does
networking contribute to the development and survival of a well-
functioning 'community', equipped with the capacity for organising
collective responses to shared problems?

Chaos in the community

Communities can be seen as complex social environments characterised by interpersonal connections that comprise fluid networks and small-scale, self-help groups alongside more formal 'anchor' organisations (Thake, 2001) and cultural practices (Blokland, 2017). Ideas from complexity theory may help us to understand some of the more puzzling features of our social and organisational world (see, for example, Gilchrist, 2000; Mitleton-Kelly, 2003; Wheatley, 2006; Byrne and Callaghan, 2014; Pflaeging, 2014; Kenny et al, 2015). Networks offer useful ways of organising within turbulent environments, managing apparent 'chaos' in ways that enhance creativity and promote innovative forms of cooperation, brokerage and leadership (Chadwick 2010; Obstfeld, 2017). As we saw in Chapter 5, organisational studies suggest that network forms of organisation are very effective at coping with high levels of uncertainty and ambiguity. Globalisation and almost universal access to online communication technologies mean that we live in a world that is more diverse and yet more connected than ever before, in which role boundaries are blurred and many personal identities have broken free from traditional social and geographical categories (Mitchell, 2003; Steen, 2010).

Most community workers would admit that many aspects of their work are unplanned or unpredictable. Happenstance encounters represent familiar but unexpected opportunities for sharing information that may lead to a change of direction or a completely new initiative:

> 'Often it's the accidental meeting in the street where something completely new comes up that wouldn't have come up in a planned way.... It's just that chance.' (KT)

It is normal for there to be an element of serendipity in community development, and unpredictable connections are apparently a reliable indicator of value (Hobsbawm, 2017). In similar ways, community workers need the flexibility and confidence to respond opportunistically to events occurring outside of their intentions or control. Developments often flow spontaneously from chance happenings:

> 'There's a strength in being organised out of informal chaos, I suppose.' (CT)

An experienced community worker will relish these kinds of situations, excited by the synergy while providing some continuity and stability for those around:

> 'People see me as that person who's always there ... as someone who holds everything together throughout masses of chaos ... you are seen as a kind of rock ... that people keep hanging onto.' (TD)

Over the years, community development has resisted predetermined targets and performance criteria, asserting that intervention strategies must be non-directive and nurture organic development rather than deliver an external agenda (see, for example, Biddle and Biddle, 1965; Batten and Batten, 1967). This is the contrast between the top-down imposition of rigid action plans with pre-set outputs versus a bottom-up approach that works with the grain of the community, mobilising assets and strengths, helping them to define and achieve their own solutions by using processes that simultaneously empower and educate. Networking prepares the ground for community-led initiatives and campaigns to *emerge* that match perceived needs and actual circumstances. The linkages between people and organisations are a vital part of a community's capacity to act collectively and engage with public decision-making bodies. A well-functioning community is vibrant, with many different groups and activities connected through a complicated lattice of organisational links and personal relationships. When this state of connectivity is reached, anything can happen, and frequently does, because a variety of experiences and interests are 'interjacent' within relatively safe environments (see Thomas, 1976). Small occurrences trigger much bigger events in ways that can be neither predicted nor controlled:

> 'I do find that you're building up [a web] in terms of your networking. It is about outreach, it is about exploration ... but I get to a point where there's suddenly a critical mass of outcomes. I think "Yes, this is making a difference".' (KT)

This unfurling of ideas and energy is a familiar, but misunderstood, feature of community development practice that is exciting, generative and mildly subversive. Change does not take place in a linear fashion which can be systematically foretold, planned and measured using scales or predetermined outputs (Byrne, 2005). Rather, incremental developments in capacity or awareness are largely invisible until a sudden leap in activity or consciousness occurs, resulting in a major shift in levels or direction of community activity. In material sciences, this abrupt change is known as a 'phase transition', and in psychosocial terms might signal a 'turning point', marking the increased propensity among a critical mass of people for community participation (Majdandzic et al, 2016). Gladwell (2000) refers to a 'tipping point', when trickles of apparently unrelated events and conversations become a torrent of coordinated behaviour. He highlights the role played by 'connectors', people who appear to 'know everyone' and act as key nodes in a vast and complex network. Popular websites and apps, such as YouTube and Twitter, generate sudden and intense flurries of interest in particular memes or videos that 'go viral' as people forward links and postings to their own contacts. Global online platforms amplify these trends. On a smaller scale, the networking approach to community development locates this connecting function at the heart of practice, with the community worker spinning and weaving many of the more fragile filaments that make up the complex fabric of community life. In effect, the community worker is shaping and facilitating a mainly informal ecosystem of people and organisations who interact to influence each other's behaviour. As a consequence, collective priorities, preferences, policies and practices emerge from a multiplicity of individual actions and attitudes. These could reflect the susceptibility of individuals to be active citizens, as well as the local traditions or conditions for civic engagement, such as a sense of collective efficacy or community empowerment. This will be shaped by the policy environment and by specific practices, including community development interventions.

Key elements of complexity theory

With this in mind, it is worth looking at theories about complex adaptive living systems. There are some interesting parallels with how communities operate, and how voluntary and community sector organisations evolve over time. Complexity arises as the 'result of a rich interaction of simple elements that only respond to the limited information each of them are presented with' (Cilliers, 1998, p 5). Complex systems are characterised as having multiple components that are connected and influence each other's behaviour. They are affected by changes in the wider environment and they also have an impact on what happens around them. The basic tenets of complexity theory were derived concurrently across different scientific fields: quantum physics, artificial intelligence, embryology, socio-biology and meteorology (Lewin, 1993). More advanced theory has developed through the study of non-linear systems in which apparently insignificant events have far-reaching, even catastrophic, consequences (Gleick, 1987). The most familiar example of this comes from meteorology and is known as the 'butterfly' effect, whereby the flap of a delicate wing is said to have the potential to precipitate a hurricane on the other side of the world. Tentative applications to human decision making and social behaviour have been used to understand reputation networks (such as used in customer ratings by eBay and AirBnB), traffic movement (Wang and Qixin, 2013), organisational team dynamics (Nooy et al, 2005; Dal Forno and Merlone, 2013), disease epidemics (Comfort et al, 2016) and large-scale financial and economic systems (Bischi et al, 2013).

Complexity theory encompasses chaos theory and is concerned with understanding how 'order' appears 'immanent' (enfolded) within apparent chaos. Complex systems comprise a multitude of units (nodes), interacting in ways that are mutually influential yet relatively 'local'. Each unit responds to signals received from its immediate neighbours, generating familiar but unique configurations known as 'strange attractors' or fractals. In nature, snowflakes are perhaps the most easily understood example. As the Japanese scientist Ukishiro Nakaya (1954) demonstrated in the 1930s, every snowflake is unique, but recognisable in its basic morphology. The exact shape is determined by an 'interplay of chance and regularity': the laws of crystallisation for water molecules and the conditions at the moment of freezing (the transition state), notably temperature and humidity.

Complexity theory assumes that transactions between elements are subject to relatively simple rules of interaction (known as Boolean logic) and that, in the absence of central control mechanisms, local clusters exhibit only limited awareness of the total system. Over time a complex system will adjust its arrangement of connections until it achieves a state of dynamic but stable equilibrium. The system has evolved, apparently spontaneously and without external interventions, from an initially random set of interacting elements, towards stable patterns of self-organisation (Jantsch, 1980; Strogatz, 2004). The actual configurations that emerge are neither arbitrary not predictable, but they invariably adopt forms that are characteristic of the system, its components and operating environment.

A state of chaos is said to exist where a large number of elements influence each other's behaviour to produce changing and unpredictable patterns of activity. Contrary to popular belief, a system in chaos is not operating at random. A fundamental feature of complex systems is the emergence of overarching properties as a result of localised interactions. Such a 'property' appears to function as some kind of integrating mechanism by which 'chaos' is averted. Thus the stunning murmuration of starlings in flight is the coordinated result of simple rules governing the behaviour and relative positions of a multitude of individual birds.

The past history of a complex system is significant because what happens in the present is influenced by constant adjustments to previous interactions. Complex systems have a capacity to process and store information from a variety of sources and are thus able to 'learn' from the past and to adapt to changing conditions. This seems to be an important feature of complex systems. The neurophysiological structure of the human brain is a prime example of a highly evolved parallel information processing system consisting of axons, dendrites and synapses forming interactive neural networks that respond with electrochemical pulses to synthesise particularly salient inputs and memories to 'produce' our perceptions and behaviour (Bechtel and Abrahamsen, 1991; Bullmore and Sporns, 2009). It has been suggested that consciousness and personal identity are the neural correlates (emergent properties) of a complex pattern of brain waves that integrates our individual experiences within the highly plastic, self-organising but functionally specialist neurophysiological structures of the brain (Dennett, 1991; Rose, 1998; Greenfield, 2008; Pinker, 2009).

In a parallel analogy, it is intuitively reasonable to locate our sense of community in the rich 'soup' of activities and interactions, the nourishing equivalent of an 'intricate network of mutual nudges' (Ball, 2004, p 135). These generate feelings of belonging and shared intelligence through a complex set of integrating processes, receiving, comparing and disseminating human knowledge and emotions. Perhaps this is what constitutes the 'wisdom of crowds', a form of intellectual social capital that can be accessed by all who are connected. In a complex social system the collective behaviour of the community is not directly deducible from the characteristics of individuals but evolves according to successive interactions between nodes in the networks (Johnson, 2007). Complex communities are characterised by modular clusters of activity, some of it formally organised, but often coordinated through informal networks of connectors. This produces the 'small world effect' by which the whole system is linked through a relatively low number of short chains. Proximity and familiarity ease this circuitry because of their low 'cost' to participants, but are not essential (Reagans, 2011).

Physics and behavioural ecology provide ideas to examine different aspects of crowdsourcing strategies, in particular the emergent behaviours and swarm intelligence that characterise 'superorganisms' (Wheeler, 1928; Wilson, 1990). These 'vivisystems', such as colonies of bees, ants or termites, are characterised by an absence of imposed central control; the (relative) autonomy but high connectivity between the sub-units; and the non-linear (web-like) influence that each creature has on its closest neighbours within the crowd (Rheingold, 2002).These models of 'social physics' explore how the 'entanglement' of individuals, their 'spin' (psychological biases) and the 'tilt' of prevailing conditions result in the emergence of self-organising phenomena such as the residential separation of slightly different populations, social 'crazes', the 'invisible hand' of markets and people's choices about what social venues to frequent (Johnson, 2001; Ball, 2004; Johnson, 2007). Our choices often reflect the opinions of people around us, a 'herding instinct' that offers a mostly valid shortcut for deciding between options. This tendency to copy and learn from our immediate contacts is influenced by two modes of thinking – the emotional 'gut reaction' and a more cognitive approach based on slow rationalisation (Kahneman, 2011). Feedback and preferences are seen to be of critical importance (about both past events and current propensities to act in certain ways), alongside levels of connectivity. It is these factors which seem to influence how sets of people behave (and think), generating order out of apparent disorder through seemingly individual decisions.

Every community is unique and operates according to different conditions, but it is not too far fetched to see communities as sharing similar characteristics, with people collectively displaying remarkable levels of coherence despite the apparent lack of organisation. Clutter and chaos in communities (as in personal life) can actually be quite productive and creative (see Abrahamson and Freedman, 2007). Bureaucracies find it difficult to deal with the inherent messiness of communities (Alter and Hage, 1993; Gilchrist, 2019), but networks are vital in enabling connections and groups to evolve without hindrance. Tendencies for cultural conformity and self-organisation appear in groups, organisations, coalitions and cliques through mutual observation and expectations. Collectivities of all kinds align, coalesce or expire in response to changes in the social, economic and political environment.

Chance encounters and unplanned interactions between people against a background of 'social jostlings' are crucial in determining the actual form (and membership) of these social configurations

(Ball, 2004). Their basic shape (or fractal) will be familiar to most community workers: the community council, the pressure group, the self-help network, the village forum and the informal clusters of neighbours and friends who come together to help each other or to pursue a mutual interest. It could be argued that community development involves 'tweaking' the conditions, the connections and, sometimes, the capacity of communities to increase the probability that certain groupings will emerge and be sustained for as long as they are useful. This includes shaping the policy and funding environments, making certain resources more available and creating opportunities that make some outcomes more likely than others. However, it is not possible to specify in detail what will happen in a given community – only to forecast likely trends (Byrne, 2005). Attempts to monitor the effectiveness of community development using prescribed targets and time-scales are therefore inappropriate, although indicators which track changes in connectivity and cohesion are probably valid (Phillips, 2005). In recent years evaluation models and theories of change have begun to incorporate ideas from complexity theory (Lowe, 2017a, 2017b) using multi-pronged web-based methods to measure the effects of complex interventions, for example in public health, education and community safety (Komro et al, 2016). It will be interesting to see if these models can be applied to community development.

A spectrum of community complexity

A system's complexity increases according to the number of elements in the system, their diversity and the levels of interconnectivity. Complex systems can be imagined as ranged along a spectrum of activity from 'stagnant' (where nothing significant happens and there are no noticeable changes) to 'chaotic' (where small incidents produce upheavals across the system) (Table 9.1).

Computer models of cell automata have been used to simulate the behaviour of complex systems. Kauffman (1995) identifies three broad bands of operation for these systems: 'frozen', 'melting' and 'chaotic'. Complexity theory suggests that systems with low levels of connectivity and highly similar elements tend to freeze. Populations that have these levels of fragmentation or homogeneity (either by choice or circumstance) struggle to innovate or to adapt to change. At the other end of the continuum, systems in which the behaviour of elements is influenced by a multitude of highly diverse connections are too volatile and cannot achieve stability. We see this in neighbourhoods

Table 9.1: Spectrum of complex social systems

➔ Increasing levels of connectivity			
	Static	**'Edge of chaos'**	**Chaos**
Nature of interactions	Frozen, stagnant	Vibrant, creative, adaptive	Unpredictable, volatile, anarchic
Level of connections	Sparse, few boundary-spanning links	Rich and diverse, plenty of 'weak ties'	Saturated, high-density networks
Community characteristics	Isolated from wider society and external influences; fragmented or homogeneous	Cohesive, social structures and informal networks are inclusive	Volatile, mobile or transient population, few linkages between clusters and sectors
Typical features	Closed, long-standing community such as a monastery; rigid structures and strong, centralised control	Multi-ethnic neighbourhood with fairly stable population, mixed-tenure housing; range of self-help community groups and umbrella organisations	Unpopular peripheral estate, housing dominated by single social landlord, transient population; absence of formal structures and community activities

with high levels of private rented properties in short-term tenancies (Robinson and Reeve, 2006).

The optimal state for a system operating in an uncertain, turbulent world is in the 'melting zone' on the 'edge of chaos', between order and disorder (Waldrop, 1992). This latter term was coined by a group of mathematicians, including Doyne Farmer and Norman Packard (Packard, 1988; Kauffman, 1995), to describe an intermediate zone of 'untidy creativity', between rigidity and chaos, where a complex system is best able to function, adjusting constantly to slight perturbations but without cataclysmic disruption. A complex system at the 'edge of chaos' has been dubbed as organisationally 'chaordic' (Hock, 1999). It is highly adaptive, maintaining itself in a state of dynamic equilibrium between regularity and randomness, through processes of self-organisation, known as *autopoiesis* (Maturana and Varela, 1987; Mingers, 1995). It is thus able to synchronise interactions and coordinate activities among individual components (Lawler et al, 2015). The emergence and experience of 'community' achieves this for human societies, through the integrating functions of informal networks. The development of 'community' as a desirable emergent property of complex social systems can be seen as the primary purpose of the networking approach to community development.

Chaordic community

The idea of 'community' as an antidote to 'chaos' was first proposed in a paper published more than half a century ago by the National Council of Social Service (White, 1950). In Greek mythology, the gods Chaos and Gaia were regarded as inseparable and complementary partners, acting in tandem to maintain the world as a self-sustaining system (see Lovelock, 1979). Using this framework, it is possible to reconceptualise the purpose of community development work as helping to achieve optimal levels of connectivity. This includes enhancing people's capacity to network individually and through their collective organisations. Traditionally in community development the emphasis has been on establishing and managing forms of associational life as goals in their own right. The 'edge of chaos' model of community suggests that the purpose of such activities is primarily to create opportunities for interaction and coordination.

The 'art of hosting' approach to community participation embraces the notion of working with 'chaos' to discover order and create unity. Practitioners using these concepts refer to a state of 'chaordism', blending characteristics of chaos and order within one organisation or community (Fitzgerald and van Eijnatten, 2002). Drawing on models of complex adaptive systems, they suggest that by 'cultivating' meaningful conversations and 'tilting' the community or organisational environment it becomes possible to perform the equivalent of 'herding cats' (Block, 2009).

Groups and organisations crystallise and evolve in an environment of complex and dynamic personal interaction, often following a life cycle that is contingent on specific conditions and responsive to the changing needs, capabilities and relations of members. Studies of local voluntary activity, social movements and the 'below the radar' community sector identify a degree of order and informal collaboration within community settings, demonstrated at organisational level through mutual affiliation and liaison, and between individuals through friendship networks and overlapping membership (Curtis and Zurcher, 1973; Chanan, 1992; Rochester, 1999, 2013; Tarrow, 2005). These mechanisms maintain a social system at the 'edge of chaos' and need to be properly understood if they are to be nurtured for collective benefit. As the biologist E.O. Wilson observed, 'by itself, emergence can be no explanation at all if you don't have any insight into the mechanics of the system' (cited in Ball, 2004, p 155).

The social mechanisms school of sociology attempts to get beyond a superficial narrative, to identify not only what is happening but how the various factors interact in causal ways (for example Hedstrom, 2005; Tindall, 2007). Passy (2003) identifies three mechanisms that encourage participation in social movements, which she terms socialisation, structural connection and decision shaping. These refer to the linkages and interactions between people which serve to draw individuals into activism (or not). In this context collective efficacy is a plausible candidate for the mechanism that translates social capital into community-led change (Ohmer and Beck, 2006). Whatever the basis for the connections between individuals, it is evident that personal networks are crucial to the development and maintenance of collective action strategies. People's sense of 'community', their social identity, derives from the unpredictable dynamics of mutual influence and interaction. This reflects real experience and emotions, encompassing the negative aspects of human relationships as well as rose-tinted notions of belonging, trust and loyalty.

Community can be seen as the 'emergent property' of a complex social system operating at the 'edge of chaos', ensuring cooperation and cohesion without imposing formal or centralised control. In this respect, 'community' is not simply equivalent to a 'social system', but is, rather, the outcome of continuous interactions within networks. 'Community' represents both the context and the process through which collective problem solving emerges, in much the same way as life forms evolved from the 'primordial soup' of previous aeons (Kauffman, 1995). The sociologist George Herbert Mead recognised this phenomenon many years previously, observing that

> when things get together, there arises something that was not there before, and that character is something that cannot be stated in terms of the elements which go to make up the combination. (Mead, 1938, p 641)

This prescient form of systems thinking recognises that different properties appear at successive levels of analysis and are the product of 'organised complexity' (Capra, 1996). Complex networks are the pattern of all living systems, in which evolution uses chance and necessity to assemble new entities and to sustain diverse and resilient eco-populations. Those combinations that best 'fit' the current environment are those that survive. In the context of human societies, the precise format and membership of these cliques, clusters and coalitions are influenced (but not determined) by factors in the environment, such as public interest, political expediency, funding regimes and the existence of similar organisations competing for the same resources (Phelps et al, 2007). A familiar range of collective entities can be discerned in the groups, forums, federations, clubs and societies that populate civil society, and the voluntary and community sector in particular. These reflect prevailing cultural expectations and local conventions, and often preserve existing differentials of power and privilege. These are the 'strange attractors' of complex mature systems that have evolved at the 'edge of chaos'.

Creating opportunities for networking

Networking is an active and ongoing process that flourishes more readily in some circumstances than in others. Traditional community work activities, such as festivals, local campaigns or support for self-help groups, are not *primarily* concerned with building relationships. Nevertheless they provide vital opportunities for informal networking and should be organised in ways that do not unintentionally exclude some people or perpetuate inequalities. Networking must therefore be based on inclusive practices that proactively address issues around access, cultural appropriateness and the assumptions and feelings that perpetuate oppression. Networking can be conceived at one level as a method of opening up and shaping communal spaces and places in order to facilitate integration and cohabitation while promoting equality and diversity (Nash and Christie, 2003). Changing the structures and cultures of an event or organisation can radically alter patterns of interaction. This could mean anything from the arrangement of chairs to form a circle at meetings to the use of ice-breakers and exercises to encourage participation (see, for example, Bradley, 2004). Some organisations host networking events that have the explicit aim of facilitating connections as efficiently as possible, including the use of 'speed networking' to encourage people to move on after just a brief encounter that may or may not be followed up. This approach allows no time to get beyond superficial impressions, let alone to build trust; nor does it address or even acknowledge power differentials.

Efforts to involve people from disadvantaged groups should be genuine and practical, not tokenistic. That may require prior work to build confidence by supporting smaller, self-organised groups until they feel able to participate equally in wider activities and partnerships. Some groups may need backing with resources and practical help so that these communities can develop the confidence and capacity needed to be influential and gain access to mainstream services and decision making. It is also likely to require tackling discriminatory attitudes and behaviours among people who assume (often unconsciously) privileged territorial 'rights' based on previous custom and practice. This can generate resentment, even outright conflict, and must be handled carefully (Gilchrist, 2007). Above all, networking should protect people's autonomy and accommodate their diversity.

Meta-networking strategies commonly involve food and entertainment. These might be regular opportunities to meet and mingle in a convivial atmosphere, such as a street party or community cooking clubs. Preparing and sharing food together is an enactment of 'communion' which epitomises the origin of the word 'community', but, as Nelson et al (2000, p 361) observe, it is also a 'gendered burden' mainly undertaken by women. Cultural and sporting events (even competitive ones) are another means of forging closer links, perhaps because of their semi-structured and yet informal nature. Team-building exercises often use communal games to create situations for improving trust and cooperation among disparate groups. Community and inclusive arts and craft activities offer reassuring and inspiring ways for people to relate to each other and share their stories, through active participation rather than passive consumption, thereby strengthening relations and revealing new perspectives on familiar mindscapes (Willats, 2012; Bell, 2017; Gulbenkian Foundation, 2017; Milling et al, 2018).

Community workers can play a role in facilitating communication and cooperation where it does not occur 'naturally', building bridges between different sections of the population while trying to create (and sometimes defend) spaces for marginalised groups to empower themselves and affirm their own identity (Chauhan, 2009). Communal spaces are where people meet regularly, exchange pleasantries and eventually begin to form low-intensity, but potentially helpful, relationships. This may explain the enduring dominance of the geographical dimension to definitions of community. It reflects the importance of 'place' as a site for unplanned, informal interaction. However, the tendency to romanticise the village or neighbourhood as the pre-eminent (if not only) basis for 'community' should be avoided. Perhaps we need to reinvent a modern equivalent of the Italian *passegiata*, a regular promenade or gathering of citizens that encourages face-to-face interchange in an environment that has open access and few rules of engagement. Unfortunately, the apparent decline in town markets and high street shopping, coinciding with the explosion of online purchases, has reduced opportunities for such encounters – although this is probably somewhat counteracted by the number of parcel deliveries that neighbours take in for each other.

Seen from this perspective, street festivals, village fetes, community open days and similar events are vital activities in the local calendar because they encourage people from different organisations and groups to work together, strengthening the trust and ties between them and reigniting community spirit (Derrett, 2003; Mellor and Stephenson, 2005). Just as significantly, such events themselves provide opportunities for 'ordinary' residents to participate in something that does not require a deep commitment but which brings them into contact with neighbours and other members of the community in a friendly, semi-structured and non-threatening environment. Street parties in urban areas create temporary 'third places' for people who are neighbours, but often unknown to each other, to come together on home ground and with minimal formal planning. Such occasions have been used effectively to develop social capital and community cohesion (Streets Alive, 2008). Community workers play a key role in helping community activists to organise (and publicise) these events and, crucially, in ensuring that they are accessible and inclusive for all residents and potential visitors. It is particularly important that people from different cultural backgrounds feel welcome, and that the access requirements of Disabled people are met. Considerable hidden work is needed to ensure that such 'open' events are genuinely comfortable and relevant to all sections of the community.

Box 9.1: Unity Streets, Birmingham

Unity Streets is based in Balsall Heath, Birmingham and is entirely run by volunteers. It was set up in 2016 by a local resident to run street parties bringing neighbours together for some family fun, with food donated by local businesses and community members. The original community group has expanded to also organise coffee mornings, barbeques and trips for children. Activities are open to anyone living in this multi-ethnic community and also involve officers from local services, such as the police.

Chantall Faure, the project's founder, uses a variety of games and 'ice-breaker' exercises at the events to actively encourage participants to talk to one another and find out what they have in common. They provide an informal opportunity for people to make connections with neighbours whom they might not normally speak to. Many young people are involved as volunteers, taking on key responsibilities and learning to become community leaders of the future.

See: https://www.facebook.com/unitystreetsbalsallheath/

Developing the well-connected community

The overall function of such interventions (whether by paid professionals, volunteers, social entrepreneurs or active citizens) is the development of a complex social system operating at the 'edge of chaos'. I term this model the well-connected community. Ideally this is based on flexible, self-reliant networks that contain, or have links to, a 'sufficient diversity' of skills, knowledge, interests and resources for the formation of any number of possible groups and collective initiatives. The primary task of the community worker is to enable people to establish these connections and maintain the web. As Zeldin notes in championing the role of intermediaries, 'respect cannot be achieved by the same methods as power. It requires not chiefs, but mediators, arbitrators, encouragers and counsellors ... whose ambition is limited to helping individuals to appreciate each other and to work together even when they are not in complete agreement' (Zeldin, 1994, p 144). How people operate as intermediaries and what they choose to do with these connections may fall into different profiles or sets of practices. Their chosen strategies (or profiles) are affected partly by individual motives, partly by local circumstances and partly by the wider social and political environment (Durose et al, 2016).

The acknowledgement of 'chance' and emotion within this process does not diminish the influence of policy makers or the skilled input of community workers. Instead it highlights the difficulties of accurate forecasting and the need for flexibility around evaluation. However, this poses some problems for implementation and evaluation because holistic, joined-up interventions in the form of whole-community (or area-based) programmes are inherently 'complicated, complex and unpredictable', due to the number of participating agencies, including community members, and the constantly changing context (Burton et al, 2006, p 302). Attempts to quantify the costs and benefits of participation have discovered both practical difficulties and professional resistance, due in part to the intangible and serendipitous nature of community-level contributions and outcomes (Andersson et al, 2007; CDF, 2014). Community development cannot be realised through business plans or the achievement of specific performance criteria. Rather, it is about helping a given population (social system) to balance at the 'edge of chaos' as a way of managing uncertainty and developing shared infrastructure. This involves the nurturing of dynamic and diverse networks to create patterns of interaction that are neither utterly confusing nor frozen rigid.

Discussion

A well-connected community is immensely capable of responding to changes in the external environment through challenge and adaptation. It is certainly not isolated from the world outside. Links that cross system boundaries offer a further advantage in allowing for the importing of new ideas and comparisons between different experiences. The well-connected community has strong internal relationships, but also benefits from useful links with people and organisations beyond its immediate borders. These give it resilience, so that it is able to recover from damage, to resist threats and to adapt to change (Innes and Jones, 2006). Weak ties provide the communication channels within communities, spanning boundaries and bridging schisms. They are often embodied in the relationships between individuals, variously termed 'switches' (Castells, 1996), 'catalysts' (Gilchrist, 1998b; Creasy et al, 2008), 'social hubs' (Gladwell, 2000), 'linkers' (Fraser et al, 2003), 'weavers' (Traynor, 2008), 'critical nodes' (Dale and Sparkes, 2008), 'civic entrepreneurs' (Durose, 2009), 'bricoleurs' (Soteri-Proctor, 2017), 'smart urban intermediaries' (Durose et al, 2016) and 'creative bureaucrats' (Landry and Caust, 2017). These connectors act as ambassadors, translators and negotiators, able to mobilise bridging and linking capital across disparate groups or organisations (Freeman, 2009).

It would be useful to enhance our understanding of the evolutionary processes of informal groups and networks, perhaps looking at the optimal relationships between size, form and purpose. Morgan (1989) suggests that networks are manageable only up to the limits of personal engagement and surveillance, and I have accumulated ample anecdotal and empirical evidence that networks function optimally with around 35–40 participating members. This observation may reflect a trade-off between the costs of maintaining this number of links and the benefits of their diverse contributions to voluntary collective action. Computer simulations of networked systems also indicate that excessive connectivity can be a problem, reducing the adaptability of the whole system (Mulgan, 1997, p 186). This has implications for online networking and suggests that, within community development, direct networking between individuals has to be tempered by some degree of formal structure, to avoid information overload and the danger of tipping a system into chaos.

The principles of empowerment and equality can easily be incorporated into a complexity-based model of community-level development (Ramalingam et al, 2008; Neely, 2015). Discrimination, prejudice and social exclusion are not just 'morally wrong'; they can be seen as dysfunctional in that they disrupt the free flow of information across the system and restrict the development of potentially advantageous collaborative arrangements. Equality issues must be addressed in order to dismantle barriers to communication and to promote diversity within the networks. Anti-oppressive practice promotes the integrity, diversity and authenticity of the whole system, guaranteeing individual rights as well as eliminating illegitimate social biases. This involves tackling institutional discrimination and attitude change, in order to develop political, practical and psychological levels of transformation.

Conclusions

Networking and meta-networking are fundamental methods of community development, and promote principles of cohesion, empowerment and inclusion. Professional practice assists individuals in making strategic and opportune connections that create and maintain collective forms of organisation. In human social systems, 'community' reflects both the objective experience and the imagined 'spirit' of complex interactions, from which emerge the familiar 'strange attractors' of self-help groups and citizens' organisations. Ideally, a sense of community expresses a dimension of our lives that is about tolerating difference, promoting equality and acknowledging mutuality. The model of the well-connected community does not, however, attempt to reinvent a nostalgic version of traditional villages or urban neighbourhoods. Instead, it proposes a vision of a complex, but integrated and dynamic, super-network of diverse connections such as depicted in the sociological revisitings of Young and Willmott's East End London (Mumford and Power, 2003; Dench et al, 2006). The purpose of community development is to support and shape formal and informal networking in order to facilitate the emergence of effective and sustainable forms of voluntary organisation and collective action. As society becomes increasingly complex, the maintenance of interlinked, flexible networks around a variety of interests and identities will constitute our best strategy for building mature, resilient and empowered communities.

QUESTIONS FOR REFLECTION AND DISCUSSION

✧ Do you know any communities that appear to you to be not functioning as well as they could be because they seem to be either 'stagnant' or 'chaotic'?

✧ Imagine yourself working in a perfectly 'chaordic' community. What does it feel like?

✧ In your experience, what gives communities their resilience and capacity to adapt with changing times?

10

Issues and implications

Where do we go from here? Chaos or community?
Martin Luther King, title of book published 1968

Community development is not a straightforward, linear process; change can happen suddenly and unevenly through shifts in consciousness or an influx of resources. Serendipitous encounters can lead to rapid alterations of course, with new connections being made, catalysing conversations, and the discovery of possibilities which did not seem to exist before. Informal networking complements formal liaison mechanisms by creating the conditions that support effective coordination across boundaries. The connections themselves appear to provide a foundation for collective and individual empowerment. Sound working relationships are vital for joint action and collaboration. They create a collective power base that enables individuals and groups in communities to influence the decisions of more powerful bodies. This emphasis on networking raises a number of questions concerning the position and function of the community worker and which have implications for policy and practice. This book has sought to demonstrate that networking should usually count as work, in the sense that it takes time, effort and practice, using a range of skills and strategies. When deployed for community development purposes, proactive interventions are needed, and so should be valued and supported. This chapter outlines a few key implications for this approach.

We have seen that internal connections and interactions are absolutely crucial to the functioning of vibrant and resourceful communities that support their members, show solidarity with others and are able to deal with differences and challenges as they arise. But, for communities to change things in order to improve their environment, services and opportunities, locally and in wider society, they need to be influential and to access resources. Collective organising and social action is effective, inclusive and sustainable if it works from a broad base and reaches out to people and organisations beyond immediate community boundaries, for example through national networks and campaigns. Community workers can help to set up and foster such links, especially if barriers, conflicts and power differentials are encountered.

It is now generally accepted that networking is essential to the community development process and that without it, other functions become difficult or impossible to carry out. Community workers frequently hold pivotal positions or play key roles in setting up and servicing network-type organisations, such as area- or issue-based multi-agency forums. They provide 'maintenance' and 'leadership' functions, sometimes chairing or facilitating meetings, organising mailings, monitoring and generally encouraging participation. In short, they establish conditions in which networking flourishes, working hard to ensure that these are inclusive, productive and equitable by paying attention to issues around access, reciprocity, diversity and power. This 'breadth of spirit' is demonstrated through compassion, tolerance and patience. Networkers show respect, not condescension, and are willing to learn from others. In many ways the competent networker will use the skills and quality of a good host at a large party: making people welcome, drawing them into conversation and introducing them to others whom they might find compatible or stimulating. Good networking should be neither too blatant nor overly focused. It is about facilitating, not controlling, interaction, helping people to make useful contacts and supporting the processes of relationship formation.

Relationships as women's work?

Commonly used metaphors for networking – spinning, weaving, netting and knitting – often refer to womanly crafts that are creative and transformative. They assemble diverse people and assets to construct something new and useful by reconfiguring and aligning connections in ways that can bring together and hold separate textures, colours and resources. Successful bricolage requires scavenging, brokering, intermediating and translating skills; a willingness to venture into unknown or uncomfortable places and then to nurture the resultant networks, or help them to 'give birth' to more formal groups and organisations.

Networking demands a complex range of capabilities, covering social, political and administrative skills. In addition it needs an appreciation of the context and a willingness to intervene actively in order to assist other people in developing their own relationships. In many informal networks there often seems to be one individual who keeps in touch with the others, who arranges get-togethers, has up-to-date news and contact details and generally ensures that everyone stays on more or less good terms. In families and friendship circles this role is often played by women, and there is evidence that women's emotional labour creates and maintains networks within other social settings, such as the workplace or within communities (Innerarity, 2003; Hochschild, 2012).

In the community development literature, networking has been referred to as a 'womanly' way of operating (Dominelli, 2006). Studies have frequently commented on the role played by women in neighbouring and informal networks (Bourke, 1994), running voluntary and community activities (Doucet, 2000; Krishnamurthy et al, 2001), participating in regeneration partnerships (May, 1997), sustaining self-help groups, building inclusive political coalitions (Fearon, 1999) and generally keeping the peace (Kolb, 1992). More controversially, Stackman and Pinder (1999) argue in their study that gender differences appear in men's and women's work-based networks, with the latter being more 'expressive' and based on relatively intense emotional ties, while men tend to cultivate fewer, but more instrumental, links with colleagues. This chimes with Ferree's (1992) view that women tend to derive their motivation and identity from the web of attachments in which they are embedded.

Women may have some advantage here, due to upbringing and social status. There is evidence that women, compared to men, may think in more fluid and lateral ways, making more effective use of intuition and inductive logic (Belenky, 1986). Gilligan (1982) suggests that this is particularly relevant to understanding gender differences in the skills and strategies that are used to manage social situations. She argues that girls learn patience, awareness of others' needs and relationship skills through childhood games that emphasise cooperation and role-playing. As a result, women have 'developed the foundations of extremely valuable psychological qualities' (Miller, 1976, p 27), including enhanced abilities in non-verbal communication and emotional perception. In addition, adults tend to praise girls for being kind and thoughtful, while boys are rewarded for behaviour that is brave and independent.

These differences become internalised as 'feminine' and 'masculine' characteristics and are translated in later life into gendered roles, styles of working and moral frameworks. These tendencies are not genetically determined and it would be invidious to over-generalise, but evidence, including the findings from the Panel Study, supports the observation that men are more achievement oriented, more instrumentalist, while women tend to see themselves as responsible for managing relationships through the expression of care and attention towards others. The suspicion that women are more diligent and proficient networkers raises issues about how the outcomes of this work are acknowledged (and rewarded), because evaluation schemes often emphasise measurable performance targets and overlook the underlying processes that have contributed to their achievement. Skill and effort underpin effective networking, and it should be celebrated as valuable, but hitherto neglected, 'women's work' developing 'community' and building social capital (Blaxter et al, 2003; Dominelli, 2006).

These abilities can be learned through observation and experience. Everyone can become more skilled and strategic in their networking. While women may not be necessarily or instinctively better networkers, it can nevertheless be argued that this work of building, maintaining and mending relationships should be more highly valued. Networking abilities are acquired in complex ways: from role models, practice situations and, possibly, formal training exercises. Simply being more aware of techniques and traits that support effective networking will encourage people to adopt this approach more explicitly in their community development work.

Spaces and opportunities for dropping in and hanging out

For diversity to flourish, communities need neutral communal spaces which are neither private nor public, where the integrative processes of community and civil society can be continually renewed (Warburton, 1998). Community development requires places and opportunities for people to meet, interact and generally get to know one another through conversations and informal exchanges. Local amenities, such as parks, libraries and playgrounds are used for hanging out, dropping by. They are familiar, communal locations for chance or scheduled encounters occurring between friends and acquaintances (Audunson et al, 2007). These 'neighbourhood level places of encounter' (Piacentini, 2018) may be particularly significant for populations at the margins of society, such as refugees. They may become the location for informal regular gatherings, but these are also associated with more formal or commercial institutions such as cafes, religious services, school collection times or business breakfasts. Community hubs and social infrastructure, such as family centres, youth clubs and the communal rooms in blocks of flats or older people's accommodation, offer vital, usually safe, places for people to gather, mingle, offer a helping hand and occasionally discover serendipitous links with one another (Percy-Smith and Matthews, 2001; Ferguson, 2016; Gregory, 2018). Community workers are often instrumental in creating and maintaining such places and occasions, and ensuring that they are safe, accessible and have a sense of local ownership or belonging so that everyone feels they can drop by, make contact or join in. Often arrangements to meet will be made via social media. This may reduce the probability of serendipitous encounters, but it seems likely that online connectivity actually encourages more face-to-face contact. For many, the functionality and friendliness of these 'landscapes of helping' and 'social platforms' in enabling 'incidental links' shapes how they experience community and access different types of support (Allen et al, 2015; Price, 2015).

Many traditional spaces for hanging out, such as shopping parades or pubs, are disappearing or have become too expensive, leading, some say, to a decline in associational life (Muir, 2012). In championing what he calls 'palaces for the people', Klinenberg (2018) argues for social infrastructure and local amenities to be protected as spaces for people to network and organise collectively against inequality and stem the tide of polarisation. These 'third places' need to be accessible and accommodating to different people: they need to feel like a 'home away from home', where there are neither guests nor hosts, simply regular users who share the space and engage with one another as and when they choose (Oldenburg, 1991). Community 'anchors' offer similar havens and may be run by volunteers or paid staff, as a statutory service, as a social business or on a commercial basis (Community Alliance, 2007; Henderson et al, 2018).

Box 10.1: Chatty cafes

Originally started by Alexandra Hoskyn in her home town of Oldham in 2017, the chatty cafe initiative aims to combat the social isolation she saw around her. She persuaded local cafes to encourage people to sit together by designating tables for 'Chatter and Natter'. These notices invite customers who come in alone or who simply want some short-term human companionship and are happy to talk to strangers. So far this simple idea for stimulating informal interaction has been well received and there are now over 400 participating cafes. The scheme has received widespread positive publicity and is being emulated across the UK.

See: https://thechattycafescheme.co.uk/

Attempts to create online 'third places' for socialising, exchange and political deliberation have included informal chat rooms, moderated discussion and decision-making forums (such as Loomis) and 'Twitter hours', but they tend to attract a vocal minority of regular users

(Albrecht, 2006; Pine and Korn, 2011; Gerbaudo, 2012; Halpern and Gibbs, 2013; Graham and Wright, 2014). While this comes across as a criticism, it could be argued that it simply reflects the offline reality.

Factors such as traffic flow through local streets can have a major impact on the level and quality of community interaction (Appleyard, 1981) and have often been the target of community campaigns. The creation of traffic-free 'home zones' should be a consideration in planning designs for sustainable neighbourhoods. Outdoor semi-mediated communal spaces, gated and gardened alleyways at the backs of urban housing rows, provide low-risk places for social interaction and encounter that are not governed by overly formal etiquette. The idea of picnics (literally and metaphorically) captures this approach – operating as they do between order and ambiguity, with important lessons for community participation (Harris, 2011). Familiarity and mutual recognition affect how users of public space relate to one another. It helps to build a sense of belonging if local interests and cultures are acknowledged, perhaps even celebrated (Worpole and Knox, 2007). Such spaces can be designed and decorated (using community art such as murals) to encourage processes of interaction that promote diversity and equality, rather than simply reflecting the dominant presence (Lownsbrough and Beunderman, 2007). Issues of perceived safety and accessibility are especially important for older people and those with reduced mobility (Connolly, 2003; Help the Aged, 2008).

How can local spaces become genuinely 'communal' as places that people use for specific purposes but where they will also encounter individuals with different needs and life-styles? Community workers can help residents and other users to share such facilities, dealing with the occasional but perhaps inevitable clashes while encouraging conversation, integration and understanding. But, as many people living in mixed neighbourhoods will testify, co-residence does not guarantee either interaction or mutual obligation (Forrest and Kearns, 2001; Madanipour, 2003; Power, 2007; Cantle, 2008).

Impact of technology

Online and mobile technologies help people to keep information on a potentially huge range of contacts. But it is not possible to sustain an unlimited number of relationships. Some will wither away unless actively maintained; and all need to be reviewed from time to time to take account of changing priorities and circumstances. Strategic judgements are made to prune or nurture parts of the network while avoiding over-attentiveness to less appropriate contacts. Differentials in access and confidence, the so-called 'digital divide', pose major problems to societies increasingly oriented towards the internet and e-citizenship (Loader and Keeble, 2004), especially with an increasing number of government services being available only online.

Deliberate efforts are needed to reach out to those on the margins of communities. In some cases, the popularity of using information technologies to connect can exacerbate this tendency, since the most vulnerable and excluded people may have limited or no access to the internet (Rheingold, 2012). This effect is likely to be countered by the near-ubiquity and increasing use of mobile devices – among people in poverty and homeless people, for example – coupled with the widespread use of social media platforms. Although disparity in access will probably diminish, economic inequalities will continue to mean that many are unable to benefit fully, even with more powerful network capabilities.

There is still room for improvement in the use of digital networking within communities and the charitable sector. Since 2015 the Centre for Acceleration of Social Technology (CAST) has been working with community and voluntary organisations to increase their use of tools that will enhance the experience of members and users for social good. In terms of active citizenship, there are moves to develop technologies that will empower residents, improve 'smart' governance and strengthen civil society (Calzada and Cobo, 2015; Knight Foundation, 2017). Experience in developing countries indicates that even the most remote and rural communities can be empowered using internet-based networks (Rahman, 2006).

Technology facilitates information flow and connections, but, it might be asked, can community informatics replicate (or even replace) the emotional basis of face-to-face interaction found in offline communities? Some have claimed that face-to-face community is somehow more valid or 'meaningful' than online community (for example Locke, 1998; Popple, 2015), or that online activities displace 'real' personal interactions (for example Nie et al, 2002). This tendency to argue in 'either/or' terms, with online regarded as inherently inferior, is unhelpful and possibly offensive (for example, to many disabled people whose lives have been enriched by web-based connectivity). It's also fair to say that rose-tinted portrayals of 'traditional' offline community as some kind of ideal, devoid of tension or conflict, hardly strengthen these claims. Reference to the emotional content found in face-to-face interaction and allegedly absent online also deserves closer scrutiny. Aside from extreme examples, it is simply not a question of 'replicating' or 'replacing' one form of communication with another, but of understanding the ideal complementarity of face-to-face and online interactions in the interests of *any* legitimate occurrence of community (see Harris, 2003, for an exploration of the issues raised in this paragraph). Mobile technologies have been used to connect with potential collaborators and to gather 'flash mobs' for mass demonstrations and generate publicity or interest. The distinction between face-to-face interaction and computer-mediated communication is becoming increasingly blurred and often depends on what is sought from the connection (Davies, 2003; Foth and Hearn, 2007; Ryberg and Larsen, 2008). Wellman (2006) refers to the rise of 'networked individualism', through which people maintain links with a variety of online communities, using these to promote themselves and meet their social needs.

Online communities

Developments in mobile and computer-based technologies have added a new (and somewhat contentious) dimension to the debate on community (Gordon, 1999; Kim, 2000; Chayko, 2002; Kennedy and Bell, 2007), raising issues around personal authenticity, virtual identities and accountability. Concerns have also been raised about the disturbing effects that concentrated attention within the two-dimensional sphere of 'smart' media and screen gaming (rather than real-world interactions) may be having on people's attentional and empathic abilities, although this may be mitigated through using 'transhuman' technologies for story sharing and virtual experiences (Greenfield, 2008; Manney, 2008). Turkle (2017) cautions against the internet culture that seduces users into addictive searching and what she calls online 'tethering' to others that is devoid of meaningful connection.

There are numerous examples of social media platforms being used to encourage communication at local level, stimulating resident interaction and civic action (Watt et al, 2002; Matthews, 2016; Turkle, 2017). Migrant and diaspora communities use the internet to exchange personal news as well as cultural ideas (Hiller and Franz, 2004; McCabe et al, 2013). Hyper-local blogs and websites have been established in many localities, adapting existing platforms (to maintain independence) or using specially designed software; for example, Nextdoor.com or, in Europe, nebenan.de (Vollman, 2018). Sites such as Harringay Online generate ongoing digital conversations about local issues, address various needs (such as enquiries about childcare or trader recommendations) and can even provide a valid channel for official consultation. A 2010 study shows that such services 'enhance the sense of belonging, democratic influence, neighbourliness and involvement in their area. Participants claim more positive attitudes towards public agencies where representatives of those agencies are engaging online' (Flouch and Harris, 2010). The research found that these forums promote positive connections between residents, in terms of both encounters and exchange.

Social media

Social media can be exploited in the interests of democracy in almost any context through its 'collective agenda-setting power' (Standage, 2013, p 239). Internationally, social media has been associated with the contestation of rights in various movements. However, the ultimate outcome of such movements, in terms of genuine empowerment, has been questioned (Harris and McCabe, 2017b).

Social media allows political participation through online commentary principally through blogs – a 'fifth estate', augmenting the 'fourth estate' of independent media channels (Dutton, 2009). Bakardjieva (2009) notes how the internet supports 'micro-discourses and practices' that relate the personal to the political and make the possibility of 'everyday' civic participation more realistic. Some commentators, however, have argued that the internet encourages the phenomenon of the 'networked democratic spectator' (Kreiss, 2015); or that it gives rise to 'clicktivism' – 'sat-at-home' online contributions through donations, signing petitions or posting 'likes', a low-cost, low-risk form of engagement that erodes and devalues 'real' activism (Morozov, 2009; Harlow and Guo, 2014). The theory of clicktivism has, however, been contested (see, for example, Fatkin and Lansdown, 2015; Schumann and Klein, 2015).

In terms of community participation, the most subtle transformation attributed to internet use may be the most significant in the long term. Several researchers suggest that there is already a reduced role for community organisations in *organising*, with a detectable shift from collective action to 'connective action' (Bennett and Segerberg, 2011, 2012; McCabe and Harris, forthcoming). Some roles traditionally carried out by groups and organisations – such as awareness raising, generating resident responses, corresponding with local politicians, officers and media and so on – are increasingly carried out by networked individuals (McCosker, 2015), with organisations staying in the background or fulfilling other functions (Theocharis et al, 2015). There is an emerging distinction between, on the one hand, collective action that is directly enabled by organisations and, on the other, self-organising networked action. The role of the 'resource-rich' organisation may be diminishing and changing because of the power of sharing through social media (Bennett and Segerberg, 2012).

The close association of social media in general, and Facebook in particular, with neoliberalism has been noted in various studies. A review of some incisive literature on this theme raises questions

> in relation to the values embedded in the systems from which enhanced levels of participation and engagement are expected to flow. It also raises questions about who benefits most from the affordances of these technologies. These questions seem not to have been expressed clearly, let alone addressed, within the sector. (Harris and McCabe, 2017a, p 15)

Emerging applications

The advent of Web 2.0 platforms has changed the way many people interact with friends, colleagues and strangers. Social networking sites such as Facebook, Twitter, Pinterest and Instagram have made it relatively easy for user-generated material (photos, messages, games, videos and so on) to be shared widely and inexpensively. These sites enable people to stay in touch with friends and family, to set up virtual communities and campaigns, to recruit and induct new employees, to search for expertise and to promote themselves (Dutton and Helsper, 2007). There is then a risk of information glut and over-absorption, with possibly damaging implications for what Hobsbawm (2017) calls our social health. Hobsbawm argues that 'knowledge, networks and time are to social health what nutrition, exercise and sleep are to physical and mental health'. Again, questions arise about the extent to which this position may overlook both the negative aspects of face-to-face interaction and the positive effects of online.

The use of WhatsApp, SMS and Twitter applications to supply a continuous news stream about people's plans and preoccupations is the 21st-century equivalent of gossip, providing a constant update on the comings and goings within loosely defined communities or the wider world. Many blogs have become dependable alternative sources for news coverage and discussion, when the official media are blocked or seen to be biased against certain views. Transactions take place through eBay and PayPal, between traders and customers who need never meet and may live on opposite sides of the globe.

Knowledge production and exchange has been democratised through compendia and open source publishing. Wikipedia, an online encyclopaedia that is collectively compiled and edited, allows all comers to contribute and to change entries (with strict controls to prevent manipulation). It is claimed that the involvement of thousands of participants in such ventures ensures that they maintain their legitimacy as trusted sources of information through feedback, corrections, reviews and reliability ratings. This 'wisdom of the crowd' is similar to the way that face-to-face communities operate, but on a much larger and more impersonal scale using 'big data' and millions of opinions (Surowiecki, 2004; Johnson, 2007; Mulgan, 2017). Models of m(obile)-learning have been put forward to enable individuals to 'swarm' towards shared learning opportunities or sources of expertise, using common wireless access to locate these and share knowledge with one another (Nalder and Dallas, 2006).

Some of these emerging technologies may fade into history or blend into different forms; others may emerge. Any single application has the potential to contribute to different kinds of communal experience, or possibly to weaken community in unanticipated ways. Reflecting on what constitutes a well-connected community should enable us to forearm ourselves by identifying potential benefits and disbenefits at an early stage.

Tensions and conflict

A culture of flexible and informal decision making is ideal for reaching people 'on the edge' and encouraging them to organise events or participate in community activities. Loose structures and informal methods of organising facilitate the flow of ideas and enable relatively disparate initiatives to emerge. Networks allow 'wild' ideas and tentative expressions of interest to crystallise into something more tangible. But for this to have a wider impact it needs coordinating, moulding into a collective demand or aspiration. Faith and favours are fine up to a point, but they are not sufficient when organisational demands exceed resources, or when there are competing external pressures and internal disputes.

Trust and understanding allow cooperative relationships to form between partners and depend on the nature of connections and exchanges. Networks provide extremely effective modes of organising and communicating in situations that are complex and uncertain, but they can also be muddled, biased and fragile. A lack of clarity over remits and responsibilities can cause problems when there is much work to be done or competition for scarce resources. This can lead to the kind of rivalry, mistrust and recriminations that beset those voluntary organisations that are overly reliant on trust and assumed common values. Networks generally have no organisational mechanisms for resolving disagreements among the contributors and this can be problematic when everyone is under pressure and nobody is willing to take a lead. Networks are sometimes expected to perform functions for which they are ill suited, such as delivering services or managing staff and resources.

Networks support organisation, but more formal procedures may be needed for decision making and unified, rather than parallel, action. This is not always acknowledged, and tensions emerge within networks when it appears that conventions or expectations are being violated, even though these are rarely made explicit. Community workers need to be aware of when networks might need to make this transition and be prepared to offer advice about how to establish more appropriate structures and procedures. This shift from informal network to formal organisation needs to be handled carefully and fully acknowledged by all concerned. Often it is not, and this can lead to confusion and disagreement over how to move forward. Ideally, the new organisation should be set up to manage formal functions while leaving the networking capacity intact, but in practice this is not always possible.

Managing roles and boundaries

Issues of boundaries and 'burn-out' are particularly relevant to a long-standing debate about whether community development work is best undertaken by people who are themselves community members or by outsiders. In many contexts it is difficult to demarcate 'work' from 'life', and some people prefer not to do this anyway; for example, those working from overtly faith or political perspectives. In most employment situations a deliberate shift to informality can be used to indicate when roles are being blurred, by changes in the style of communication, relaxing of dress codes and using alternative settings or timings. Within most professions and bureaucracies, work conventions are recognised and generally adhered to, and so this switch from formal to informal is obvious. But community workers have no 'uniform', often work unconventional hours, occupy no fixed 'workplace', may themselves be members of the community and would normally converse in everyday language. Experienced community workers develop tactics and algorithms to distinguish between their professional roles and personal lives. At an interpersonal level it is probably acceptable to slacken role boundaries but not to ignore them altogether.

Good community development requires the maintenance of real and reciprocal relationships. Networking has been portrayed as an activity in which people engage as 'themselves', and the importance of 'authentic' relationships has been constantly emphasised. But, like any other occupation, community workers need to maintain their accountability and professional standards vis-à-vis colleagues, employers and community members. As we have seen, trust and informality are important aspects of networking. Good practice must also consider issues around power, role boundaries and impact. Sustainable networks have to be based on genuine commitment and mutual interests. Community workers use 'themselves' but should not lose sight of their responsibilities as agents representing their employers or as accountable to funders and different sections of the community.

Networking is effective for community development *because* it is personal, involving more than superficial connections devoid of emotional content. Networking is not about exploiting contacts in a manipulative or selfish way, but about establishing levels of trust, goodwill and mutual respect that run deeper than a sporadic and perfunctory exchange of information, business cards or 'likes' on social media. Personal relationships make it easier to make requests and suggestions, especially when these are inconvenient, complicated or hazardous:

> 'The personal touches are so important. If the personal stuff and the foundations are right, then I think the work will come out of it, because people will have such faith in you.' (TD)

This is particularly important when working with disadvantaged and oppressed people, who may feel more vulnerable and more suspicious of professional interventions. It is vital not to let people down or to deceive them. Being 'oneself' is crucial, while also taking care to negotiate and maintain roles – an essential but delicate balancing act. Adequate supervision and training would ease this, helping workers to be more conscious of role boundaries and better able to assert or, at least, manage these. Cross-sectoral and multi-layered partnerships have accentuated this issue, making it ever more important that community workers are able to work across organisational boundaries while maintaining both personal integrity and accountability. But networking carried out in one's professional capacity usually needs to stop short of friendship and personal intimacy. This applies to most colleagues as well as to community members, so as to minimise difficulties around confidentiality or misplaced loyalty that could distort decision making:

> 'I try to make sure that I don't take advantage of somebody, because it's easy to mislead people into thinking you're developing what could be a friendship with them, when really what in fact you're doing is developing a working relationship. I find this especially so in the mental health field, or [with] people who are unemployed or just vulnerable for whatever reason.' (TD)

Constantly 'being oneself' means that it is difficult to change or lower one's standards without being seen as hypocritical. The chameleon-like nature of networking also creates strain, in that "you can't be all things to all people all of the time" (PH).

Sustainability and accountability

This aspect of networking is often overlooked, and is the most probable cause of burn-out so often encountered in this type of work (Maslach, 1982). Burn-out is very common in community development and appears to be the consequence of a mismatch between expectations and what can actually be achieved by the worker (Fernet et al, 2004; Briner et al, 2008). It is characterised by emotional exhaustion and a reduced sense of personal accomplishment, possibly because the demands on well-connected community workers can come from anywhere in their extensive networks, and because networking seems so much to involve using one's own character and beliefs to build and maintain relationships. This can amount to a kind of 'prostitution of the personality', trying to be endlessly helpful, kind and caring to any and every member of the community. It may be helpful for workers if they can find mentors within their networks who can keep them focused and professional.

Notions of good practice include operating as transparently as possible, maintaining accountability and ensuring that relationships are reciprocal and non-dependent:

> 'Networking needs to take place at all levels [so that it is] mutual, it's supportive, it's not exclusive [and] must involve all sections of the community with different levels of

experience. It needs to occur purposefully and explicitly.' (CT)

This can create an additional burden for community workers in that this work is hidden from public view and can be taken for granted by others. It is not always appreciated that someone's capacity to provide relevant information and contacts has probably required a great deal of time and attention in acquiring (and storing) that knowledge in the first place. Practitioners usually work hard at cultivating the less convenient or more uncomfortable links in their networks. This involves making efforts to stay in touch, to send apologies and to show a continuing interest in different projects and communities. Networking can be stressful and tiring, creating invisible or unnegotiated accountability webs that are sometimes confusing and onerous.

Occasionally it may be expedient to dissolve the boundaries between paid and unpaid time, between activist and professional roles, and it is common for people in community development to be 'wearing several hats' at once. This multiplicity of ties and roles can be useful in terms of gaining access to different networks and building credibility. It may, however, create confusion around mutual expectations, confidentiality and professional accountability, especially when your friends and colleagues also have formal responsibilities as your employers and managers, as is often the case in communities and the voluntary sector.

When participating in networks, especially ones that are semi-formalised, paid community workers need to be clear about their role as members or representatives of organisations, especially within interdisciplinary teams or partnerships. They also need to take into account any relevant stated values or assumed goals and conventions.

'Networks have aims, have policies and so if I'm in a network I take very much on board what their aims and objectives are, what their policies are and I try and work within those.' (KT)

Nevertheless, participation in a network allows one to enjoy a degree of autonomy to make suggestions and take stances that might not be possible within a more rigid organisational framework.

However, there are clearly limits to the amount of time community workers can spend simply tending relationships. Managers and funders expect outcomes and often need these delivered across a range of issues and within a given time-scale. Job constraints necessitate a division of labour, and it is useful to keep strategic links with a variety of networks

183

in order to stay in touch with areas of policy where direct involvement is limited or precluded.

In addition, networking provides informal mechanisms of accountability. It allows people to monitor their own performance and credibility, while simultaneously providing a means of informal reporting. Managers should help community workers to clarify their roles and to review on a regular basis the effectiveness of their networking by asking people to examine how their relationships with people in the community are developing and being maintained. Otherwise the almost infinite complexity of informal networking can be somewhat bewildering for the workers and those they work with (Gilchrist, 2003; 2016, p 18).

Personal preferences and power differentials

In his examination of personal networks, Heald (1983, p 213) suggests that the 'art of networking is to do it naturally and with pleasure', but professional community workers cannot allow personal preferences to wholly determine the nature or content of their professional relations. This poses something of a dilemma: networking is easier and more enjoyable where there are common interests and mutual affinity. People tend to associate with people who are like themselves, and this dimension of networking could militate against inclusion and equality of opportunity. In some situations, the worker's identity (as perceived by others) may be a block to forming relationships, especially if differences in status or background are involved. The characteristics and capabilities of the community worker may be a factor in negotiating access to certain communities or self-organising groups, such as transgender or specific ethnic populations.

Understandably, people will seek company and stimulation where they feel appreciated or comfortable, and this also applies to 'off-duty' community workers. Individual preferences should not be underestimated as a source of inequality in networks, and this can have an unacceptable impact on community participation and joint working. The effect of envy, anxiety, resentment and fear on personal and professional networks is rarely considered, but these negative emotions obviously affect the availability of ideas and resources within the community and voluntary sector. Private affiliations and antagonisms are endemic in community networks and may create a quandary for people who are committed to principles of equal opportunity and democracy.

This gives rise to major issues around power and dependency in relation to networking activities. All too often, strategic and decision-making networks simply reflect and preserve existing privileges, perpetuating inequalities and social exclusion. An important role for the community worker is to expose and challenge semi-covert 'wheeling and dealing' by cliques operating in the 'corridors of power'. Community development's commitment to empowerment means that effective networking must span institutional boundaries and counter discrimination within organisations and communities.

Dominance by paid workers can present a problem, especially in situations where the pace of change is prescribed by external factors, such as funding programmes or performance criteria. Community development also operates within political systems, where staff can be persuasive either because of their position in the networks or because of their professional status. Practitioners must acknowledge their own influence, while working to reduce power differentials.

Monitoring and evaluation: measuring impact

Some thought should be given to assessing the overall impact of networking on the development of community benefits, as well as wider social outcomes. Networking interactions are often informal and happenstance. The gossamer-like threads set up are so fine that they are sometimes not even recognised as connections and are barely noted. Networking rarely has tangible or attributable 'outputs' and, consequently, funders and managers often do not appreciate its value:

> 'It's quite difficult to justify the fact that networking is an efficient way of achieving something, because a lot of people don't think it is; a lot of people think it's just chatting and wasting time.' (TD)

Attempts to evaluate the benefits of networking are clumsy by comparison, especially where monitoring procedures detect only predetermined performance criteria or quantifiable measures. In reviewing networks it is important to examine which sets of linkages may need strengthening or repairing, and which might be allowed to lapse or lie fallow for a while. The mental map needs constantly updating in the light of changes to organisations, policies or personnel.

The essence of good networking practice lies in balanced and recurrent interaction, rather than transitory and purely instrumental contact. Most forms of evaluation fail to acknowledge the 'serendipity' factor in community work, notably that many perfectly useful and decent developments are not planned, nor even sometimes imagined. They arise instead from opportune synchronicity to be found in everyday interactions (Cohen and Stewart, 1994). The complexity of context and interventions must be considered in thinking about communities as open, adaptive systems in which a number of initiatives (and their interactions) influence what happens in unpredictable ways (Barnes et al, 2003; Byrne, 2005; Burton et al, 2006).

Some versions of 'social capital' emphasise the importance of networks over norms of trust, and this approach has generated useful methods of measurement, as well as some methodological challenges (Coffé and Geys, 2007). Possibilities emerge from the concept of 'network capital' propounded by Wellman (2000, 2006). The RSA's 'connected communities' programme paid close attention to the growth of 'community capital' as a desired outcome from the various wellbeing interventions it introduced (Parsfield et al, 2015).

In the professional field of community work there has been an overemphasis on 'process' rather than product, and it is right that this apparent lack of accountability has been challenged (CD Challenge Group, 2006). It should be possible to devise evaluation frameworks that capture the hidden benefits of networking. The Achieving Better Community Development (ABCD) approach, first developed in Northern Ireland, provides a realistic and credible model for evaluating community development interventions, identifying informal networks as an important feature of community life:

> As well as tangible assets, communities are in one sense a sum of interpersonal and inter-group relationships. In a well-functioning community these will be well established ... and a crucial part of how the community actually works. (Barr and Hashagen, 2000, p 56)

The challenge of assessing the effectiveness of networks is addressed sometimes as a measure of community strengths (Skinner and Wilson, 2002), but more evidence is needed on whether there is an optimal level of connectivity for communities (equivalent to the 'chaordic' state). In the past, community development work has been reluctant to demonstrate (and claim) its impact in tackling problems and achieving results. The well-connected community model set out in this book deems 'community' to be the primary outcome emerging as a result of networking using various mechanisms of interaction, relationship building, cooperation and exchange.

A particular focus on the effectiveness of informal arrangements for organising social action may reveal the delicate practice and judgements made by those who are facilitating these encounters and relationships so that we can learn more about what works, and why. The evaluations carried out by learning advisors for funding programmes draw out useful lessons and identify positive, if sometimes intangible, outcomes, even though they do not purport to provide rigorous assessments of impact. Good ideas are often generated and spread informally but can become diluted in the process, losing the key principles or features that have made the model so inspiring. However, it is rarely possible to predict the exact consequences of community development, and in any case the requirement to do so risks stifling the initiative, creativity and synergy that networking can generate.

The benefits of networking should be viewed over the long term, but networking without eventual outcomes can also be criticised. At some stage there have to be results in terms of things actually happening – new projects, enhanced services, proposals agreed, funding secured and so on. The less visible improvements should also be recognised, such as increased cooperation among agencies, better representation on forums or consultative bodies and more subtle changes in relationships and attitudes:

> 'The things that I try to get done can't get done unless people invested personal commitments, so they're proof of whether networks have come alive, or whether things have been done well.... In the course of achieving the different practical results you do kind of note whether there are shifts in the tone of relationships between yourself and other people.' (MW)

Community workers know their networking to be effective when they are in demand. Other people hear of their work and they are invited to contribute to joint initiatives, their suggestions are taken up and implemented, they are used by others as an information resource and as a point of access into other networks:

> 'People say directly to you things like "you've got an amazing network" ... or, more to the point (the real test of it), they send other people, particularly new people, new workers coming into the borough ... You do feel a sense of being appreciated. That's the main thing that indicates that I'm there as a resource person.' (GrS)

Box 10.2: Grapevine Revaluation

Grapevine is a Warwickshire-based charity that focuses on developing projects that connect residents, disabled people, people with long-term health conditions, migrants and young people as 'co-producers' and activists, rather than being dependent on services. One of these was the Good to Go platform that organised inclusive fitness activities (swimming, cycling, group walks and such like) and now operates independently. It adopted a 'living systems' approach by involving everyone who might have a role to play in public health. The organisation works with people to develop their own solutions to shared problems and is currently using the Connecting for Good platform that enables participants to exchange skills and resources so as to be innovative in achieving 'positivity' in their lives.

The highly participative Revaluation model was used to evaluate their work because it aims to measure inputs and outcomes that contribute to developing the capacity of complex systems. A report concluded that 'Deep, extensive, networked relationships have been created that provide the infrastructure for innovation, and naturally regenerate in the face of challenges and in response to demand' (Harrison and Darnton, 2017).

See: www.grapevinecovandwarks.org and https.www.connectingforgoodcov.com

Time and trouble

Community workers should be encouraged to experiment, to take risks and invest time in building up relationships within the community and with colleagues in organisations that they are likely to be working with. Giving time is an expression of commitment and respect. This should be acknowledged as 'work' invested in building social capital, even if it does not appear to have immediate or tangible results. Due to austerity cuts and changing ideologies there has been a lack of investment in intensive, long-term community development that would allow workers to build up and maintain their contacts in an area. As a result, spontaneity and flexibility have been 'squeezed out' of many community development activities. This clearly has an impact on community workers' capacity to respond sensitively and strategically to needs and aspirations arising from community members, either collectively or as individuals:

> 'What you're trying to do is to build up the ability of local people, the organisations that they create to shape their lives

as much as possible … the process is in some ways more
important than the outcomes. It's never one thing or another.
A process is pointless if it isn't generating outcomes but in
a way it's more important to get the process right.' (MW)

Time is needed to establish credibility and to develop a mental map of
the relevant community and social networks, as well as keeping it up
to date. This may stretch over several years, often through a number
of successive or overlapping jobs. Good networkers are recognised as
a stable feature of the social and professional environment, operating
as a 'rock' during times of upheaval, a 'fulcrum' to provide leverage,
a 'fountain' of useful information and the 'key link' between separate
networks.

Short-term funding for projects that are 'parachuted' into areas from
national agencies with externally imposed performance criteria can
result in less efficient inter-agency working, strained relationships,
frustration and a growing sense of isolation. Until recently, networking
has been insufficiently supported or recognised by employers, and
often relies on the dedication of individuals either by default or
because they have a particular talent or inclination. Time is needed
for relationships to unfurl or grow. We use the phrase 'give it time',
in the expectation that difficulties will resolve or diminish simply as a
result of time passing but this is not always the case (Gilchrist, 2016).

Opportunities for unplanned networking need to be preserved within
busy work programmes. Long-term investment in potentially useful
relationships is more difficult to justify, and yet this is just as necessary.
These informal connections provide vital channels for information,
resources and energy to flow through the circuits of civil society,
linking community groups, local government politicians and officers,
funding bodies and the array of voluntary organisations. Networking
takes time, but time to network has become an increasingly scarce
commodity for practitioners faced with the imperatives of targets and
project deadlines:

'Giving time is a very valuable thing. But you've got to be
strong to do it. To hold out against all the pressures … and
try and keep an eye on the overall plan, but when it's really
appropriate being able to make a critical judgement, [that]
this person needs the time.' (KT)

Time for social interaction can be woven sensitively and creatively into
or alongside formal proceedings so that people find enjoyment as well as

purpose from their involvement in community activities. The 'leading lights' of community organisations are often very busy people and they want to see that their efforts and time are well used. The same applies to those who represent their communities on area forums or similar.

Reciprocity

The 'give and take' of informal sharing or swapping is a familiar aspect of neighbourliness and community action, through networks of trust and solidarity. Informal gifts and favours are an investment for an unpredictable future return (Gray, 2003). These tend to be subconsciously monitored for fairness and to maintain a sense of reciprocity. The costs of networking are often invisible or absorbed by a few individuals. They need to be recognised and shared more fairly, with attention paid to gender and role issues. This is important not only on grounds of equity, but also to ensure that power (administrative, organisational and emotional) does not accumulate to a small, unrepresentative clique. There needs to be greater acknowledgement by managers and funders that sustainable networking requires reciprocity – you have to give in order to get. Helping out another organisation with a temporary problem, taking a turn to do the minutes of a meeting, offering advice or a sympathetic ear to a colleague, 'lending' the use of a meeting room or photocopying facilities – all detract from one's own work in the short term, but lay a longer-term foundation for mutual support, respect and trust. The benefits of this work for the individual or the organisation rarely register in balance sheets or records of achievement, and yet are valuable contributions to community development.

Box 10.3: Vibe & Tone

Vibe & Tone hosts the entrepreneurial network NVærk, located in Copenhagen's Nordvest district. NVærk is open to anyone who is passionate about creating a neighbourhood where residents can fulfil their potential and where the local conditions are good for communities. NVærk wants to combat the rampant 'what's-in-it-for-me' mentality, so, instead, NVærk builds on the principles that create a good potluck supper (*sammenskudsgilde*) namely, that:

• all participants must contribute more than they take;
• there must be diversity in the network;
• the network is led by the good host.

The participants in the NVærk meetings are a very diverse group of local organisations, companies, citizens, associations and enthusiasts who want to make a difference in the district. There are always current topics on the agenda, concrete projects, such as: the Nordvest Festival, the Christmas market and the Cherry Caravan. The meetings are held at different locations in Nordvest, and therefore have rotating hosts who report on their recent efforts in the district.

Vibe & Tone also acts as a sparring partner and inspiration for other networks and organisations in and around Copenhagen. A large part of Vibe & Tone's DNA is in meeting with other people. They believe that everything happens in the meeting. Ideas and agreements are developed so that understanding and relationships are created. Vibe & Tone describes itself as a small, agile unit that can move out of the office at any time, using walking and cycling to move through the city.

(Thanks to Mads Mazanti for sharing this example.)

Being seen as human, even slightly vulnerable, helps to build genuine links with others. So does generosity in sharing resources, time, skills and knowledge. People in the 'helping' professions need to remember that for networking to be effective and sustainable, it is as important to receive as well as to give in order to maintain reciprocity with colleagues and 'clients'. It is therefore helpful to create opportunities for community members to be givers and contributors, rather than always the recipients of services or charity (Gilchrist, 2006b).

Acquisition of networking capability

Networking requires high levels of intuition. Some people feel that it involves skills that cannot be taught through formal training, but must be learned through experience and from observing role models. Studies of professional competence emphasise the intuitive aspects of professional practice that are evident in an ability to deal with complex and dynamic problems in 'situations of uncertainty, instability, uniqueness and value conflict' (Schön, 1990, p 49). But how are these acquired?

> 'Maybe it stems right the way back as to how you were brought up in the first place … in the sense that you accept people for what they are, you're no better or worse than anybody else, that we're all there to help each other … maybe there's that in the background that comes over to other people.' (LM)

Training in feeling and expressing empathy has been suggested as a way of enhancing attention and sensitivity to other people's feelings, though some individuals are said to be natural 'empaths', absorbing emotions from their environment. Similarly, being immersed in collective activities is a chance to learn skills in organising, communication and social interaction. In the Panel Study, community workers referred to adults, especially their female relatives, as important role models. Kinship or community networks were described that provided a stable background in which trust, diversity and a sense of community were key components. Most of the Panel thought that their capacity to network was based on a subconscious 'inclination' or predisposition, rather than requiring specific knowledge and skills. And yet there was also a suggestion that networking was a 'trick of the trade', a knack which could be acquired through experience, observation, practice and even training.

Workshops can make people more aware of the strategic nature of effective networking, and more willing to develop skills in establishing, maintaining and using their connections proactively. Early childhood shapes our personalities through a process of socialisation – observation, action and selective reinforcement. We acquire those attitudes and abilities that are rewarded, and we seek out or create situations where we can exhibit behaviours that gain approval and tangible benefits. However, by understanding these influences and identifying traits that seem to support good networking, it is possible to adopt practices that make it easier to develop links with others and to be clearer about how to present one's 'self' in different arenas (see Goffman, 1959). Anyone who is willing to put in time and effort, as well as to listen to feedback from others, can improve their networking skills.

Discussion

For a profession that asserts that participation should be open, fair and equal (Banks and Westoby, 2019), it might seem strange, even heretical, to promote networking as a core method of community development. Networking itself is a neutral tool and can have 'good' or 'bad' consequences, depending on circumstance and motivation. It needs to balance ethics and efficiency and therefore be underpinned by the values and commitments set out in Chapter 3. The term 'networking' has been used disparagingly to refer to tokenistic interactions that are short term, superficial, expedient and often elitist. 'Bad' networking takes many forms. It might involve poor communication between individuals or a failure to understand how information will spread through a network. Networking can be both ineffective and unethical if it does not involve some gain for participants, and if it is not based on a level of genuine commitment. This is a superficial, complacent and unsustainable form of community development. 'Bad' networking pays insufficient attention to gaps and inequalities, maintaining only connections that are comfortable or convenient. Priorities and positive action to ensure equal opportunity within networks must be considered in order to minimise unconscious or deliberate biases.

Conclusions

This chapter has explored some of the challenges associated with a networking approach to community development. Practitioners – people working with communities – are aware of the complexities and ambiguities in the community development role, and need to be prepared to manage their personal and professional networks in ways that promote cooperation and participation. Issues around power, equality and diversity need to be addressed constantly in order that communities themselves develop their own connections, capacity and confidence. Being able to maintain, extend and use networks is vital to managing internal tensions and having influence over decisions that affect their circumstances and choices. Being 'well connected' can only be an advantage in today's complex but unequal society, so investment in authentic relationships and face-to-face interactions is time well spent.

QUESTIONS FOR REFLECTION AND DISCUSSION

✧ How do you maintain your own networks?

✧ What strategies do you use for encouraging others to network, thinking especially about connections with people from other communities or sectors?

✧ How do you manage your different roles and accountabilities?

✧ How do you achieve a balance between online networking and face-to-face interactions?

11

Developing the well-connected community

> Only connect! That was the whole sum of her sermon.
> E.M. Forster, *Howards End*, 1910, p 188

This book has sought to demonstrate the value of networks and the importance of networking practices for community development. It has argued that community workers can play an active role in weaving and repairing the fabric of society: creating new ties and consolidating relationships. This contributes to the development of well-connected communities through nurturing internal bonds and associations, while also setting up and strengthening ties that bridge across community boundaries and link up with external agencies.

Over the years since this book was first published (2004) the significance of connectedness has been recognised increasingly as contributing to individual wellbeing, promoting community health and ensuring that civil society functions more or less democratically and coherently. Being well connected is not just about the number of links in our networks but about the quality of those relationships and how interactions help us to 'get by' and to 'get on'. The idea of social solidarity rejects the spurious dichotomy between the individual citizen or resident and 'community' belonging. Rather, it is based on combining emotional and political dimensions of rights, civic responsibilities, mutuality and emotional attachments (Lawrence, 2018; 2019). Many forms of social and community capital are needed for people to thrive.

As earlier chapters have demonstrated, the 'bonding' capital of interpersonal networks provides internal structure, enabling information sharing, mutual support and collective action at grassroots level. A community with good 'bridging' connections is likely to be more cohesive: able to adapt to change and deal with differences more effectively. But communities cannot flourish if they are not also well connected with effective links to outside influences and resources.

The latest government strategy for the future of civil society (Cabinet Office, 2018) shapes its vision around a 'connected, resourceful society'. It sets direction and principles for policies that it hopes will decentralise power and create conditions for the creation of 'social value' and thriving communities. Like much government thinking before, it envisages a strong role for community and voluntary organisations taking responsibility for some complex problems that the state has been unable to solve. The strategy places its faith in collaboration between citizens and the three key sectors: statutory, voluntary and private bodies working together to commission and deliver services through contracts, with a welcome revival of grant funding as a complementary form of financial support. At local level, community organisers will help people to connect and devise solutions to the problems they identify for themselves, including exercising 'rights' to take over the management of community assets and services. The strategy acknowledges that deprivation and turbulence will affect the ability (and possibly willingness) of communities to rise to these challenges, but sadly promises no more than to 'take steps' to address these inequalities.

This all sounds familiar. It is a continuation of the community development story, but without adequate funding for what many believe are essential resources for national and local infrastructure, long-term investment in training, generic community work teams or networking opportunities for workers and citizen activists. With many of the smaller community and voluntary organisations starved of core funding and a steady, though slight, decline in formal and informal volunteering, increased agility and adaption are appearing at grassroots levels, with networks as the new mode of organising (Macmillan and Ellis Paine, 2018). 'The challenge is to enable and support these networks and get behind the individuals who are connectors' (Scott, 2018, p 52). This final chapter considers how community development might continue to do just this.

Strategic networking

The complexity model of community development suggests that an important outcome of the community worker's interventions is being overlooked – namely, the extent to which community networks are strengthened and diversified. Crucial aspects of community development can be reconceptualised as 'meta-networking': the maintenance and coordination of interpersonal and inter-organisational relationships within complex systems of interaction (Gilchrist, 1999). Community workers perform an undervalued function in facilitating interdisciplinary and cross-sectoral partnerships, with a particular role in identifying and supporting community members to work with others around shared issues and goals (for example, Oladipo Fiki et al, 2007).

The community worker frequently performs the boundary-spanning function, being the person who is able to operate within different settings and constituencies, acting as broker or interpreter, especially in situations of misunderstanding or conflict (Taylor et al, 2007). The community worker has a crucial role in 'networking the networks'. They spin and mend strands across the web: putting people in touch with one another, helping them to communicate effectively and generally supporting the more problematic or tenuous links – the ones blocked by organisational barriers, misunderstandings or prejudice. When performed well, this is a strategic function involving a myriad of micro-decisions about where to be, whom to speak with, what to say, what connections to make, what information to convey and so on. Sometimes the community worker may simply operate as a go-between, keeping the pathway open as a route for future cooperation.

The community worker often acts as an important node in community and cross-sectoral networks: a source of information that others can use to make connections or to obtain resources. The Panel Study identified specific strategies and outcomes that were achieved through networking, and these form the basis for a model of 'good networking practice'. This includes recommendations for community development work as an occupation in terms of core principles, role management, training and support structures. Table 11.1 summarises the key recommendations and explains why they are important.

Practitioner and activists networks

Networking enhances the quality of community development and service delivery generally. The morale and knowledge of individual staff are improved because practitioners benefit from critical discussion with colleagues by developing a sharper, more reflective analysis of their work. These networks operate as a kind of informal community of practice (Wenger et al, 2002). These facilitated networks allow participants to explore contentious issues, upgrade their professional knowledge and reflect critically on their own practice. Informal comparisons and discussions encourage people to keep their ideas fresh, to stay informed, to review their work, to maintain key principles and to challenge poor standards and complacency. This is how 'promising practice' can be examined and consolidated so that theories may develop as to why some approaches work better than others. Networks are a source of friendly support that recognise and reinforce commitment to the job, without which many community development practitioners might become isolated and discouraged.

Table 11.1: Summary of key recommendations

Recommendation	Explanation
1. Networking should be explicitly acknowledged as a core activity within community development practice.	Its inclusion in national occupational standards should inform job descriptions, person specifications, work programmes and funding applications.
2. Networking should be better monitored and managed through work reports which identify informal interaction with key or new contacts as well as formal, inter-organisational liaison.	An index of effective networking practice could include criteria for performance appraisal. This could incorporate short-term impact measures, as well as longer-term outcomes.
3. The meta-networking aspect of generic community work should be incorporated into employment conditions through long-term contracts with secure funding.	Supervision and training should be available to community development workers (and others) to improve their networking abilities and to recognise the difficulties and dilemmas inherent in networking approaches.
4. The less tangible aspects of human interaction, derived from intuition and informal networking, should be recognised and valued as important ways of working with people to develop collective action and multi-agency initiatives.	Greater flexibility in work programmes allows for experimentation and unexpected developments that emerge as a result of networking activities.
5. The importance of networking as a foundation for partnership arrangements needs to be recognised in the time-scales for developing bids, delivery plans and formal management structures.	Partners need time together to develop a shared vision, to build trust, to deal with disagreements and to address power differentials. Team-building exercises may help, as will informal social activities.
6. A code of good practice in networking may need to be established, setting out ethical standards.	This should cover issues around role boundaries, reciprocity, accountability, confidentiality, equal opportunities and covert influence.

(continued)

Table 11.1: Summary of key recommendations (continued)

Recommendation	Explanation
7. Opportunities for informal networking should be included (and sometimes facilitated) within formal events, such as conferences, training courses or inter-agency meetings.	A balance is needed between structured time at events, and time when participants can make contact and informally follow up discussions with one another.
8. The function of intermediary bodies in helping community and voluntary organisations to develop cooperative and 'learningful' connections across identity and geographic boundaries should be strengthened.	Umbrella bodies, such as Councils for Voluntary Service or specialist forums, provide vital opportunities for information exchange and debate across the whole sector and need support to make sure their facilities are accessible to all sections of the sector.
9. Techniques of network analysis should provide a baseline 'snapshot' of how communities are operating.	This could provide a good opportunity for participatory appraisal research involving community members in identifying changes to networks.
10. Evaluation of community development programmes should include outcomes that relate to improved relationships and connections within communities, and between communities and organisations in other sectors.	Longitudinal network-mapping exercises should indicate how the linkages between groups and organisations within communities change as a result of community development interventions and show in graphic form any isolated clusters and gaps in communication.

Networking with other community workers creates opportunities for informal support, coaching, advice and mentoring. In the absence of formal supervision arrangements and in-service training, this form of peer education enables community workers (who are often in lone or peripheral posts) to cope with stress and to manage what are often quite complicated work programmes. Networks provide a useful sounding board at moments of crisis and an occasional shoulder to cry on. Feedback from informal mentors and trusted allies is an important source of constructive criticism, enabling people to examine the validity of their own ideas and to consider alternative perspectives, correcting and adjusting their plans accordingly. Informal networking creates safe and supportive environments where practitioners can talk things through with sympathetic colleagues.

Just as other forms of identity are forged through relationships with others, so occupational identity is reconfigured and preserved through our interactions and observations of colleagues, creating a form of 'connected identity' (Oliver, 2007). Fellow practitioners appear to exhibit similar sets of values and techniques, which are discovered and reinforced through networking. Learning in these communities of practice helps to build a strong collective identity, but can also lead to collusion and complacency if discussions are confined only to like-minded people. This can be especially unproductive during times of transition or organisational restructuring when a 'democratic discourse' is crucial for 'an open flow of ideas' and critical reflection (Oliver, 2006). Nevertheless, as we saw in Chapter 2, the social support provided by peer relationships can be crucial to survival, job satisfaction and success, helping people to cope in environments that are unfamiliar, precarious or threatening.

For communities, and perhaps for society as a whole, interventions targeted at well-connected individuals produce positive effects that ripple out to enhance hope, health and happiness, spreading positive mood, determination and confidence among those connected (Fowler and Christakis, 2008; Christakis and Fowler, 2009). This emotional contagion may contribute to the subjective and relational aspects of collective efficacy, community cohesion and social identity, through an overall sense of belonging.

Skilled networking

Professional community development involves proficient, sometimes expert, networking, requiring intelligence and ingenuity. It requires thoughtful self-presentation, preparation and exploration of the 'lay of the land'. Effective networking is skilled, strategic and sustainable. It can be improved through observation, reflection and practice. Networking involves two layers of competence. The first refers to the maintenance of relationships between the worker and others. The second aspect, here termed meta-networking, is about supporting and shaping the connections that weave across communities and link them into the wider world. Meta-networking involves the usual skills and processes of networking, such as making contact, finding commonalities, crossing boundaries, building relationships and interpersonal communication. It also requires an ability to facilitate the resultant network of relationships as a resource that others can make use of. This is difficult because the links themselves are multifaceted and delicate, while the web as a whole comprises a complex system of intricate connections.

It is possible to increase people's capacity to network by improving awareness, practice and incentives. Bubb and Davidson (2004) identify eight networking competences: openness, organisational ability, strategic ability, communications, social skills, personal branding, supporting and tenacity. Twelvetrees (2017), in the latest edition of his classic text on community work, sets out six rules for networking, in which he recommends opportunism, integrity, empathy, active listening, reciprocity and scepticism as key qualities for effective grassroots practice.

The ability to develop and maintain relationships with a range of people, and to communicate in a variety of modes, has been given insufficient recognition as a necessary competence and this could easily be improved by encouraging community development trainees to gain experience in a wider range of practice situations than is currently the norm. Motivation is an important factor and most good networkers seem to possess a genuine curiosity about other people and other cultures.

To be effective, the successful networker needs to be able to acquire, assimilate and access information, preferably in a form that will benefit those who might need it most. This requires good administrative and organisational skills, notably some kind of system for storing and retrieving information. For some this might be an excellent memory, but it may also be wise to use notes, a computer database or all three. Knowledge management is not simply about information processing. Community workers analyse, interpret, evaluate and synthesise ideas from an extraordinary range of sources. This flow of information includes official statistics, gossip, rumour, policy statements, ideological dogma, legal documents, political demands, cries for help, dreams, aspirations, half-remembered impressions and formal reports. The effective networker is able, somehow, to make sense of this kaleidoscope of inconsistent and incomplete versions of the world, assemble some kind of coherent assessment and help others to interpret and consider various perspectives. This requires complex cognitive processes by which patterns and congruencies are identified amid apparently contradictory opinions, facts and beliefs. Community workers network to develop insights and intuition. They should be able to fairly and accurately present opposing views and make sensible forecasts of future developments based on their knowledge of past and current events. The good networker must therefore develop and exercise a political analysis of situations, taking account of power dynamics and personal interests, alongside their own ideologies and role status.

Mapping diverse connections

Adaptable communication skills are needed so that the community worker can understand and interpret messages and impressions across cultural and institutional boundaries. People from different organisations and communities think in different ways and may use language differently, including diverse non-verbal forms of communication. It is therefore important to understand how body language carries different significance in different settings and cultures, and to behave accordingly. Good networkers need to be alert to potential misunderstandings and anticipate friction among people from different backgrounds, whether this is about working with people from different sectors or from different parts of the world. It is useful to have an understanding of the varied conventions and traditions in complex social or organisational environments.

An important component of networking capacity is an overview of the environment in which one is operating, including an up-to-date 'map' of the organisational landscape (and the relationships that weave across it). Network analysis or web-mapping exercises (for example, Pharoah and Hopwood, 2013) enable people to discover or be more aware of nodes and links among communities, and more explicit about how they use (or could use) these connections with other individuals or agencies. By identifying actual and potential forms of cooperation, people can become more proactive, and consequently more effective, in their networking.

Organisational diagrams are helpful in conflict situations because they encourage participants to interrogate (and adjust) network relationships rather than antagonise each other. Similarly, power mapping has been used in developing countries and in the UK to trace and, where possible, 'unscramble' divergent interests (Estrella and Gaventa, 1998). Understanding how the people one is working with are connected (or not) and how this affects the organisation of collective activities is crucial to all successful community development strategies. Computer simulations, network analysis and visualisation programs are being developed to promote, manage and evaluate organisational change, but have only rarely been systematically applied to community development (Huisman and van Duijn, 2005; Ennis and West, 2012).

Resources for networking

Informal networks create a foundation for effective collective action and the empowerment of disadvantaged communities. The networking approach to community development argues that a core function of practice is to help individuals and organisations to establish and make use of connections that reach across boundaries. Networking, therefore, is not an incidental or peripheral activity. It must become more strategic, more skilful, better managed and more realistically funded.

Core funding for long-term community development posts would be helpful, allowing workers to understand and engage with community dynamics, build meaningful relationships and respond to issues identified by community members themselves. As the evaluation of the community organisers programmes indicated, effective social action relies on networks and these are often sustained only with external support (Cameron et al, 2015). Community participation and collective empowerment emerge from a complex infrastructure of informal networks and self-organising groups developed through extended collective organising (McInroy, 2004). It is this layer of interaction and confidence that is neglected by, and yet essential to, successful community-led regeneration programmes and neighbourhood management (Taylor, 2007). It needs to be supported both by generic community-work posts and by adequately funded, but independent, umbrella bodies. The decline in numbers and capacity of intermediary bodies undermines networking between the smaller charities and informal community groups that support self-help and collective action at town and neighbourhood levels (NAVCA, 2015).

Further emphasis on partnership and 'joined up' working has been accompanied by a growing understanding that this requires capacity building and social mobilisation in order to make and maintain the requisite connections. While there is still a tendency to assume that the deficit lies with local communities rather than the officers and institutions of the private and statutory partners, there is evidence that shared capacity-building programmes (where all partners train together) are most effective in promoting learning and trust (Scott et al, 2002).

Community initiatives and networking processes are organic, needing space and support to grow. Voluntary sector umbrella bodies provide both the trellises and the nutrients for this growth, but are under threat from reduced local authority funding. Intermediary agencies often act as social relays and brokers, enabling smaller organisations to network with one another and connecting informal networks into more formal partnerships. Local forums and federations provide a similar service, sometimes with paid administrative support, but more often reliant on the dedication of a few hard-pressed individuals who are able (just about) to undertake these tasks on top of other work commitments.

Studies of multi-agency collaboration invariably find relationships and informal networks to have a major (and not always positive) impact on the quality of decision making and cooperation (Adamson and Bromiley, 2008). Partnerships tend to involve prominent and well-connected key players: community leaders, voluntary sector professionals or local authority officers who are able to influence decisions through their contacts with politicians and funders. Access to such networks is rarely either transparent or equitable, and can be a major source of resentment and cynicism. Community development can help to open up such policy networks to community participation and wider scrutiny.

Community involvement in government initiatives depends on a foundation of community sector activity that may be low profile, but somehow enduring over time (Chanan, 2003). Supporting this 'below the radar' layer of active citizenship, self-help and collective action is a core function of community development, which should be better supported whether by paid professionals or by unpaid volunteer activists (Packham, 2008; Richardson, 2008).

The tendency for government and grant-giving bodies to prefer new or innovative projects has distorted community work practice and undermined the basis for creative thinking and genuine community participation. Nonetheless, there appears to be an increased willingness among politicians and policy makers to trust agencies and professions that are not under their immediate control and to acknowledge that risk, discretion and occasional failure are inevitable corollaries of strategies that urge community enterprise and innovation. If these approaches are to be successful, community development needs space and opportunity for informal and serendipitous activities to operate alongside more formal, task-related projects.

Collective efficacy

Collective efficacy describes the sense of control that communities feel about issues that affect them and their capacity (skills, knowledge and confidence) to take action to address these (Bandura, 2001; Sampson et al, 2002). The concept has been developed as a way of explaining the shared belief that, by working together, people can change situations and challenge injustices. Their combined experience, shared and reinforced through community networks, creates a virtuous spiral of learning, confidence and mutuality. Informal relationships make it easier for people to communicate and cooperate with one another. They create the conditions for collective action, enabling people to work together to achieve (or defend) common interests (Lowndes et al, 2006). Those communities that are well connected have an advantage when it comes to organising themselves for whatever purpose. Endogenous community action (that initiated by communities themselves) is more likely and more sustainable when people have strong social assets in the form of networks of relationships with others who share similar experiences (Burkett and Bedi, 2006).

There is strong evidence from studies of community participation that behaviours such as helping neighbours or attending local events are the precursors for informal networks, which in turn result in strong governance and collective efficacy (Perkins et al, 1996; Wollebaek and Selle, 2002). Robust and diverse community networks are vital for effective and inclusive empowerment because they encourage a wider range of people to become active citizens and take on civic roles.

A new paradigm for sustainable wellness

The terms 'sustainability' and 'wellbeing' reflect two policy agendas aimed at improving the quality of life, while making sure that gains in one area of policy do not jeopardise the achievement of other goals. This includes strategies for protecting the planet from the existential threat of climate change (Church, 2008; Harley and Scandrett, 2019). Sustainability is also concerned with ensuring the continuing effectiveness of development initiatives through changes to mainstream services. If funding is for projects, then it is vital that the methods used to plan, implement and evaluate these encourage the formation of relations and linkages between stakeholders and communities that can sustain a lasting mutual commitment.

The recession of 2008 shaped the economic and political landscape, with austerity policies driving substantial cuts in public spending, especially at local authority levels. There are now fewer staff employed to run, manage and monitor services and a greater reliance on voluntary labour and community assets. Increasingly, projects previously run by council staff are being delivered and overseen by volunteers, including youth clubs and advice services. Direct support to communities through grants, community development officers and infrastructure organisations has been particularly hard hit, while at the same time citizens are being expected to take on more and more responsibilities. The rationale for these developments across the UK is both political and economic, but the situation is not completely bleak and there are fiscal as well as democratic benefits to be gained. For example, Milne and Rankin (2013) examined a number of case studies of devolved and flexible decision making in Scotland and found that not only had relations improved between communities and the local state, but public money had been saved.

Well-functioning communities need both 'weak' and 'strong' ties. Higher-level networks, such as federations or forums that link together smaller community-based organisations, are useful in scaling up the efforts and achievements of the smaller groups, enabling them to have more impact and to build alliances for future campaigns (Donelson, 2004; Opare, 2007). This is particularly important for oppressed and minority groups where resources are limited, and yet there is an urgent need to influence policy. It is vital to provide channels for marginalised and dissenting voices to be heard and to create cross-cutting forums that encourage discussion, democratic decision making and collective problem solving.

Back to the future

Community development is fundamentally concerned with long-term wellbeing and social justice. Networks are vital to maintaining the first and achieving the second but this is not a new insight. Butcher (1993, p 17) saw the end product of community practice as a 'neighbourhood alive with activity and cross-cut with networks of relationships, providing a locus for informal support and mutual aid', to which might be added 'and for collective organising'. In many respects, the model of the well-connected community presented in this book was pre-empted long ago by Flecknoe and McLellan, who recognised in their introduction to neighbourhood work that:

> The community development process sets out to create the context within which meaningful relationships can be formed and through which people have the spaces to grow and change, and fulfil their potential.... A high quality of relationships is the foundation for all community development work. Unless people are able to trust in others and share a part of their lives, collective activity is impossible.... 'Community' is that web of personal relationships, group networks, traditions and patterns of behaviour that develop against the backdrop of the physical neighbourhood and its socio-economic situation. Community development aims to enrich that web and make its threads stronger. (Flecknoe and McLellan, 1994, pp 7–8)

As we saw in Chapter 9, complexity theory provides an explanation of why networks form the basis for an optimally functioning social system. These can be characterised by mildly 'chaotic' interactions, leading to the evolution of collective forms of organising that adapt or die according to changes in the social environment. The model of the well-connected community sees 'community' as neither a place nor an agent of change, nor even a fuzzy set of characters. Community is conceptualised as an experience or capacity that emerges as a result of the interactions within a complex open system of overlapping networks. The development of community is an aspiration, a principle and an outcome. Managing the web of interpersonal and inter-organisational linkages is a primary function for community development. For large-scale urban environments it is even more important to acknowledge the diversity, the difficulties and the dynamism of communities as crucial features of complex systems (Batty, 2007; 2019).

While it is true that a proportion of the work is conducted through one-to-one conversations, assistance and support, networking for community development is not primarily about helping people to form connections that will be beneficial to them personally. Rather, it is about strategies for overcoming psychological and other barriers so as to facilitate their participation in broader activities and decision making. Work with individuals is a necessary, but not sufficient, contribution to the establishment and maintenance of groups, organisations and coalitions. Thomas (1995, p 15) refers to this as the 'lost meaning' of community development, the work that 'strengthens the social resources and processes in a community by developing those *contacts, relationships, networks, agreements and activities* outside the household' (emphasis in original). The paradigm set out in this book seeks to restore the value of this work by locating networking at the heart of community development.

Conclusions

Collective action and partnership working rely on and are enhanced by largely unacknowledged networking. Much of this takes place informally through face-to-face conversation and mutual cooperation. Networking requires knowledge of local customs, organisational structures and cultural institutions, as well as a commitment to building trust and respect across community and sectoral boundaries relating to ethnicity, class and other dimensions of difference in society. Networking offers an effective tool for honouring diversity and promoting equality to achieve empowerment and cohesion.

The model of the well-connected community and the idea of meta-networking are core to community development practice, which is fundamentally about nurturing informal social, political and professional networks using interpersonal links and organisational liaison. Well-connected communities attain a sufficient level of self-organisation, in which individuals become aligned through clusters of interaction (networks, groups and organisations) and achieve the critical mass of 'received wisdom' and shared motivation necessary for collective action. Intervention is necessary to create 'order from chaos' in a complex system. In some circumstances, the commitment and connections supplied by community workers are crucial in helping the well-connected community to adapt to changing conditions in its organisational and political environment. The community worker as meta-networker must be both strategic and opportunistic. They need to maintain a balance between the formal and informal aspects of community life, operating within a complex accountability matrix in a context that is shaped by political, cultural and psychological processes. They are both catalyst and connector (Gilchrist, 1998b).

The networking approach to community development opens up access and communication routes across the social landscape, by making use of personal habits, local conventions and institutional power in order to improve the quality of life for communities and create mechanisms for collective empowerment. Complexity theory suggests that a community poised at the 'edge of chaos' is able to survive in turbulent times because it evolves forms of collective organisation that fit the environmental conditions. If, as I am suggesting, meta-networking is a key professional function, then we need to find ways of evaluating community development in terms of improvements to interpersonal and inter-organisational links within wider networks. This involves looking at the intricacy and effectiveness of the individual relationships as well as levels of diversity and connectedness across the whole web, including interactions beyond the immediate locality.

Morrissey (2000) reports on an action research study to evaluate citizen participation and learning that included as progress indicators: 'development of new networks', 'levels of trust', 'alliances among organisations', 'organisations with networks formed' and (for individuals) 'expanded network of relationships' and 'learning the importance of networking'. Community indicators that measure the feel-good factors of community life offer further possibilities (Walker et al, 2000; Chanan, 2004), as do the relational audits suggested by the Relationship Foundation (Baker, 1996).

In particular, it will be important to develop ways of assessing the robustness of networks and measuring the 'interconnectivity' between individuals and organisations (Skinner and Wilson, 2002, pp 152–4). More work is needed to establish the link between networking practice and community development outcomes, perhaps using social network analysis and the growing interest in evaluating complex interventions, indicated in Chapter 9. This would be well suited to an action research approach using participatory enquiry methods (for example Burns, 2007).

The well-connected community will demonstrate insight and imagination, responding to local or external perturbations and accommodating internal diversity. It will develop 'collective efficacy' by learning from experience and developing strategies for dealing with unusual situations and eventualities (Morgan, 1989; Capra, 1996; Sampson, 2004). Networks help to reconcile individual interests with the common good through the development of locally appropriate problem-solving strategies. Complexity theory encourages us to see informal and inter-organisational networks as an extended communal 'brain', processing information intelligently to construct a resilient body of knowledge and generating a collective consciousness at the same time (Rose, 1998). As Wilson (1998, p 106) observes, 'the brain is a machine assembled not to understand itself, but to survive.... The brain's true meaning is hidden in its microscopic detail. Its fluffy mass is an intricately wired system.' By analogy, the capacity of a community to respond creatively to change and ambiguity is to be found in its web of connections and relationships, rather than in either the heads of individuals or the formal structures of voluntary bodies. A well-connected community is able to solve problems through reasoning, experimentation and strategic engagement with external bodies, not just trial and error.

The starting point for this book was a recognition that 'things' happen as a result of informal interactions, even though these often failed to register in formal auditing, monitoring and evaluation procedures. Social relations and networks represent intangible resources in people's lives that can either be nurtured or allowed to wither through neglect. Networking ensures that connections and trust are generated and maintained within communities. In a world characterised by uncertainty and diversity, the networking approach enables people to make links, to share resources and to learn from each other without the costs and constraints of formal organisational structures. Empowerment is a collective process, achieved through compassion, communication and connections. This book is a contribution to the discussion on how community development uses networking to develop community and to promote 'strength through diversity'.

QUESTIONS FOR REFLECTION AND DISCUSSION

✧ Think about a community that you feel works well. How might you describe the connections that it has?

✧ How do you see the future for networking?

Suggested further reading

Banks, S., Butcher, H., Henderson, P. and Robertson, J. (2007) *Critical community practice*, Bristol: Policy Press.

Bartley, T. (2003) *Holding up the sky*, London: Community Links.

Beck, D. and Purcell, R. (2013) *International community organising: taking power, making change*, Bristol: Policy Press.

Blokland, T. (2017) *Community as urban practice*, Cambridge: Polity Press.

Caldarelli, G. and Catanzaro, M. (2012) *Networks: A very short introduction*, Oxford: Oxford University Press.

Chambers, R. (1983) *Rural development: Putting the last first*, Harlow: Longman.

Cohen, S., Fuhr, C. and Bock, J-J. (2018) (eds) *Austerity, community action and the future of citizenship in Europe*, Bristol: Policy Press.

Craig, G., Mayo, M., Popple, K., Shaw, M. and Taylor, M. (2011) *The community development reader*, Bristol: Policy Press.

DeFilippis, J. and Saegert, S. (2008) (eds) *The community development reader* (2nd edn), New York: Routledge

Gilchrist, A. and Taylor, M. (2016) *The short guide to community development* (2nd edn), Bristol: The Policy Press.

McCabe, A. and Phillimore, J. (2017) *Community groups in context: Local activities and actions*, Bristol: Policy Press.

Ledwith, M. (2019) *Community development: A critical approach* (3rd edn) Bristol: Policy Press.

Meade, R., Shaw, M. and Banks, S. (2016) *Politics, power and community development*, Bristol: Policy Press.

Newman, M. (2010) *Networks: an introduction*, Oxford: Oxford University Press.

Obstfeld, D. (2017) *Getting new things done: Networks, brokerage and the assembly of innovative action*, Stanford: Stanford University Press.

Shaw, M. and Mayo, M. (2016) *Class, inequality and community development*, Bristol: Policy Press.

Taylor, M. (2011) *Public policy in the community*, Basingstoke: Palgrave Macmillan.

Twelvetrees, A. (2017) *Community development, social action and social planning*, Basingstoke: Palgrave Macmillan.

References

Abrahamson, E. and Freedman, D. (2007) *A perfect mess: The hidden benefits of disorder*, London: Little, Brown & Company.

Abrams, D. and Hogg, M.A. (1990) *Social identity theory*, Hemel Hempstead: Harvester Wheatsheaf.

ACW (Association of Community Workers) (1975) *Knowledge and skills for community work*, London: ACW.

Adams, D. and Hess, M. (2006) 'New research instruments for government: measuring community engagement', in C. Duke, L. Doyal and B. Wilson (eds) *Making knowledge work: Sustaining learning communities and regions*, Leicester: NIACE.

Adamson, D. and Bromiley, R. (2008) *Community empowerment in practice: Lessons from Communities First*, York: Joseph Rowntree Foundation.

Adhikari, A. and Taylor, P. (2016) 'Transformative education and community development: shared learning to challenge inequality', in M. Shaw and M. Mayo (eds) *Class, inequality and community development*, Bristol: Policy Press, pp 189–203.

Afridi, A. and Warmington, J. (2009) *Managing competing equality claims*, London: Equality and Diversity Forum.

Ager, A. and Strang, A. (2008) 'Understanding integration: a conceptual framework', *Journal of Refugee Studies*, 21 (2): 166–91.

Agranoff, R. and McGuire, M. (2001) 'Big questions in public network management research', *Journal of Public Administration Research and Theory*, 3: 295–326.

Aiken, M. (2014) *Ordinary glory: The changing shape of voluntary services: How this affects volunteer based community groups*, London: NCIA Inquiry into the Future of Voluntary Services Working Paper 2.

Albrecht, S. (2006) 'Whose voice is heard in online deliberation? A study of participation and representation in political debates on the internet', *Information, Communication & Society*, 9 (1): 62–82.

Aldridge, J. (2016) *Participatory research: Working with vulnerable groups in research and practice*, Bristol: Policy Press.

Alexander, C. (2000) *The Asian gang: Ethnicity, identity, masculinity*, Oxford: Berg.

Alinsky, S. (1969) *Reveille for radicals*, New York: Vintage Books.

Alinsky, S. (1972) *Rules for radicals*, New York: Vintage Books.

Allen, M. Clement, S. and Prendergast, Y. (2014) *A 'can do' approach to community action: What role for risk, trust and confidence?*, York: Joseph Rowntree Foundation.

Allen, M., Spandler, H., Prendergast, Y. and Froggett, L. (2015) *Landscapes of helping: Kindliness in neighbourhoods and communities*, York: Joseph Rowntree Foundation.

Alsop, R., Bertelson, M.F. and Holland, J. (2005) *Empowerment in practice: From analysis to implementation*, Washington, DC: World Bank.

Alston, P. (2018) 'Statement on visit to the United Kingdom, by United Nations Special Rapporteur on extreme poverty and human rights', London: United Nations.

Alter, C. and Hage, J. (1993) *Organizations working together: Coordination in inter-organizational networks*, Newbury Park, CA: Sage Publications.

AMA (Association of Metropolitan Authorities) (1993) *Local authorities and community development: A strategic opportunity for the 1990s*, London: AMA.

Amin, A. (2002) *Ethnicity and the multi-cultural city: Living with diversity*, Swindon: Economic and Social Research Council.

Amnesty International (2018) *Trapped in the matrix: Secrecy, stigma, and bias in the Met's Gangs Database*, London: Amnesty International UK Section.

Anastacio, J., Gidley, B., Hart, L., Keith, M., Mayo, M. and Korwarzik, V. (2000) *Reflecting realities: Participants' perspectives on integrated communities and sustainable development*, Bristol/York: Policy Press/ Joseph Rowntree Foundation.

Anderson, B. (1983) *Imagined communities: Reflections on the origin and spread of nationalism*, London: Verso.

Anderson, J. (1995) *How to make an American quilt screenplay*, Los Angeles, CA: Universal City Studios.

Anderson, R. (2013) *Doing emotion, doing policy: The emotional role of 'grassroots' community activists in poverty policy-making*, Working Paper 96, Birmingham: Third Sector Research Centre, University of Birmingham.

Anderson, S., Brownlie, J. and Milne, E.J. (2015) *The Liveable Lives Study: Understanding everyday help and support*, York: Joseph Rowntree Foundation.

Andersson, E., Warburton, D. and Wilson, R. (2007) 'The true costs of public participation', in T. Brannan, P. John and G. Stoker (eds) *Re-energising citizenship: Strategies for civil renewal*, Basingstoke: Palgrave Macmillan.

Andrew, F.A. and Lukajo, N.M. (2005) 'Golden opportunities – myth and reality? Horn of Africa female migrants, refugees and asylum seekers in the Netherlands', *Community Development Journal*, 40: 224–31.

Anklam, P. (2007) *Net work: A practical guide to creating and sustaining networks at work and in the world*, Oxford: Butterworth-Heinemann.

Anwar, M. (1985) *Pakistanis in Britain: A sociological study*, London: New Century.

Appleyard, D. (1981) *Liveable streets*, Berkeley, CA: University of California Press.

Argyle, M. (1996) *The social psychology of leisure*, Harmondsworth: Penguin.

Arnold, S., Coote, A., Harrison, T., Scurrah, E. and Stephens, L. (2018) *Health as a social movement: Theory into practice. Programme report*, London: RSA/nef.

Arrandon, G. and Wyler, S. (2008) *What role for community enterprises in tackling poverty?*, York: Joseph Rowntree Foundation.

Atran, S. (2011) *Talking to the enemy: Violent extremism, sacred values and what it means to be human*, London: Allen Lane.

Audunson, R., Varheim, A., Aabo, S. and Holm, E.D. (2007) 'Public libraries, social capital, and low intensive meeting places', *Information Research*, 12: 4.

Back, L. (1996) *New ethnicities and urban culture*, London: UCL Press.

Bacon, N. (2013) *Turning strangers into neighbours*, London: RSA.

Bagnall, A-M., South, J., Di Martino, S., Southby, K., Pilkington, G., Mitchell, B., Pennington, G. and Corcoran, R. (2018) *Places, spaces, people and wellbeing: Full review: a systematic review of interventions to boost social relations through improvements in community infrastructure (places and spaces)*, London: What Works Centre for Well-being.

Bakardjieva, M. (2009) 'Subactivism: lifeworld and politics in the age of the internet', *The Information Society*, 25 (2): 91–104.

Baker, C. (2018) 'Aiming for re-connection: responsible citizenship', in S. Cohen, C. Fuhr and J.-J. Bock (eds) *Austerity, community action and the future of citizenship in Europe*, Bristol: Policy Press.

Baker, N. (ed) (1996) *Building a relational society: New priorities for public policy*, Aldershot: Arena.

Baker, N. (2014) *Peer-to-peer leadership: Why the network is the leader*, San Francisco, CA: Berrett-Koehler.

Baker, W. (1994) *Networking smart: How to build relationships for personal and organisational success*, New York: McGraw-Hill.

Baker, L. and Taylor, M. (2018) *The future for communities – perspectives on power (final research report)*, London: Local Trust.

Baker, L., Hennessy, C. and Taylor, M. (2013) *Big Local: What's new?*, https://www.ivar.org.uk/research-report/big-local-whats-new-and-different/.

Ball, P. (2004) *Critical mass: How one thing leads to another*, London: Arrow Books.

Bandura, A. (2001) 'Social cognitive theory: an agentic perspective', *Annual Review of Psychology*, 52: 1–26.

Banks, S. and Orton, A. (2007) 'The grit in the oyster: community development workers in a modernising authority', *Community Development Journal*, 42: 97–113.

Banks, S. and Westoby, P. (2019) *Ethics, equity and community development*, Bristol: Policy Press.

Banks, S., Butcher, H., Henderson, P. and Robertson, J. (2007) *Critical community practice*, Bristol: Policy Press.

Banks, S., Butcher, H., Henderson, P. and Robertson, J. (eds) (2013) *Managing community practice: Principles, policies and programmes* (2nd edn), Bristol: The Policy Press.

Banks, S., Hart, A., Pahl, K. and Ward, P. (eds) (2018) *Co-producing research: A community development approach*, Bristol: Policy Press.

Barabási, A.L. (2014) *Linked: The new science of networks*, Philadelphia, PA: Basic Books.

Barnes, M., Matka, E. and Sullivan, H. (2003) 'Evidence, understanding and complexity', *Evaluation*, 9: 265–84.

Barnes, M., Newman, J. and Sullivan, H. (2004) 'Power, participation, and political renewal: theoretical perspectives on public participation under New Labour in Britain', *Social Politics: International Studies in Gender, State and Society*, 11: 267–79.

Barnes, M., Newman, J. and Sullivan, H. (2007) *Power, participation and political renewal: Case studies in public participation*, Bristol: Policy Press.

Barnes, M., Skelcher, C., Beirens, H., Dalziel, R., Jeffares, S. and Wilson, L. (2008) *Designing citizen-centred governance*, York: Joseph Rowntree Foundation.

Barnett, S.A. (1888) 'Charity up to date', in S. Barnett (ed) *Practicable socialism*, London: Longmans Green and Co.

Barr, A. (2014) *Community development: Everyone's business?*, Glasgow: SCDC, CDA and SCDN.

Barr, A. and Hashagen, S. (2000) *ABCD handbook: A framework for evaluating community development*, London: Community Development Foundation.

Barth, F. (1998) *Ethnic groups and boundaries: The social organisation of cultural difference*, Long Grove: Waveland Press.

Bateson, N. (2016) *Small arcs of larger circles*, Bridport: Triarchy Press.

Batten, T.R. and Batten, M. (1967) *The non-directive approach in group and community work*, London: Oxford University Press.

Batty, M. (2007) *Cities and complexity: Understanding cities with cellular automata, agent-based models, and fractals*, Cambridge, MA: MIT Press.

Batty, M. (2019) *Inventing future cities*, Cambridge, MA: Press.

Bauman, Z. (2000) *Liquid modernity*, Cambridge: Polity Press.

Bauman, Z. (2001) *Community: Seeking safety in an insecure world*, Cambridge: Polity Press.

Bauman, Z. (2003) *Liquid love: On the frailty of human bonds*, Cambridge: Polity Press.

Bayley, M. (1997) 'Empowering and relationships', in P. Ramcharan (ed) *Empowerment in everyday life: Learning disability*, London: Jessica Kingsley.

Bechtel, W. and Abrahamsen, A. (1991) *Connectionism and the mind: An introduction to parallel processing in networks*, Oxford: Blackwell.

Beck, D. and Purcell, R. (2010) *Popular education practice for youth and community development work*, Exeter: Learning Matters.

Beck, D. and Purcell, R. (2013) *International community organising: Taking power, making change*, Bristol: Policy Press.

Beck, D. and Purcell, R. (2015) 'Everyday experience and community development practice', *Radical Community Work Journal*, 1 (1).

Beirens, H., Hughes, N., Hek, R. and Spicer, N. (2007) 'Preventing social exclusion of refugees and asylum seeking children: building new networks', *Social Policy and Society*, 6: 219–29.

Belenky, M. (1986) *Women's way of knowing: The development of self, voice and mind*, New York: Basic Books.

Bell, D.M. (2017) 'The politics of participatory art', *Political Studies Review*, 15 (1): 73–83.

Bell, J. (1992) *Community development team work: Measuring the impact*, London: Community Development Foundation.

Bell, C. and Newby, H. (1971) 'Community studies, community power and community conflict', in C. Bell and C. Newby (eds) *Community studies*, London: George Allen and Unwin.

Bell, D., Pool, S., Streets, K., Walton, N. and Pahl, K. (2019) 'How does arts practice inform a community development approach to the co-production of research?' in S. Banks, A. Hart, K. Pahl and P. Ward (eds) *Co-producing research*, Bristol: Policy Press, pp 95–114.

Benkler, Y. (2006) *The wealth of networks: How social production transforms markets and freedom*, New Haven, CT: Yale University Press.

Bennett, W.L. and Segerberg, A. (2011) 'Digital media and the personalization of collective action: social technology and the organization of protests against the global economic crisis', *Information, Communication & Society*, 14 (6): 770–99.

Bennett, W.L. and Segerberg, A. (2012) 'The logic of connective action: digital media and the personalization of contentious politics', *Information, Communication & Society*, 15 (5): 739–68.

Benson, J.K. (1975) 'The inter-organisational network as a political economy', *Administrative Science Quarterly*, 20: 229–49.

Bentley, T. (2005) *Everyday democracy: Why we get the politicians we deserve*, London: Demos.

Bhavnani, R., Mirza, H.S. and Meetoo, V. (2006) *Tackling the roots of racism: Lessons for success*, Bristol: Policy Press.

Biddle, W.W. and Biddle, L.J. (1965) *The community development process*, New York: Holt, Rinehart and Winston.

Bigby, C. (2008) 'Known well by no-one: Trends in the informal social networks of middle-aged and older people with intellectual disability five years after moving to the community', *Journal of Intellectual and Developmental Disability*, 3: 148–57.

Billis, D. (2010) 'Towards a theory of hybrid organisations', in D. Billis (ed) *Hybrid organizations and the third sector: Challenges for practice, theory and policy*, Basingstoke: Palgrave Macmillan.

Bischi, G., Chiarella, C. and Shusko, I. (2013) *Global analysis of dynamic models in economics and finance*, New York: Springer-Verlag.

Blake, G., Diamond, J., Foot, J., Gidley, B., Mayo, M., Shukra, K. and Yarnit, M. (2008) *Governance and diversity: Fluid communities, solid structures*, York: Joseph Rowntree Foundation.

Blaxter, L., Farnell, R. and Watts, J. (2003) 'Difference, ambiguity and the potential for learning: local communities working in partnership with local government', *Community Development Journal*, 38: 130–9.

Block, P. (2009) *Community: The structure of belonging*, San Francisco: Berrett-Koehler.

Blokland, T. (2017) *Community as urban practice*, Cambridge: Polity Press.

Blunkett, D. (2001) *Politics and progress: Renewing democracy and civil society*, London: Demos, Politico's Publishing.

Bock, J.-J. and Cohen, S. (2018) 'Conclusion: citizenship, community and solidarity', in S. Cohen, C. Fuhr and J.-J. Bock (eds) *Austerity, community action and the future of citizenship in Europe*, Bristol: Policy Press, pp 277–88.

Boeck, T., Fleming, J. and Kemshall, H. (2006) 'The context of risk decisions: does social capital make a difference?', *Forum: Qualitative Social Research*, 7 (1), Art 17.

Boissevain, J. (1974) *Friends of friends: Networks, manipulators and coalitions*, Oxford: Blackwell.

Bollier, D. and Helfrich, S. (eds) (2012) *The wealth of the commons: A world beyond market and state*, Amherst, MA: The Levellers Press.

Bollobás, B. (2001) *Random graphs* (2nd edn), Cambridge: Cambridge University Press.

Bolton, M. (2017) *How to resist: Turn protest to power*, Bloomsbury: London.

Borgatti, S.P., Everett, M.G. and Freeman, L.C. (2002) *Ucinet for Windows: Software for social network analysis*, Harvard, MA: Analytic Technologies.

Botsman, R. and Rogers, R. (2010) *What's mine is yours: The rise of collaborative consumption*, New York: HarperCollins.

Bott, E. (1957) *Family and social networks*, London: Tavistock.

Bourdieu, P. (1986) 'The forms of capital', in J.G. Richardson (ed) *Handbook of theory and research for the sociology of education*, New York: Greenwood Press.

Bourke, J. (1994) *Working class cultures in Britain, 1890–1960*, London: Routledge.

Bovaird, A., Van Ryzin, G.G., Loeffler, E. and Parrado, S. (2015) 'Activating citizens to participate in collective coproduction of public services', *Journal of Social Policy*, 44 (1): 1–23.

Bowen, G.A. (2008) 'An analysis of citizen participation in anti-poverty programmes', *Community Development Journal*, 43: 65–78.

Boyle, D., Slay, J. and Stephens, L. (2011) *Public services inside out: Putting co-production into practice*, London: National Endowment for Science Technology and the Arts.

BRAC (1980) *The net: Power structure in ten villages*, Dacca: Bangladesh Rural Advancement Committee.

Bradley, D. (2004) *Participatory approaches: A facilitator's guide*, London: Voluntary Services Overseas.

Bragman, P., Penner, S. and Wilcock, A. (2017) 'A tool to reducing group and gang violence in London', *Community Development Society*, 21: 24–31.

Brah, A. (2007) 'Non-binarised identities of similarity and difference', in M. Wetherell, M. Lafleche and R. Berkeley (eds) *Identity, ethnic diversity and community cohesion*, London: Sage Publications.

Brannan, T., John, P. and Stoker, G. (2006) 'Active citizenship and effective public services and programmes: how can we know what really works?', *Urban Studies*, 43: 993–1008.

Briggs, X. (1997) 'Social capital and the cities: advice to change agents', *National Civic Review*, 86: 111–17.

Briner, R., Poppleton, S., Owens, S. and Kiefer, T. (2008) *The nature, causes and consequences of harm in emotionally demanding occupations,* Norwich: HMSO, Health and Safety Executive.

Britton, T. (2017) *Online guide to Participatory Cities,* www.participatorycity.org/every-one-every-day/.

Bronfenbrenner, U. (1979) *The ecology of human development: Experiments by nature and design,* Cambridge, MA: Harvard University Press.

Brown, L.D. (2015) 'Bridge-building for social transformation', *Stanford Social Innovation Review,* Winter 2015.

Brownett, T. (2018) 'Social capital and participation: the role of community arts festivals for generating wellbeing', *Journal of Applied Arts and Health,* 9 (1): 71–84.

Brownlie, J. (2014) *Ordinary relationships: A sociological study of emotions, reflexivity and culture,* Basingstoke: Palgrave MacMillan.

Bruegel, I. (2005) 'Social capital and feminist critique', in J. Franklin (ed) *Women and social capital,* Working Paper No 12, London: South Bank University.

Bubb, S. and Davidson, H. (2004) *Only connect: A leader's guide to networking,* London: ACEVO.

Buchanan, M. (2003) *Nexus: Small worlds and the ground breaking theory of networks,* New York: Norton Books.

Buckingham, H. (2018) 'Faith-based social engagement: what's changed, what's stayed the same?', in A. McCabe (ed) *Ten years below the radar: Reflections on voluntary and community action 2008–2018,* Working Paper 143, Birmingham: Third Sector Research Centre, University of Birmingham.

Bullmore, E. and Sporns, O. (2009) 'Complex brain networks: graph theoretical analysis of structural and functional systems', *Nature Reviews Neuroscience,* 10: 186–98.

Bunch, C. with Antrobus, P., Frost, S. and Reilly, N. (2001) 'International networking for women's human rights', in M. Edwards and J. Gaventa (eds) *Global citizen action,* Boulder, CO: Lynne Rienner Publishers, pp 217–29.

Buonfino, A. with Thomson, L. (2007) *Belonging in contemporary Britain,* London: Young Foundation.

Burkett, I. and Bedi, H. (2006) *What in the world … Global lessons, inspirations and experiences in community development,* Falkland, Fife: International Association for Community Development.

Burnage, A. (2010) *Understanding the transfer of resources within and between below the radar groups using social network analysis – methodological issues,* Birmingham: Third Sector Research Centre, University of Birmingham.

Burns, D. (2007) *Systemic action research*, Bristol: Policy Press.

Burns, D., Williams, C.C. and Windebank, J. (2004) *Community self-help*, Basingstoke: Palgrave.

Burrell, S. (2015) *Room for a view: Democracy as a deliberative system*, London: Involve.

Burt, R. (1992) *Structural holes*, Chicago, IL: University of Chicago Press.

Burt, R. (2000) 'The network structure of social capital', in B.M. Staw and R.I. Sutton (eds) *Research in organizational behavior*, New York: Elsevier, pp 345–423.

Burton, P., Goodlad, R. and Croft, J. (2006) 'How would we know what works? Context and complexity in the evaluation of community involvement', *Evaluation*, 12: 294–312.

Butcher, H. (1993) 'Introduction: some examples and definitions', in H. Butcher, A. Glen, P. Henderson and J. Smith (eds) *Community and public policy*, London: Pluto Press.

Byrne, D. (2005) 'Complexity, configurations and cases', *Theory, Culture & Society*, 22: 95–111.

Byrne, D. and Callaghan, G. (2014) *Complexity theory and the social sciences*, Abingdon: Routledge.

Cabinet Office (2018) *Civil society strategy: Building a future that works for everyone*, London: HMSO.

Cacioppo, J.T. and Patrick, B. (2008) *Loneliness: Human nature and the need for social connection*, New York: W.W. Norton and Company.

Calzada, I. and Cobo, C. (2015) 'Unplugging: deconstructing the smart city', *Journal of Urban Technology*, 22 (1): 23–43.

Cameron, D., Rennick, K. and MacGuire, R. (2015) *Community Organisers Programme – evaluation report*, London: Ipsos-MORI/nef.

Campbell, E., Pahl, K., Pente, E. and Rasool, Z. (eds) (2018) *Re-imagining contested communities*, Bristol: Policy Press.

Cantle, T. (2005) *The End of Parallel Lives? The Report of the Community Cohesion Panel*, London: Home Office.

Cantle, T. (2008) *Community cohesion: A new framework for race and diversity* (2nd edn), Basingstoke: Palgrave Macmillan.

Cantle, T. (2012) *Interculturalism: The new era of cohesion and diversity*, Basingstoke: Palgrave Macmillan.

Capra, F. (1996) *The web of life: A new synthesis of mind and matter*, London: HarperCollins.

Castells, M. (1996) *The rise of the network society: The information age: Economy, society and culture*, Oxford: Blackwell.

Castells, M. (2001) *The internet galaxy*, New York: Oxford University Press.

Castells, M. (2012) *Networks of outrage and hope: Social movements in the internet age*, Cambridge: Polity Press.

Catalani, C. and Minkler, M. (2010) 'Photovoice: a review of the literature in health and public health', *Health Education Behavior*, 37 (3): 424–51.

Cattell, V. (2001) 'Poor people, poor places and poor health: the mediating role of social networks and social capital', *Social Sciences and Medicine*, 52: 1501–16.

CD Challenge Group (2006) *The Community Development Challenge report*, London: Department for Communities and Local Government.

CDF (Community Development Foundation) (2014) *Tailor-made research*, http://tailor-made.cdf.org.uk/.

CDFA (Community Development Finance Association) (2012) *Just finance: Capitalising communities, strengthening local economies*, London: CDFA.

CDP (Community Development Project) (1974) *Inter-project report*, London: Community Development Project Information Intelligence Unit.

CDP (1977) *Gilding the ghetto: The state and the poverty experiment*, London: Community Development Project Information Intelligence Unit.

Cemlyn, S., Greenfields, M., Burnett, S., Matthews, Z. and Whitwell, C. (2009) *Inequalities experienced by Gypsy and Traveller communities*, London: EHRC.

Chadwick, M.M. (2010) 'Creating order out of chaos: a leadership approach', *AORN Journal*, 91 (1): 154–70.

Chambers, E. (2010) *Roots for radicals: Organising for power, action and justice*, New York: Continuum International Publishing Group.

Chambers, R. (1983) *Rural development: Putting the last first*, Harlow: Longman.

Chanan, G. (1992) *Out of the shadows*, Dublin: European Foundation for the Improvement of Living and Working Conditions.

Chanan, G. (2003) *Searching for solid foundations: Community involvement and urban policy*, London: ODPM.

Chanan, G. (2004) *Measures of community*, London: ODPM.

Chanan, G. and Fisher, B. (2018) *Commissioning community development for health: A concise handbook*, London: Coalition for Collaborative Care.

Chanan, G. and Miller, C. (2013) *Rethinking community practice: Developing transformative neighbourhoods*, Bristol: Policy Press.

Chauhan, V. (2009) *Creating spaces: Community development approaches to building stronger communities*, London: Community Development Foundation.

Chayko, M. (2002) *Connecting: How we form social bonds and communities in the internet age*, Albany, NY: State University of New York Press.

Chomsky, N. (2012) *Occupy*, London: Penguin.

Christakis, N. (2010) 'Does this social network make me look fat?' Interview in *Wired: Business*, 1 December.

Christakis, N. and Fowler, J. (2009) *Connected: The surprising power of our social networks and how they shape our lives*, London: Harper Press.

Christie, C. (2011) *Christie Commission on the future delivery of public services*, Edinburgh: Scottish Government.

Church, C. (2008) *Better places, better planet*, London: Community Development Foundation.

Cialdini, R.B. (1993) *Influence: The psychology of persuasion*, New York: William Morrow.

Cilliers, P. (1998) *Complexity and post-modernism*, London: Routledge.

Civil Society Futures (2018) *The story of our times: Shifting power, bridging divides and transforming society*, https://civilsocietyfutures. shorthandstories.com/the-story-of-our-future/index.html.

Clark, C. (2018) 'Water justice struggles as a process of commoning', *Community Development Journal*, bsy052, https://doi.org/10.1093/cdj/bsy052.

Clark, G. and Greenfields, M. (eds) (2006) *Here to stay*, Hatfield: University of Hertfordshire Press.

Clark, T. and Heath, A. (2014) *Hard times: The divisive toll of the economic slump*, New Haven and London: Yale University Press.

Clarke, T. (1963) *Working with communities*, London: National Council of Social Services.

Clarke, S., Gilmour, R. and Garner, S. (2007) 'Home, identity and community cohesion', in M. Wetherell, M. Lafleche and R. Berkeley (eds) *Identity, ethnic diversity and community cohesion*, London: Sage Publications, pp 87–101.

Clarke, S., Hoggett, P. and Thompson, S. (eds) (2006) *Emotions, politics and society*, Basingstoke: Palgrave Macmillan.

Clegg, S. (1989) *Frameworks of power*, London: Sage Publications.

Cobble, D.S. (2004) *The other women's movement: Workplace justice and social rights in modern America*, Princeton, NJ: Princeton University Press.

COC (2018) *Community organising framework*, https://www.corganisers. org.uk/wp-content/uploads/2018/08/Community-Organisers-Ltd-Framework.pdf

Coetzer, M.F., Bussin, M. and Geldenhuys, M. (2017) 'The functions of a servant leader', *Administrative Sciences*, 7 (1): 6.

Coffé, H. and Geys, B. (2007) 'Toward an empirical characterization of bridging and bonding social capital', *Non-profit and Voluntary Sector Quarterly*, 36: 121–39.

Cohen, A. (1985) *The symbolic construction of community*, London: Routledge.

Cohen, J. and Stewart, I. (1994) *The collapse of chaos: Discovering simplicity in a complex world*, New York: Viking.

Coker, E.M. (2008) 'Religion, ethnicity, and community mental health: service provision and identity politics in an unplanned Egyptian community', *Community Development Journal*, 43: 79–92.

Cole, K.C. (1984) *Sympathetic vibrations: Reflections on physics as a way of life*, New York: Bantam Books.

Coleman, J. (1990) *Foundations of social theory*, Cambridge, MA: Harvard University Press.

Comfort, L.K., Burt, J. and Song, J.E. (2016) 'Wicked problems in real time: uncertainty, information, and the escalation of Ebola', *Information Polity*, 21 (3): 273–89.

Commission on Strengthening Local Democracy (2014) *Effective democracy: Re-connecting with communities*, www.localdemocracy.info/wp-content/uploads/2014/08/Final-Report-August-2014.pdf

Commission on the Future of Localism (2018) *People power*, London: Locality.

Community Alliance (2007) *An ever-evolving story: How community anchor organisations are making a difference*, London: Community Alliance.

Conn, E. (2011) 'Community engagement in the social eco-system dance', in A. Tait and K.A. Richardson (eds), *Moving forward with complexity*, Litchfield Park, AZ: Emergent Publications.

Connolly, P. (2003) *Liveable London: The need for a walkable neighbourhood: Older and disabled people have their say*, London: Living Streets.

Considine, M. (2003) 'Networks and inter-activity: making sense of front-line governance in the United Kingdom, the Netherlands and Australia', *Journal of European Public Policy*, 10: 46–58.

Cook, K., Burt, R.S. and Lin, N. (2001) *Social capital: Theory and practice*, Edison, NJ: Aldine Transaction.

Cooke, B. and Kothari, U. (eds) (2001) *Participation: The new tyranny?*, London: Zed Books.

Cornwall, A. (2008) 'Unpacking "participation": models, meanings and practices', *Community Development Journal*, 43: 269–83.

Cowley, J. (ed) (1977) *Community or class struggle?*, London: Stage One.

Cox, E. (2006) *Empowering neighbourhoods: Going beyond the double devolution deal*, London: Local Government Information Unit.

Craig, G. (2007) 'Something old, something new …?', *Critical Social Policy*, 38: 335–59.

Craig, G. (2012) 'The history and pattern of settlement of the UK's black and minority ethnic communities', in G. Craig, K. Atkin, S. Chattoo and R. Flynn (eds) *Understanding race and ethnicity*, Bristol: Policy Press, pp 41–69.

Craig, G. (2016) 'Community development in the UK: whatever happened to class? A historical analysis', in M. Shaw and M. Mayo (eds) *Class, inequality and community development*, Bristol: Policy Press, pp 39–55.

Craig, G. (2017) *Community organising against racism: 'Race', ethnicity and community development*, Bristol: Policy Press.

Craig, G. (2018) Foreword to A. McCabe (ed) *Ten years below the radar: Reflections on voluntary and community action 2008–2018*, Working Paper 143, Birmingham: Third Sector Research Centre, University of Birmingham.

Craig, G., Burchardt, T. and Gordon, D. (2008) *Social justice and public policy*, Bristol: Policy Press.

Craig, G., Mayo, M., Popple, K., Shaw, M. and Taylor, M. (eds) (2011a) *Community development in the United Kingdom 1950–2010*, Bristol: Policy Press.

Craig, G., Mayo, M., Popple, K., Shaw, M. and Taylor, M. (eds) (2011b) *The community development reader*, Bristol: Policy Press.

Creasy, S., Gavelin, K. and Potter, D. (2008) *Everybody needs good neighbours? A study of the link between public participation and community cohesion*, London: Involve.

Cresswell, T. (2010) 'Towards a politics of mobility', *Environment and Planning D: Society and Space*, 28: 17–31.

Cross, R. and Parker, A. (2004) *The hidden power of networks: Understanding how work really gets done in organisations*, Boston, MA: Harvard Business School Press.

Crow, G. (2002) *Social solidarities*, Buckingham: Open University Press.

Crow, G. and Allan, G. (1994) *Community life*, Hemel Hempstead: Harvester Wheatsheaf.

Crowe, D. (2012) *Catalyst councils: A new future for local public service delivery*, London: Localis.

Crowther, J., Galloway, V. and Martin, I. (2005) *Popular education: Engaging the academy*, Leicester: NIACE.

Curtis, R.L. and Zurcher, L.A. (1973) 'Stable resources of protest movements: the multi-organisational field', *Social Forces*, 52: 53–61.

Dal Forno, A. and Merlone, U. (2013) 'Nonlinear dynamics in work groups with Bion's basic assumptions', *Nonlinear Dynamics, Psychology, and Life Sciences*, 17 (2): 295–315.

Dale, A. and Sparkes, J. (2008) 'Protecting ecosystems: network structure and social capital mobilization', *Community Development Journal*, 43: 143–56.

Damasio, A. (2006) *Descartes' error: Emotion, reason and the human brain*, London: Vintage.

Darroch, S., Laflamme, M. and Wagner, P.J. (2018) 'High ecological complexity in benthic Ediacaran communities', *Nature Ecology & Evolution*, 2: 1541–47.

Davies, J. (2011) *Challenging governance theory: From networks to hegemony*, Bristol: Policy Press.

Davies, W. (2003) *You don't know me but ... : Social capital and social software*, London: The Work Foundation.

Davies, J. and Spicer, A. (2015) 'Interrogating networks: towards an agnostic perspective on governance research', *Environment and Planning C: Government and Policy*, 33: 223–238.

Day, G. (2006) *Community and everyday life*, Abingdon: Routledge.

DCMS (Department of Culture, Media and Sport) (2018) *Community Life survey*, London: DCMS.

Deakin, N. (2014) *Making good: The future of the voluntary sector*, London: Civil Exchange.

De Angelis, M. (2012) 'Crisis, capital and co-optation: does capitalism need a commons fix', in D. Bollier and S. Helfrich (eds) *The wealth of the commons: A world beyond market and state*, Amherst, MA: The Levellers Press, pp 184–91.

DeFilippis, J. (2008) 'Community control and development: the long view', in J. DeFilippis and S. Saegert (eds) *The community development reader*, New York: Routledge, pp 30–5.

Defourney, J. and Nyssens, M. (2012) 'Conceptions of social enterprise in Europe: a comparative perspective with the United States', in B. Gidron and Y. Hasenfeld (eds) *Social enterprise: An organisational perspective*, Basingstoke: Palgrave, pp 71–89.

Dekker, P. and Uslaner, E.M. (eds) (2001) *Social capital and participation in everyday life*, London: Routledge.

Del Castillo, J., Khan, H., Nicholas, L. and Finnis, A. (2016) *Health as a social movement: The power of people in movements*, London: Nesta.

Dench, G., Gavron, K. and Young, M. (2006) *The new East End: Kinship, race and conflict*, London: Profile.

Dennett, D. (1991) *Consciousness explained*, London: Little Brown.

Derounian, J. (2018) 'Rural community organising: going, going … gone?', in A. McCabe (ed) *Ten years below the radar: Reflections on voluntary and community action 2008–2018*, Working Paper 143, Birmingham: Third Sector Research Centre, University of Birmingham.

Derrett, R. (2003) 'Making sense of how festivals demonstrate a community's sense of place', *Event Management*, 8: 49–58.

Dharamsi, F., Edmonds, G., Filkin, E., Headley, C., Jones, P., Naish, M., Scott, I., Smith, H. and Williams, J. (1979) *Community work and caring for children*, Ilkley: Owen Wells.

DiFonzo, N. (2008) *The water cooler effect: A psychologist explores the extraordinary power of rumours*, New York: Avery Publishing.

Dinham, A. (2005) 'Empowered or over-powered? The real experiences of local participation in the UK's New Deal for Communities', *Community Development Journal*, 40: 301–12.

Dinham, A. (2007) 'Raising expectations or dashing hopes? Well-being and participation in disadvantaged areas', *Community Development Journal*, 42: 181–93.

Dinham, A. (2012) *Faith and social capital after the debt crisis*, Basingstoke: Palgrave Macmillan.

Dinham, A., Furbey, R. and Lowndes, V. (eds) (2009) *Faith in the public realm: Controversies, policies and practices*, Bristol: Policy Press.

Dobson, J. (2018) *New seeds beneath the snow*, London: Local Trust.

Dominelli, L. (2006) *Women and community action* (2nd edn), Bristol: Policy Press.

Donelson, A. (2004) 'The role of NGOs and NGO networks in meeting the needs of US *colonias*', *Community Development Journal*, 39: 332–44.

Dorling, D. (2015) *Injustice: Why social inequality persists* (2nd edn), Bristol: Policy Press.

Dorling, D. (2018) *Peak inequality: Britain's ticking time bomb*, Bristol: Policy Press.

Doucet, A. (2000) '"There's a huge gulf between me as a male carer and women": gender domestic responsibility and the community as an institutional arena', *Community, Work and Family*, 3 (3): 163–84.

Douglass, F. (1857) 'No progress without struggle!', An address on West Indian Emancipation (4 August).

Dreyfus, H.L. and Dreyfus, S.E. (1986) *Mind over machine: The power of intuition and expertise in the era of the computer*, New York: The Free Press.

Duck, S. (2007) *Human relationships*, London: Sage Publications.

Duerden, N. (2018) *Life is lonely: What we can all do to lead more connected, kinder lives*, London: Bloomsbury.

Dunbar, R. (1996) *Grooming, gossip and the evolution of language*, London: Faber and Faber.

Dunbar, R. (2010) *How many friends does one person need?*, London: Faber and Faber.

Durkheim, E. (1893) *The division of labour in society*, London: Macmillan.

Durose, C. (2009) 'Front-line workers and "local knowledge": neighbourhood stories in contemporary UK local governance', *Public Administration*, 87 (1): 35–49.

Durose, C. and Richardson, L. (2015) *Rethinking public policy-making: Why co-production matters*, Bristol: Policy Press.

Durose, C., van Hulst, M., Jeffares, S., Escobar, O., Agger, A., and de Graaf, L. (2016) 'Five ways to make a difference: perceptions of practitioners working in urban neighbourhoods', *Public Administration Review*, 76 (4): 576–86.

du Toit, A.-M. (1998) 'Building cultural synergy and peace in South Africa', *Community Development Journal*, 33 (2): 80–90.

Dutton, W.H. (2009) 'The fifth estate emerging through the network of networks', *Prometheus*, 27 (1): 1–15.

Dutton, W. and Helsper, E.J. (2007) *The internet in Britain*, Oxford: University of Oxford.

Easley, D. and Kleinberg, J. (2010) *Networks, crowds and markets: Reasoning about a highly connected world*, Cambridge: Cambridge University Press.

Eckert, P. and McConnell-Ginet, S. (1998) 'Communities of practice: where language, gender and power all live', in J. Coates (ed) *Language and gender: A reader*, Oxford: Blackwell, pp 89–99.

Edwards, M. and Gaventa, J. (eds) (2001) *Global citizen action*, Boulder, CO: Lynne Rienner Publishers.

Eguren, I.R. (2008) 'Moving up and down the ladder: community-based participation in public dialogue and deliberation in Bolivia and Guatemala', *Community Development Journal*, 43: 312–28.

Elgenius, G. (2018) 'Social division and resentment in the aftermath of the economic slump', in S. Cohen, C. Fuhr and J.-J. Bock (eds) *Austerity, community action and the future of citizenship in Europe*, Bristol: Policy Press, pp 39–62.

Elsdon, K., Reynolds, J. and Stewart, S. (1995) *Voluntary organisations: Citizenship, learning and change*, Leicester: National Institute of Adult and Community Education.

Elvidge, J. (2014) *A routemap to an enabling state*, Fife: Carnegie UK Trust.

Elworthy, S. (1996) *Power and sex: A book about women*, Shaftesbury: Element Books.

Emejulu, A. (2015) *Community development as micropolitics: Comparing theories, policies and politics in America and Britain*, Bristol: Policy Press.

Emery, F.E. and Trist, E.L. (1965) 'The causal texture of organisational environments', *Human Relations*, 18: 21–31.

Ennis, G. and West, D. (2012) 'Using social network analysis in community development practice and research: a case study', *Community Development Journal*, 48(1): 40–57.

ESB (Endorsement and Quality Standards Board for Community Development Learning) (2015) *Community Development National Occupational Standards*, www.esbendorsement.org.uk/index.php/nos-2015-guidance-from-esb/

ESB (2017) *Current community development practice and learning: A snapshot*, http://esbendorsement.org.uk/index.php/nos-2015-guidance-from-esb/download-file?path=ESB+Research+FULL+Report+April+2017+web.pdf

Esteva, G. (2014) 'Commoning in the new society', *Community Development Journal*, 49, (1): 144–59.

Estrella, M. and Gaventa, J. (1998) *Who counts reality? Participatory monitoring and evaluation: A literature review*, Brighton: Institute of Development Studies, University of Sussex.

Etzioni, A. (1993) *The spirit of community*, New York: Crown Books.

Evans, S. (2009) *Community and ageing: Maintaining quality of life in housing with care settings*, Bristol: Policy Press.

Eversley, J. (2019) *Social and community development: An introduction*, London: Red Globe Press.

Facer, K. and Pahl, K. (2017) *Valuing interdisciplinary collaborative research: Beyond impact*, Bristol: Policy Press.

Fanshawe, S. and Sriskandarajah, D. (2010) *You can't put me in a box: Super diversity and the end of identity politics*, London: Institute for Public Policy Research.

Fatkin, J.-M. and Lansdown, T.C. (2015) 'Prosocial media in action', *Computers in Human Behavior*, 48, 581–6.

Fearon, K. (1999) *Women's work: The study of the Northern Ireland Women's Coalition*, Belfast: Blackstaff Press.

Featherstone, D., Ince, A., Mackinnon, D., Strauss, K. and Cumbers, A. (2012) 'Progressive localism and the construction of political alternatives', *Transactions of British Geographers*, 37: 177–82.

Fehr, B. (1996) *Friendship processes*, London: Sage Publications.

Feldman, P. (2009) *Unmasking the state: A rough guide to real democracy*, London: A world to win.

Ferguson, K. (1984) *The feminist case against bureaucracy*, Philadelphia, PA: Temple University Press.

Ferguson, Z. (2016) *Kinder communities: The power of everyday relationships*, Fife: Carnegie Trust.

Ferguson, Z. (2017) *The place of kindness: Combating loneliness and building stronger communities*, Fife: Carnegie Trust.

Fernet, C., Guay, F. and Senecal, C. (2004) 'Adjusting to job demands; the role of work self-determination and job control in predicting burnout', *Journal of Vocational Behavior*, 65: 39–56.

Ferree, M.M. (1992) 'The political context of rationality: rational choice theory and resource mobilisation', in A.D. Morris and C. McClurg Mueller (eds) *Frontiers in social movement theory*, New Haven, CT: Yale University Press.

Fieldhouse, E. (2008) 'Social capital and ethnic diversity', in N. Johnson (ed) *Citizenship, cohesion and solidarity*, London: The Smith Institute.

Fildes, D., Cass, Y. and Wallner, F. (2010) 'Shedding light on men: the Building Healthy Men project', *Journal of Men's Health*, 7 (3): 233–40.

Finnegan, R. (1989) *The hidden musicians*, Cambridge: Cambridge University Press.

Finney, N. and Simpson, L. (2009) *Sleepwalking to segregation? Challenging myths about race and migration*, Bristol: Policy Press.

Fischer, C. (1982) *To dwell amongst friends: Personal networks in town and city*, Chicago, IL: University of Chicago Press.

Fitzgerald, L. and van Eijnatten, F. (2002) 'Chaos speak: a glossary of chaordic terms and phrases', *Journal of Organizational Change Management*, 15 (4): 412–23.

Flam, H. and King, D. (eds) (2005) *Emotions and social movements*, London: Routledge.

Flecknoe, C. and McLellan, N. (1994) *The what, how and why of neighbourhood community development* (3rd edn), London: Community Matters.

Flint, J. and Robinson, D. (2008) *Community cohesion in crisis? New dimensions of diversity and difference*, Bristol: Policy Press.

Flouch, H. and Harris, K. (2010) *The online neighbourhood networks study*, The Networked Neighbourhoods Group, www.networkedneighbourhoods.com/wp-content/uploads/2011/04/Online-Nhood-Networks-4-page-summary-web-rev-1.pdf.

Flynn, R. and Craig, G. (2012) 'Policy, politics and practice: a historical review and its relevance to current debates' in G. Craig, K. Atkin, S. Chattoo and R. Flynn (eds) *Understanding race and ethnicity*, Bristol: Policy Press, pp 71–94.

Foot, J. (2010) *A glass half full*, London: IDEA.

Foresight Future Identities (2013) *Final report*, London: Government Office for Science.

Forrest, R. and Kearns, A. (2001) *Social cohesion, social capital and neighbourhood change*, Bristol/York: Policy Press/Joseph Rowntree Foundation.

Forster, E.M. (1910) *Howards End*, London: Edward Arnold.

Foth, M. and Hearn, G. (2007) 'Networked individualism of urban residents: discovering the communicative ecology in inner-city apartment buildings', *Information, Communication & Society*, 10: 749–72.

Foucault, M. (1977) *Discipline and punish*, Harmondsworth: Penguin.

Fowler, J.H. and Christakis, N.A. (2008) 'Dynamic spread of happiness in a large social network: longitudinal analysis over 20 years in the Framingham Heart Study', *British Medical Journal*, 337: 2338.

Frances, J., Levacic, R., Mitchell, J. and Thompson, G. (1991) 'Introduction', in G. Thompson, J. Frances, R. Levacic and J. Mitchell (eds) *Markets, hierarchies and networks: The co-ordination of social life*, London: Sage Publications.

Francis, D., Henderson, P. and Thomas, D. (1984) *A survey of community development workers in the United Kingdom*, London: NISW.

Frankenberg, R. (1966) *Communities in Britain: Social life in town and country*, Harmondsworth: Penguin.

Fraser, H. (2005) 'Four different approaches to community participation', *Community Development Journal*, 40: 286–300.

Fraser, E., Thirkell, A. and McKay, A. (2003) *Tapping into existing social capital: Rich networks, poor connections*, London: Department for International Development.

Freeman, J. (1973) *The tyranny of structurelessness*, New York: Falling Wall Press.

Freeman, L. (2000) 'Visualising social networks', *Journal of Social Structure*, 1 (1).

Freeman, R. (2009) 'What is "translation"?', *Evidence and Policy*, 5(4): 429–47.

Freire, P. (1972) *Pedagogy of the oppressed*, Harmondsworth: Penguin.

Fujimoto, I. (1992) 'Lessons from abroad in rural community revitalisation; the one village, one product', *Community Development Journal*, 27: 10–20.

Fung, K.K. (2016) 'Community development and class in the context of an East Asian productivist welfare regime', in M. Shaw and M. Mayo (eds) *Class, inequality and community development*, Bristol: Policy Press, pp 205–18.

Furbey, R., Dinham, A., Farnell, R., Finneron, D. and Wilkinson, G. with Howarth, C., Hussain, D. and Palmer, S. (2006) *Faith as social capital: Connecting or dividing?*, Bristol: Policy Press.

Gallup Poll (2017) *Global Emotions report*, https://news.gallup.com/reports/212648/gallup-global-emotions-report-2017.aspx.

Gamble, C. (1999) *The paleolithic societies of Europe*, Cambridge: Cambridge University Press.

Gandolfi, F., Stone, S. and Deno, F. (2017) 'Servant leadership: an ancient style with 21st century relevance', *Revista de Management Comparat International*, 18 (4): 350-61.

Gaventa, J. (2006) *Finding the spaces for change*, https://www.powercube.net/wp-content/uploads/2009/12/finding_spaces_for_change.pdf

Geertz, C. (1973) *The interpretation of cultures*, New York: Basic Books.

Gerbaudo, P. (2012) *Tweets and the streets: Social media and contemporary activism*, London: Pluto Press.

Giarchi, G. (2001) 'Caught in the nets: a critical examination of the use of the concept of "networks" in community development studies', *Community Development Journal*, 36: 63–71.

Gibson, T. (1996) *The power in our hands: Neighbourhood-based world shaking*, Charlbury: Jon Carpenter.

Gilchrist, A. (1994) *Report and evaluation of the Bristol Festival Against Racism*, Bristol: Avon Race Equality Unit.

Gilchrist, A. (1995) *Community development and networking*, London: Community Development Foundation.

Gilchrist, A. (1998a) ' "A more excellent way": developing coalitions and consensus through informal networking', *Community Development Journal*, 33 (2): 100–8.

Gilchrist, A. (1998b) 'Connectors and catalysts', *SCCD News*, 18: 18–20.

Gilchrist, A. (1999) 'Serendipity and the snowflakes', *SCCD News*, 19: 7–10.

Gilchrist, A. (2000) 'The well-connected community: networking to the "edge of chaos"', *Community Development Journal*, 35: 264–75.

Gilchrist, A. (2001) 'Strength through diversity: a networking approach to community development', unpublished PhD thesis, University of Bristol.

Gilchrist, A. (2003) 'Linking partnerships and networks', in S. Banks, H. Butcher, P. Henderson and J. Robertson (eds) *Managing community practice*, Bristol: Policy Press, pp 35–54.

Gilchrist, A. (2004) *Community cohesion and community development: Bridges or barricades?*, London: Community Development Foundation.

Gilchrist, A. (2006a) 'Partnership and participation: power in process', *Public Policy and Administration*, 21: 70–85.

Gilchrist, A. (2006b) 'Community development and networking for health', in J. Orme, M. Grey, T. Harrison, J. Powell and P. Taylor (eds) *Public health for the 21st century: Policy, participation and practice*, Basingstoke: Open University Press/McGraw Hill Education.

Gilchrist, A. (2007) *Equalities and communities: Challenge, choice and change*, London: Community Development Foundation.

Gilchrist, A. (2016) *Blending, braiding, balancing: Strategies for managing the interplay between formal and informal ways of working with communities*, Working Paper 136, Birmingham: Third Sector Research Centre, University of Birmingham.

Gilchrist, A. (2019) 'Blending, braiding, balancing: strategies for managing the interplay between formal and informal ways of working with communities', in B. Pratten (ed) *The Plowden papers: Rethinking governance?*, London: NCVO, pp 29–38.

Gilchrist, A. and Taylor, M. (1997) 'Community networking: developing strength through diversity', in P. Hoggett (ed) *Contested communities: Experiences, struggles, policies*, Bristol: The Policy Press, pp 165–79.

Gilchrist, A. and Taylor, M. (2016) *The short guide to community development* (2nd edn), Bristol: Policy Press.

Gilchrist, A., Wetherell, M. and Bowles, M. (2010) *Social action and identities: connecting communities for a change*, Basingstoke: Open University Press.

Gilligan, C. (1982) *In a different voice: Psychological theory and women's development*, Cambridge, MA: Harvard University Press.

Gladwell, M. (2000) *The tipping point: How little things can make a big difference*, London: Little Brown.

Gleick, J. (1987) *Chaos: Making a new science*, New York: Viking.

Godfrey, M., Townsend, J. and Denby, T. (2004) *Building a good life for older people in local communities: The experience of ageing in time and place*, York: Joseph Rowntree Foundation.

Goetschius, G.W. (1969) *Working with community groups*, London: Routledge and Kegan Paul.

Goffman, E. (1959) *The presentation of self in everyday life*, New York: Doubleday.

Goldstein, N.J., Martin, S.M. and Cialdini, R.B. (2008) *Yes! 50 scientifically proven ways to be persuasive*, Cambridge, MA: Simon and Schuster.

Goligoski, E. (2018) 'Join the club: how Burning Man festival and co-ops are helping shape journalism', *The Guardian*, 28 September, https://www.theguardian.com/membership/2018/sep/08/membership-puzzle-burning-man-co-ops-journalism.

Goodwin, M. (2011) *New British fascism: The rise of the British National Party*, London: Routledge.

Gordon, G. (1999) *The internet: A philosophical inquiry*, London: Routledge.

Graham T. and Wright, S. (2014) 'Analysing "super-participation" in online third spaces', in M. Cantijoch, R. Gibson and S. Ward (eds) *Analyzing social media data and web networks*, London: Palgrave Macmillan, pp 197–215.

Gramsci, A. (1971) *Selections from the prison notebooks*, London: Lawrence and Wishart.

Granovetter, M. (1973) 'The strength of weak ties', *American Journal of Sociology*, 78: 1360–80.

Granovetter, M. (1978) 'Threshold models of collective behaviour', *American Journal of Sociology*, 78: 1420–43.

Granovetter, M. (1985) 'Economic action and social structure: the problem of embeddedness', *American Journal of Sociology*, 9: 481–510.

Grapevine (2017) *A revaluation of Grapevine: Good to go*, Coventry: Grapevine.

Gratton, L. (2008) *Hot spots: Why some companies buzz with energy and innovation – and others don't*, Harlow: Pearson Educational.

Gray, A. (2003) *Towards a conceptual framework for studying time and social capital*, London: South Bank University.

Green, G. and Haines, A. (2015) *Asset building and community development*, London: Sage.

Green, A. and White, R.J. (2007) *Attachment to place: Social networks, mobility and prospects of young people*, York: Joseph Rowntree Foundation.

Greenfield, S. (2008) *ID: The quest for identity in the 21st century*, London: Sceptre.

Gregory, D. (2018) *Skittled out*, London: Local Trust.

Gregory, L. (2015) *Trading time: Can exchange lead to social change?*, Bristol: Policy Press.

Guijt, I. and Shah, M.K. (1998) *The myth of community: Gender issues in participatory development*, London: Intermediate Technology Publications.

Gulbenkian Foundation (2017) *Rethinking relationships: Phase one of the Inquiry into the Civic Role of Arts Organisations*, London: Calouste Gulbenkian Foundation.

Gunaratne, R. (2005) 'International and regional implications of the Sri Lankan Tamil insurgency', in R. Soysa (ed) *Peace in Sri Lanka: Obstacles and opportunities*, London: World Alliance for Peace in Sri Lanka (WAPS).

Guy, M.E., Newman, M.A. and Mastracci, S.H. (2008) *Emotional labor: Putting the service in public service*, Abingdon: Routledge.

Hacker, K. (2013) *Community-based participatory research*, Los Angeles: Sage.

Hall, S. (1990) 'Cultural identity and diaspora', in J. Rutherford (ed) *Identity: Community, culture, difference*, London: Lawrence and Wishart, pp 222–37.

Hall, T. and Smith, R. (2015) 'Care and repair and the politics of urban kindness', *Sociology*, 49 (1): 3–18.

Halpern, D. (2005) *Social capital*, Cambridge: Polity Press.

Halpern, D. (2009) *The wealth of nations*, Cambridge: Polity Press.

Halpern, D. and Gibbs, J. (2013) 'Social media as a catalyst for online deliberation? Exploring the affordances of Facebook and YouTube for political expression', *Computers in Human Behavior*, 29 (3): 1159–68.

Hampton, K. (2003) 'Grieving for a lost network: collective action in a wired suburb', *The Information Society*, 19 (5): 1–13.

Hampton, K. (2007) 'Neighbourhoods in the network society: the e-neighbours study', *Information, Communication and Society*, 10: 714–48.

Hampton, K., Shin, I. and Lu, W. (2017) 'Social media and political discussion: when online presence silences offline conversation', *Information, Communication & Society*, 20 (7): 1090–107.

Handy, C. (1988) *Understanding voluntary organisations*, Harmondsworth: Penguin.

Hanifan, L.J. (1916) 'The rural school community centre', *Annals of the American Academy of Political and Social Science*, 67: 130–8.

Hari, J. (2018) *Lost connections: Uncovering the real cause of depression – and the unexpected solutions*, London: Bloomsbury.

Harley, A. and Scandrett, E. (2019) *Environmental justice, popular struggle and community development*, Bristol: Policy Press.

Harlow, S., and Guo, L. (2014) 'Will the revolution be tweeted or Facebooked? Using digital communication tools in immigrant activism', *Journal of Computer-Mediated Communication*, 19 (3): 463–78.

Harris, K. (2003) 'Keep your distance: remote communication, face-to-face and the nature of community', *Journal of Community Work and Development*, 1 (4): 5–28.

Harris, K. (2008) *Neighbouring and older people: An enfolding community?*, London: Community Development Foundation.

Harris, K. (2011) *Picnic: Order, ambiguity and community*, Bushey: Local Level.

Harris, K. and McCabe, A. (2017a) *Community action and social media: A review of the literature*, Working Paper 139, Birmingham: Third Sector Research Centre , University of Birmingham.

Harris, K. and McCabe, A. (2017b) *Community action and social media: Trouble in Utopia*, Birmingham: Third Sector Research Centre, University of Birmingham.

Harris, M. and Young, T. (2009) *Bridging community divides: Impact of grassroots bridge building activities*, London: Institute for Voluntary Action Research (IVAR).

Harrison, A. and Darnton, A. (2017) 'Revaluation: measuring value, making value', London: Tavistock Institute, https://www.tavinstitute.org/projects/revaluation-measuring-value-making-value/.

Harrow, J. and Bogdanova, M. (2006) *Sink or SWiM: Towards a 21st century community sector*, London: bassac.

Hart, A., Davies, C., Aumann, K., Wenger, E., Aranda, K., Heaver, B. and Wolff, D. (2013) 'Mobilising knowledge in community-university partnerships: what does a community of practice approach contribute?', *Contemporary Social Science*, 8 (3): 278–91.

Hastings, A., Bailey, N., Besemer, K., Bramley, G., Gannon, M., Watkins, D. (2015) *The cost of the cuts? The impact on local government and poorer communities*, York: Joseph Rowntree Foundation.

Hastings, C. (1993) *The new organisation: Growing the culture of organizational networking*, Maidenhead: McGraw-Hill.

Heald, T. (1983) *Networks: Who we know and how we use them*, London: Hodder and Stoughton.

Hedstrom, P. (2005) *Dissecting the social: On the principles of analytical sociology*, Cambridge: Cambridge University Press.

Helgesen, S. (1990) *The female advantage: Women's ways of leadership*, New York: Doubleday.

Helliwell, J. and Putnam, R. (2006) 'The social context of well-being', in F. Huppert, N. Baylis and B. Keverne (eds) *The science of well-being*, Oxford: Oxford University Press, pp 435–59.

Help the Aged (2008) *Towards common ground: The Help the Aged manifesto for lifetime neighbourhoods*, London: Help the Aged.

Henderson J., Revell, P. and Escobar, O. (2018) *Transforming communities? Exploring the roles of community anchor organisations in public service reform, local democracy, community resilience and social change*, Edinburgh: What Works Scotland.

Henderson, P. (2005) *Including the excluded: From practice to policy in European community development*, Bristol: The Policy Press.

Henderson, P. and Salmon, H. (2001) *Social exclusion and community development*, London: Community Development Foundation.

Henderson, P. and Thomas, D.N. (1980) *Skills in neighbourhood work* (1st edn), London: Allen and Unwin.

Henderson, P. and Thomas, D.N. (1987) *Skills in neighbourhood work* (2nd edn), London: Allen and Unwin.

Henderson, P. and Thomas, D.N. (2002) *Skills in neighbourhood work* (3rd edn), London: Routledge.

Henning, C. and Lieberg, M. (1996) 'Strong ties or weak ties? Neighbourhood networks in a new perspective', *Scandinavian Housing and Planning Research*, 13 (1): 3–26.

Heraud, B. (1975) 'The new towns: a philosophy of community', in P. Leonard (ed) *The sociology of community action*, Keele: Sociological Review, pp 39-55.

Hero, R.E. (2007) *Racial diversity and social capital: Equality and community in America*, Cambridge: Cambridge University Press.

Heron, J. (1996) *Co-operative inquiry: Research into the human condition*, London: Sage Publications.

Hickey, S. (2004) *Participation: From tyranny to transformation exploring new approaches to participation in development*, London: Zed Books.

Hickman, P., Batty, E., Dayson, C. and Muir, J. (2014) *'Getting-by', coping and resilience in difficult times*, Sheffield: Centre for Regional Economic and Social Research.

Hicks, J. and Myeni, S. (2016) 'The impact of gender, race and class on women's political participation in post-apartheid South Africa: challenges for community development', in M. Shaw and M. Mayo (eds) *Class, inequality and community development*, Bristol: Policy Press, pp 107–20.

Hill, K., Barton, M. and Hurtado, A.M. (2009) 'The emergence of human uniqueness: underlying characteristics of behavioral modernity', *Evolutionary Anthropology*, 18: 187–200.

Hill-Collins, P. (2009) *Black feminist thought: Knowledge, consciousness and the politics of empowerment*, London: Routledge.

Hiller, H. and Franz, T. (2004) 'New ties, old ties and lost ties: the use of the internet in diaspora', *New Media and Society*, 6: 731–52.

Hillery, G. (1955) 'Definitions of community: areas of agreement', *Rural Sociology*, 20: 111–23.

Hindess, B. (1996) *Discourse of power: From Hobbes to Foucault*, Oxford: Blackwell.

Hirsch, A. (2018) *Brit(ish): On race, identity and belonging*, London: Jonathan Cape/Vintage.

Hobsbawm, J. (2017) *Fully connected: Surviving and thriving in an age of overload*, London: Bloomsbury.

Hochschild, A.R. (2012) *The managed heart: Commercialization of human feeling* (3rd edn), Berkeley, CA: University of California Press.

Hock, D. (1999) *Birth of the chaordic age*, San Francisco: Berrett-Koehler.

Hoerr, J. (1993) 'Solidaritas at Harvard: organising in a different voice', *The American Prospectus*, 14: 67–82.

Hoggart, R. (1957) *The uses of literacy: Aspects of working class life*, Harmondsworth: Penguin.

Hoggett, P. (2000) *Emotional life and the politics of welfare*, Basingstoke: Macmillan.

Hoggett, P. (2006) 'Pity, compassion, solidarity', in S. Clarke, P. Hoggett and S. Thompson (eds) *Emotions, politics and society*, Basingstoke: Palgrave Macmillan, pp 145–61.

Hoggett, P. (2009) *Politics, identity and emotion*, Boulder, CO: Paradigm.

Hoggett, P., Mayo, M. and Miller, C. (2008) *The dilemmas of development work*, Bristol: Policy Press.

Holgate, J. (2009) 'Contested terrain: London's living wage campaign and the tension between community and union organising', in J. McBride and I. Greenwood (eds) *Community unions: A comparative analysis of concepts and contexts*, Basingstoke: Palgrave Macmillan, pp 49-74.

Holley, J. (2012) *The network weaving handbook: A guide to transformational networks*, https://networkweaver.com/network-weaving-handbook

Holt-Lunstad, J., Smith, T., Baker, M., Harris, T. and Stephenson, D. (2015) 'Loneliness and social isolation as risk factors for mortality: a meta-analytic review', *Perspectives on Psychological Science*, 10 (2): 227–37.

Hope, A. and Timmel, S. (2013) *Training for transformation in practice*, Rugby: Practical Action Publishing.

Hopkins, R. (2008) *The transition handbook: From oil dependency to local resilience*, Dartington: Green Books.

Hothi, M. with Bacon, N., Brophy, M. and Mulgan, G. (2008) *Neighbourliness + empowerment = well being: Is there a formula for happy communities?*, London: Young Foundation/IDeA.

Hudson, M. and Netto, G. et al (2013) *In-work poverty, ethnicity and workplace cultures*, York: Joseph Rowntree Foundation.

Hudson, M., Phillips, J., Ray, K. and Barnes, H. (2007) *Social cohesion in diverse communities*, York: Joseph Rowntree Foundation.

Huisman, M. and van Duijn, M.A.J. (2005) 'Software for social network analysis', in P.J. Carrington, J. Scott and S. Wasserman (eds) *Models and methods in social network analysis*, Cambridge: Cambridge University Press, pp 270–316.

Humphries, B. and Martin, M. (2000) 'Unsettling the learning community: from "dialogue" to "difference"', *Community, Work and Family*, 3: 279–95.

Hunter, F. (1953) *Community power structure*, Chapel Hill, NC: University of North Carolina Press.

Hunter, A. and Staggenborg, S. (1988) 'Local communities and organised action', in C. Milofsky (ed) *Community organisations: Studies in resource mobilisation and exchange*, New York: Oxford University Press.

Hussein, D. (2007) 'Identity formation among British Muslims', in M. Wetherell, M. Lafleche and R. Berkeley (eds) *Identity, ethnic diversity and community cohesion*, London: Sage Publications.

Hustedde, R. and King, B. (2002) 'Rituals: emotions, community faith in soul and the messiness of life', *Community Development Journal*, 37: 338–48.

IACD (International Association for Community Development) (2018) *Towards shared international standards for community development practice*, Glasgow: International Association for Community Development.

Ife, J. (2009) *Human rights from below: Achieving rights through community development*, Melbourne, Australia: Cambridge University Press.

Ife, J. (2013) *Community development in an uncertain world: Vision, analysis and practice*, Melbourne, Australia: Cambridge University Press.

Illich, I. (1973) *Deschooling society*, Harmondsworth: Penguin.

Illich, I. (1975) *Tools for conviviality*, London: Fontana.

Imagine (2015) *Community Organisers Programme legacy report*, London: Locality.

Innerarity, F. (2003) *Gender dimensions of social capital in the Caribbean*, Kingston, Jamaica: University of West Indies Press.

Innes, M. and Jones, V. (2006) *Neighbourhood security and urban change: Risk, resilience and recovery*, York: Joseph Rowntree Foundation.

Isen, A. and Levin, P. (1972) 'Effect of feeling good on helping: cookies and kindness', *Journal of Personality and Social Psychology*, 21: 384–8.

Ishkanian, A. and Szreter, S. (2012) *The Big Society debate: A new agenda for social welfare?* Cheltenham: Edward Elgar.

Jacobs, J. (1961) *The death and life of great American cities*, London: Cape.

James, D. et al (2014) *Big Local: The early years – evaluation report*, London: NCVO.

Jantsch, E. (1980) *The self-organising universe*, Oxford: Pergamon Press.

Jason, L.A., Light, J. and Callahan, S. (2016) 'Dynamic social networks', in L.A. Jason and D.S. Glenwick (eds) *Handbook of methodological approaches to community based research: Qualitative, quantitative and mixed methods*, New York: Oxford University Press, ch 22.

Jeffs, T. and Smith, M.K. (2005) *Informal education: Conversation, democracy and learning*, Ticknall: Education Now.

Jeffers, S., Hoggett, P. and Harrison, L. (1996) 'Race, ethnicity and community in three localities', *New Community*, 22: 111–26.

Johnson, N. (2007) *Two's company, three is complexity*, Oxford: Oneworld.

Johnson, S. (2001) *Emergence: The connected lives of ants, brains, cities and software*, New York: Scribner.

Jones, T. (2007) *Utopian dreams: In search of the good life*, London: Faber and Faber.

Jopling, K. (2017) *Combatting loneliness one conversation at a time: A call to action*, London: Jo Cox Commission on Loneliness.

Journard, R. (2010) *Awra Amba, an Ethiopian utopia*. Original French version: http://local.attac.org/rhone/article.php3?id_article=1489

Judis, J.B. (2016) *The populist explosion: How the great recession transformed American and European politics*, New York: Columbia Global Reports.

Jupp, E. (2013) '"I feel more at home here than in my own community": approaching the emotional geographies of neighbourhood policy', *Critical Social Policy*, 33: 532–53.

Kagan, C. (2006) *Making a difference: Participation and wellbeing*, Manchester: RENEW Intelligence Report.

Kagan, C. and Duggan, K. (2011) 'Creating community cohesion. The power of using innovative methods to facilitate engagement and genuine partnership', *Social Policy and Society*, 10: 393–404.

Kagan, C., Burton, M., Duckett, P., Lawthom, R. and Siddiquee, A. (2011) *Critical community psychology: Critical action and social change*, Chichester: BPS Blackwell.

Kahneman, D. (2011) *Thinking, fast and slow*, London: Macmillan.

Kane, L. (2008) 'The World Bank, community development and education for social justice', *Community Development Journal*, 43: 194–209.

Kanter, R. (1983) *The changemasters*, New York: Simon and Schuster.

Kastelle, T. and Steen, M. (2014) 'Networks of innovation', in M. Dodgson, D. Gann, and N. Phillips (eds) *The Oxford handbook of innovation management*, Oxford: Oxford University Press, Ch 6.

Kauffman, S. (1995) *At home in the universe: The search for the laws of complexity*, London: Penguin.

Kawachi, I., Kennedy, B.P., Lochner, K. and Prothrow-Stith, D. (1997) 'Social capital, income inequality, and mortality', *American Journal of Public Health*, 87 (9): 1491–8.

Kelly, J. (2006) *Being ecological: An expedition into community psychology*, New York: Oxford University Press.

Kennedy, B.M. and Bell, D. (eds) (2007) *The cybercultures reader* (2nd edn), London: Routledge.

Kenny, S. (2017) 'Community development and populism', *New Community*, 15 (57–58): 25–8.

Kenny, S., Taylor, M., Onyx, J. and Mayo, M. (2015) 'Active citizenship and the emergence of networks', in *Challenging the third sector: Global prospects for active citizenship*, Bristol: Policy Press.

Kenny, S., Ife, J. and Westoby, P. (forthcoming) *Populism, democracy and community development*, Bristol: Policy Press.

Khan, O. (2007) 'Policy, identity and community cohesion', in M. Wetherell, M. Lafleche and R. Berkeley (eds) *Identity, ethnic diversity and community cohesion*, London: Sage Publications, pp 40–58.

Kim, A.J. (2000) *Community building on the web*, Berkeley, CA: Peachpit Press.

Kim, J. (2006) 'Networks, network governance, and networked networks', *International Review of Public Administration*, 11 (1): 19–34.

Kimberlee, R. (2016) 'What is the value of social prescribing?', *Advances in Social Sciences Research Journal*, 3 (3): 29–35.

Kindler, M., Ratcheva, V. and Piechowska, M. (2015) *Social networks, social capital and migrant integration at local level*, IRiS Working Paper Series, No 6/2015, Birmingham: Institute for Research into Superdiversity.

Kindon, S., Pain, R. and Kesby, M. (2010) *Participatory action research approaches and methods: Connecting people, participation and place*, London: Routledge.

King, M.L. (1968) *Chaos or community? Where do we go from here?*, London: Hodder and Stoughton.

Klandermans, B. (1997) *The social psychology of protest*, Oxford: Blackwell.

Klein, J. (1973) *Training for the new helping professions*, London: Goldsmiths College.

Klinenberg, E. (2018) *Palaces for the people*, New York: Random House.

Knapp, M., Bauer, M., Perkins, M. and Snell, T. (2013) 'Building community capital in social care: is there an economic case?', *Community Development Journal*, 48 (2): 313–31.

Knifton, L. (2015) 'Collective wellbeing in public mental health', *Perspectives in Public Health*, 135 (1): 24–6.

Knight Foundation (2017) *Scaling civic tech: Paths to a sustainable future*, Miami: Knight Foundation and Princeton, NJ: Rita Allen Foundation.

Knoke, D. (1990a) *Organising for collective action: The political economies of association*, New York: Aldine de Gruyter.

Knoke, D. (1990b) *Political networks: The structural perspective*, Cambridge: Cambridge University Press.

Kohn, M. (2009) *Trust: Self-interest and the common good*, Oxford: Oxford University Press.

Kolb, D. (1992) 'Women's work: peacemaking in organisations', in D. Kolb and J.M. Bartunek (eds) *Hidden conflict in organisations: Uncovering behind the scenes disputes*, Newbury Park, CA: Sage Publications.

Komro, K.A., Flay, B.R., Biglan, A. and Wagenaar, A.C. (2016) 'Research design issues for evaluating complex multicomponent interventions in neighborhoods and communities', *Translational Behavioural Medicine*, 6 (1): 153–9.

Kottegoda, S. (2004) *Negotiating household politics: Women's strategies in urban Sri Lanka*, Colombo: Social Scientists' Association.

Kratzwald, B. (2016) 'Community development and commons: on the road to alternative economics', in R. Meade, M. Shaw, and S. Banks (eds) *Politics, power and community development*, Bristol: Policy Press, pp 235–51.

Kreiss, D. (2015) 'The networked democratic spectator', *Social Media + Society*, 1 (1).

Kretzmann, J. and McKnight, J. (1993) *Building communities from the inside out: A path toward finding and mobilizing a community's assets*, Evanston, IL: Institute for Policy Research, Northwestern University.

Krishnamurthy, A., Prime, D. and Zimmeck, M. (2001) *Voluntary and community activities: Findings from the British Crime Survey 2000*, London: ACU research team, Home Office.

Kubisch, A.C., Brown, P., Chaskin, R., Fullbright-Anderson, K. and Hamilton, R. (2002) 'Strengthening the connexions between communities and external resources', in A.C. Kubisch (ed) *Voices from the field 2: Reflections on comprehensive community change*, Washington: The Aspen Institute.

Laerhoven, F. van and Barnes, C. (2014) 'Communities and commons: the role of community development support in sustaining the commons', *Community Development Journal*, 49 (1): 118–32.

Laguerre, M.S. (1994) *The informal city*, Basingstoke: Macmillan.

Landry, C. and Caust, M. (2017) *The creative bureaucracy and its radical common sense*, Gloucestershire: Comedia.

Laumann, E. and Pappi, F. (1976) *Networks of collective action: A perspective on community influence systems*, New York: Academic Press.

Laurence, J. and Heath, A. (2008) *Predictors of community cohesion: Multi-level modelling of the 2005 Citizenship Survey*, London: Department for Communities and Local Government.

Lawler, E., Thye, S. and Yoon, J. (2015) *Order on the edge of chaos: Social psychology and the problem of social order*, Cambridge: Cambridge University Press.

Lawrence, J. (2018) 'Individualism and community in historical perspective', in S. Cohen, C. Fuhr and J-J. Bock (eds) *Austerity, community action and the future of citizenship in Europe*, Bristol: Policy Press, pp 239–54.

Lawrence, J. (2019) *Me, me, me: The search for community in post-war England*, Oxford: Oxford University Press.

Lawrence, J. and Lim, C. (2015) 'Doing good when times are bad: volunteering behaviour in economic hard times', *British Journal of Sociology*, 6: 319–44.

Layard, R. (2005) *Happiness: Lessons from a new science*, London: Penguin.

Ledwith, M. (1997) *Participating in transformation: Towards a working model of community empowerment*, Birmingham: Venture Press.

Ledwith, M. (2006) *Community development*, Bristol: Policy Press/ BASW.

Ledwith, M. (2015) *Community development in action: Putting Freire into practice*, Bristol: Policy Press.

Ledwith, M. (2019) *Community development: A critical approach* (3rd edn), Bristol: Policy Press.

Ledwith, M. and Asgill, P. (2000) 'Critical alliance: black and white women working together for social justice', *Community Development Journal*, 35: 290–9.

Ledwith, M. and Springett, J. (2009) *Participatory practice: Community-based action for transformative change*, Bristol: Policy Press.

Lees, R. and Mayo, M. (1984) *Community action for change*, London: Routledge and Kegan Paul.

Leissner, A. (1975) 'Models for community work and community and youth workers', *Social Work Today*, 5 (22): 669–75.

Levitas, R. (2013) *Utopia as method: The imaginary reconstitution of society*, Basingstoke: Palgrave Macmillan.

Lewin, R. (1993) *Complexity: Life on the edge of chaos*, London: Phoenix.

Lewis, M. (2005) *Asylum: Understanding public attitudes*, London: IPPR.

LEWRG (London Edinburgh Weekend Return Group) (1979) *In and against the state*, London: Pluto Press.

LGA (Local Government Association) (2002) *Guidance on community cohesion*, London: LGA.

Liebler, C. and Ferri, M. (2004) 'NGO networks: building capacity in a changing world', Paper presented to the Office of Private and Voluntary Co-operation for USAID.

Lin, N. (2002) *Social capital: A theory of social structure and action*, Cambridge: Cambridge University Press.

Lindsey, R. and Mohan, J. (2019) *Continuity and change in voluntary action: Patterns, trends and understandings*, Bristol: Policy Press.

Lipsky, M. (1969) *Toward a theory of street-level bureaucracy*, IRP Discussion Papers Nos 48–69, Madison, WI: Institute for Research on Poverty (IRP), University of Wisconsin, p 45.

Livingstone, M., Bailey, N. and Kearns, A. (2008) *People's attachment to place: The influence of neighbourhood deprivation*, York: Joseph Rowntree Foundation.

Loader, B. and Keeble, L. (2004) *A literature review of community informatics initiatives*, York: Joseph Rowntree Foundation.

Local Trust (2017) 'Partnership survey results', http://localtrust.or.guk/library/blogs/are-residents-leading-big-local.

Locke, J.L. (1998) *The de-voicing of society: Why we don't talk to each other anymore*, New York: Simon and Schuster.

Loney, M. (1983) *Community against government*, London: Heinemann.

Lovelock, J. (1979) *Gaia*, Oxford: Oxford University Press.

Lowe, T. (2017a) 'Debate: complexity and the performance of social interventions', *Public Money and Management*, 37 (2): 79–80.

Lowe, T. (2017b) 'Performance management in the voluntary sector: responding to complexity', *Voluntary Sector Review*, 8 (3): 319–31.

Lowndes, V. and Sullivan, H. (2004) 'Like a horse and carriage or a fish on a bicycle: how well do local partnerships and public participation go together?', *Local Government Studies*, 30: 51–73.

Lowndes, V., Pratchett, L. and Stoker, G. (2006) *Locality matters: Making participation count in local politics*, London: Institute for Public Policy Research.

Lownsbrough, H. and Beunderman, J. (2007) *Equally spaced? Public space and interaction between diverse communities*, London: Demos.

Lukes, S. (1974) *Power: A radical view*, Basingstoke: Macmillan.

Lyons, J. (2007) *Place-shaping: A shared ambition for the future of local government*, London: HMSO.

MacGillivray, A., Conaty, P. and Wadhams, C. (2001) *Low flying heroes: Micro-social enterprises below the radar screen*, London: New Economics Foundation.

MacLean, D. and MacIntosh, R. (2003) 'Complex adaptive systems: towards a theory for practice', in E. Mitleton-Kelly (ed) *Complex systems and evolutionary perspectives on organisations: The application of complexity theory to organisations*, London: Pergamon, pp 149–66.

Macmillan, R. and Ellis Paine, A. (2018) 'Real time change: reflections from qualitative longitudinal research on voluntary action', in A. McCabe (ed) *Ten Years Below the Radar: Reflections on Voluntary and Community Action 2008–2018*, Working Paper 143, Birmingham: Third Sector Research Centre, University of Birmingham, pp 56–60.

Madanipour, A. (2003) *Public and private spaces of the city*, London: Routledge.

Maffesoli, M. (1996) *The time of the tribes: The decline of individualism in mass society*, London: Sage Publications.

Majdandzic, A., Braunstein, L., Curme, C., Vodenska, I., Levy-Carciente, S., Eugene S.H. and Havlin, S. (2016) 'Multiple tipping points and optimal repairing in interacting networks', *Nature Communications*, 7: 10850.

Manney, P.J. (2008) 'Empathy in the time of technology: how storytelling is the key to empathy', *Journal of Evolution and Technology*, 19 (1): 51–61.

Marjoribanks, D. and Darnell Bradley, A. (2017) *The way we are now: The state of the UK's relationships*, London: Relate and Relationships Scotland.

Marmot, M. (2015) *The health gap: The challenge of an unequal world*, London: Bloomsbury.

Marwell, G. and Oliver, P. (1993) *The critical mass in collective action: A micro-social theory*, Cambridge: Cambridge University Press.

Maslach, C. (1982) *Burnout: The cost of caring*, Englewood Cliffs, NJ: Prentice Hall.

Mathers, J., Parry, J. and Jones, S. (2008) 'Exploring resident (non-)participation in the UK New Deal for Communities regeneration programme', *Urban Studies*, 45: 591–606.

Matthews, P. (2016) 'Social media, community development and social capital', *Community Development Journal*, 51 (3): 419–35.

Matthews, P. and Besemer, K. (2014) *Poverty and social networks: Evidence review*, York: Joseph Rowntree Foundation.

Matthews, P. and Besemer, K. (2015) 'Social networks, social capital and poverty: panacea or placebo?', *Journal of Poverty and Social Justice*, 23 (3): 189–201.

Maturana, H.R. and Varela, F.J. (1987) *The tree of knowledge: The biological roots of human understanding*, Boston, MA: Shambhala.

May, N. (1997) *Challenging assumptions: Gender considerations in urban regeneration in the UK*, York: Joseph Rowntree Foundation.

May, R.M. (2001) *Stability and complexity in model ecosystems*, Princeton, NJ: Princeton University Press.

Mayo, M. (1979) 'Radical politics and community action', in M. Loney and M. Allen (eds) *The crisis in the inner-city*, London: Macmillan, pp 131–48.

Mayo, M. (2005) *Global citizens: Social movements and the challenge of globalization*, London: Zed Books.

Mayo, M. (2008) 'Community development, contestations, continuities and change', in G. Craig, K. Popple and M. Shaw (eds) *Community development in theory and practice: An international reader*, Nottingham: Spokesman, pp 13–27.

Mayo, M. (forthcoming) 'Community development and popular education in populist times', in S. Kenny, J. Ife and P. Westoby (eds) *Populism, democracy and community development*, Bristol: Policy Press.

Mayo, M. and Annette, J. (eds) (2010) *Taking part: Active learning for active citizenship and beyond?*, Leicester: NIACE Publications.

Mayo, M. and Rooke, A. (2006) *Evaluation of the active learning for active citizenship*, London: Department of Communities and Local Government.

Mayo, M. and Taylor, M. (2001) 'Partnership and power in community regeneration', in S. Balloch and M. Taylor (eds) *Partnership working*, Bristol: Policy Press, pp 39–56 .

Mayo, M., Tucker, P. and Danaher, M. (2016) 'Community unionism; looking backwards, looking forwards', in M. Shaw and M. Mayo (eds) *Class, inequality and community development*, Bristol: Policy Press, pp 235-50.

McCabe, A. (2018) 'Introduction', in A. McCabe (ed) *Ten Years Below the Radar: Reflections on Voluntary and Community Action 2008–2018*, Working Paper 143, Birmingham: Third Sector Research Centre, University of Birmingham, p 6.

McCabe, A. and Burnage, A. (2015) *Developing street associations in low income neighbourhoods, final evaluation report*, Birmingham: Third Sector Research Centre and Barrow Cadbury Trust.

McCabe, A. and Harris, K. (forthcoming) 'Community organisations and social media: from collective to connective action?', *Community Development Journal*.

McCabe, A. and Phillimore, J. (2017) 'Are we different? Claims for distinctiveness in voluntary and community action', in A. McCabe and J. Phillimore (eds) *Community groups in context*, Bristol: Policy Press, pp 51–70.

McCabe, A., Wilson, M. and Macmillan, R. (2019) *Big Local: Reflections on community leadership*, www.ourbiggerstory.com/2018_OBS_ leadership_paper.pdf

McCabe, A., Gilchrist, A., Harris, K., Afridi, A. and Kyprianou, P. (2013) *Making the links: Poverty, ethnicity and social networks*, York: Joseph Rowntree Foundation.

McCabe, A., Wilson, M. and Macmillan, R. with Morgans, P. and Edwards, M. (2017) *Big Local: Beyond the early years – our bigger story: The longitudinal multi media evaluation of Big Local 2015–2016*, http:// localtrust.org.uk/assets/downloads/documents/OBS%20Beyond%20 the%20Early%20Years%20Full%20Report%20Final.pdf

McCosker, A. (2015) 'Social media activism at the margins: managing visibility, voice and vitality affects', *Social Media + Society*, 1 (2).

McInroy, N. (2004) 'Working with complexity: the key to effective regeneration', *Local Work*, 59 (September), Manchester: CLES.

McKenzie, K. and Harphan, T. (eds) (2006) *Social capital and mental health*, London: Jessica Kingsley.

McKnight, J. and Block, P. (2012) *The abundant community: Awakening the power of families and neighborhoods*, San Francisco: Berrett-Koehler.

McPherson, K., Kerr, S., McGee, E., Cheater, F. and Morgan, A. (2013) *The role and impact of social capital on the health and wellbeing of children and adolescents: A systematic review*, Glasgow: Glasgow Centre for Population Health.

Mead, G.H. (1938) *The philosophy of the act*, ed C.W. Morris, Chicago, IL: Chicago University Press.

Meade, R., Shaw, M. and Banks, S. (2016) *Politics, power and community development*, Bristol: Policy Press.

Measor, L. (2006) 'Young women, community safety and informal cultures,, in P. Squires (ed) *Community safety: Critical perspectives on policy and practice*, Bristol: Policy Press, pp 181–200.

Meijl, T. van (2011) 'Community development as fantasy? A case study of contemporary Maori society', in Y. Musharbash and M. Barber (eds) *Ethnography and the production of anthropological knowledge*, Canberra, ACT: ANU E Press, pp 133–46 .

Mellor, M. and Stephenson, C. (2005) 'The Durham miners' gala and the spirit of community', *Community Development Journal*, 40: 343–51.

Melucci, A. (1996) *Challenging codes: Collective action in the information age*, Cambridge: Cambridge University Press.

Middleton, A., Murie, A. and Groves, R. (2005) 'Social capital and neighbourhoods that work', *Urban Studies*, 42: 1711–38.

Milbourne, L. (2013) *Voluntary sector in transition: Hard times or new opportunities?*, Bristol: Policy Press.

Milgram, S. (1967) 'The small world problem', *Psychology Today*, 2: 60–7.

Milgram, S. (1977) *The individual in a social world*, Reading, MA: Addison-Wesley.

Mill, J.S. (1848) *Principles of political economy*, London: John W. Parker.

Miller, J.B. (1976) *Towards a new psychology of women*, Boston, MA: Beacon Press.

Miller, P. (2004) 'The rise of network campaigning', in H. McCarthy, P. Miller and P. Skidmore (eds) *Network logic: Who governs in an interconnected world?*, London: Demos, pp 205-17.

Miller, K. and Rasco, L. (2004) *The mental health of refugees: Ecological approaches to healing and adaptation*, Mahwah, NJ: Lawrence Erlbaum Associates.

Milling, J. Simpson, R. and Ramsden, H. (2018) 'Grassroots and voluntary arts: Looking back, imagining the future', in A. McCabe (ed) *Ten years below the radar: Reflections on voluntary and community action 2008–2018*, Working Paper 143, Birmingham: Third Sector Research Centre, University of Birmingham.

Milne, A. and Rankin, D. (2013) *Reality, resources, resilience: Regeneration in a recession*, York: Joseph Rowntree Foundation.

Milofsky, C. (1987) 'Neighbourhood-based organisations: a market analogy', in W.W. Powell (ed) *The non-profit sector: A research handbook*, New Haven, CT: Yale University Press, pp 277–95.

Milofsky, C. (1988) 'Introduction: networks, markets, cultures and contracts: understanding community organisations', in C. Milofsky (ed) *Community organisations: Studies in resource mobilisation and exchange*, New York: Oxford University Press, pp 3–15.

Mingers, J. (1995) *Self-producing systems: Implications and applications of autopoiesis*, New York: Plenum Press.

Misztal, B. (2000) *Informality: Social theory and contemporary practice*, London: Routledge.

Mitchell, J.C. (ed) (1969) *Social networks in urban situations: Analyses of personal relationships in central African towns*, Manchester: Manchester University Press.

Mitchell, W.J. (2003) *Me++: The cyborg self and the networked city*, Cambridge, MA: MIT Press.

Mitleton-Kelly, E. (ed) (2003) *Complex systems and evolutionary perspectives on organisations: The application of complexity theory to organisations*, London: Pergamon.

Mlodinow, L. (2018) *Plastic: The power of flexible thinking*, London: Penguin.

Modood, T. (2003) 'New forms of Britishness: post-immigration ethnicity and hybridity in Britain', in R. Sackmann, B. Peters and T. Faust (eds) *Identity and integration: Migrants in Western Europe*, Aldershot: Ashgate.

Modood, T. (2007) *Multiculturalism: A civic idea*, Cambridge: Polity Press.

Mogus, J. and Liacas, T. (2016) *Networked change: How progressive campaigns are won in the 21st century*, http://netchange.co/report.

Mohan, J. and Bulloch, S. (2012) *The idea of a 'civic core': What are the overlaps between charitable giving, volunteering, and civic participation in England and Wales?*, Birmingham: Third Sector Research Centre, University of Birmingham.

Morgan, D. (2009) *Acquaintances: The space between intimates and strangers*, Maidenhead: Open University Press.

Morgan, G. (1989) *Creative organisation theory: A resource book*, London: Sage Publications.

Morgan-Trimmer, S. (2014) '"It's who you know": community empowerment through network brokers', *Community Development Journal*, 49: 458–72.

Morozov, E. (2009) 'The brave new world of slacktivism', *Foreign Policy* blog, 19 May, https://foreignpolicy.com/2009/05/19/the-brave-new-world-of-slacktivism/

Morris, J., Cobbing, P., Leach, K. and Conaty, P. (2013) *Mainstreaming community economic development*, Birmingham: Localise West Midlands.

Morrison, T. (2019) *Mouth full of blood: Essays, speeches, meditations*, London: Vintage.

Morrissey, J. (2000) 'Indicators of citizen participation: lessons from learning teams in rural EZ/EC communities', *Community Development Journal*, 35 (1): 59–74.

Muir, R. (2012) *Pubs and places: The social value of community pubs*, London: IPPR.

Mulgan, G. (1997) *Connexity: How to live in a connected world*, London: Chatto and Windus.

Mulgan, G. (2017) *Big mind: How collective intelligence can change the world*, Princeton, NJ: Princeton University Press.

Mumford, K. and Power, A. (2003) *East Enders: Family and community in east London*, Bristol: Policy Press.

Murtagh, B. and Goggin, N. (2015) 'Finance, social economics and community development', *Community Development Journal*, 50 (3): 494–509.

Muslim Council of Britain (2018) *Our shared British future: Muslims and integration in the UK*, London: Muslim Council of Britain.

Nakaya, U. (1954) *Snow crystals: Natural and artificial*, Boston, MA: Harvard University Press.

Nalder, G. and Dallas, A. (2006) 'Personalized profiling and self-organization as strategies for the formation and support of open m-learning communities', in *Across generations and cultures: Proceedings of the 5th World Conference on Mobile Learning*, Banff: Athabasca University.

Narayan, D. (2002) *Empowerment and poverty reduction: A source book*, Washington, DC: World Bank.

Nash, V. and Christie, I. (2003) *Making sense of community*, London: IPPR.

Navarro, A. (2006) *Refugee integration and cohesive communities: Community development in practice*, London: Community Development Foundation.

NAVCA (2015) *Change for good: Report of the independent commission on the future of local infrastructure*, Sheffield: National Association for Voluntary and Community Action.

NCIA (2015) *Fight or fright: Voluntary services in 2015*, London: National Coalition for Independent Action.

Neely, K. (2015) 'Complex adaptive systems as a valid framework for understanding community level development', *Development in Practice*, 25 (6): 785–97.

Nelson, C., Dickinson, S., Beetham, M. and Batsleer, J. (2000) 'Border crossings/translations: resources of hope in community work with women in Greater Manchester', *Community, Work and Family*, 3: 349–62.

Newman, K. (2016) 'Reconciling participation and power in international development: a case study', in M. Shaw and M. Mayo (eds), *Class, inequality and community development*, Bristol: Policy Press, pp 171–87.

Newman, I. and Geddes, M. (2001) 'Developing local strategies for social inclusion', Paper presented to Local Authorities and Social Exclusion programme, Local Government Centre, Warwick University, March.

Newman, J. (2012) *Working the spaces of power*, London: Bloomsbury.

Newman, M. (2010) *Networks: An introduction*, Oxford: Oxford University Press.

Nextdoor (2016) *One Poll Survey*, https://nextdoor.co.uk/

NICE (2016) *Community engagement: Improving health and wellbeing and reducing health inequalities*, London: National Institute for Health and Care Excellence.

Nie, N., Sunshine, H., Hillygus, D. and Erbring, L. (2002) 'Internet use, interpersonal relations, and sociability', in B. Wellman and C. Haythornthwaite (eds) *The internet in everyday life*, Oxford: Blackwell, pp 215–43.

Nietzsche, F. (1878) *Thus spake Zarathustra*, trans A. Tille (1960), London: J.M. Dent and Sons.

Nisbet, R.A. (1953) *The quest for community*, Oxford: Oxford University Press.

Nooy, W. de, Mrvar, A. and Batagelj, V. (2005) *Exploratory social network analysis with Pajek*, Cambridge: Cambridge University Press.

Nowak, M. and Highfield, R. (2011) *Superco-operators: Evolution, altruism and human behaviour*, Edinburgh: Canongate Books.

Obstfeld, D. (2017) *Getting new things done: Networks, brokerage and the assembly of innovative action*, Stanford: Stanford University Press.

Offer, S. (2012) 'The burden of reciprocity: Processes of exclusion and withdrawal from personal networks among low-income families', *Current Sociology*, 60 (6): 788–805.

Office of the Third Sector (2007) *The future role of the third sector in social and economic regeneration: Final report*, Cm 7189, Norwich: HM Treasury and the Cabinet Office.

Ogden, C. (2018) 'What is network leadership?', *Education Week* blog, 17 April, http://blogs.edweek.org/edweek/next_gen_learning/2018/04/what_is_network_leadership.html

Ohmer, M. and Beck, E. (2006) 'Citizen participation in neighbourhood organizations in poor communities and its relationship to neighbourhood and organizational collective efficacy', *Journal of Sociology and Social Welfare*, 33 (1): 179–202.

Ohri, A. (1998) *The world in our neighbourhood*, London: Development Education Association.

O'Keeffe, G.S. and Clarke Pearson, K. (2011) 'The impact of social media on children, adolescents, and families', *Paediatrics*, 127 (4): 800–4.

Oladipo Fiki, C., Amupitan, J., Dabi, D. and Nyong, A. (2007) 'From disciplinary to interdisciplinary community development: the Joss-McMaster drought and rural water use project', *Journal of Community Practice*, 15: 147–70.

Oldenburg, R. (1991) *The great good place: Cafes, coffee shops, community centres, beauty parlours, general stores, bars, hangouts, and how they get you through the day*, New York: Paragon House.

Oliver, B. (2006) 'Identity and change: youth working in transition', *Youth & Policy*, 93: 5–19.

Oliver, B. (2007) 'Connected identities: youth working in transition', unpublished Ed.D. thesis, University of Sussex.

Oliver, M. (1996) *Understanding disability*, London: Macmillan.

Oliver, B. and Pitt, B. (2013) *Engaging communities and service users: Context, themes and methods*, London: Red Globe.

Onyx, J. and Leonard, R. (2011) 'Complex systems leadership in emergent community projects', *Community Development Journal*, 46: 493–510.

Opare, S. (2007) 'Strengthening community-based organisations for the challenge of rural development', *Community Development Journal*, 42: 251–64.

Ouchi, W.G. (1980) 'Markets, bureaucracies and clans', *Administrative Science Quarterly*, 25: 129–41.

Packham, C. (2008) *Active citizenship and community learning*, Exeter: Learning Matters.

Packard, N. (1988) *Adaptation toward the edge of chaos*, Urbana-Champaign: University of Illinois, Center for Complex Systems Research.

Park, R. (ed) (1925) *The city*, Chicago, IL: University of Chicago Press.

Park, R. (1929) *Human communities: The city and human ecology*, Glencoe, IL: Free Press.

Parkinson, J. and Mansbridge, J. (2012) *Deliberative systems: Deliberative democracy at the large scale*, Cambridge: Cambridge University Press.

Parsfield, M., Morris, D., Bola, M., Knapp, M. Yoshioka, M. and Marcus, G. (2015) *Community capital: The value of connected communities*, London: RSA.

Passy, F. (2003) 'Social networks matter. But how?', in M. Diani and D. McAdam (eds) *Social movements and networks: Relational approaches to collective action*, Oxford: Oxford University Press.

Percy-Smith, B. and Matthews, H. (2001) 'Tyrannical spaces: young people, bullying and urban neighbourhoods', *Local Environment*, 6: 49–63.

Perkins, D.D., Brown, B.B. and Taylor, R.B. (1996) 'The ecology of empowerment', *Journal of Social Issues*, 52: 85–110.

Perrow, C. (1992) 'Small firm networks', in N. Nohria and R. Eccles (eds) *Networks and organisations*, Boston, MA: Harvard Business School Press, pp 445–70.

Pflaeging, N. (2014) *Organize for complexity: How to get life back into work to build the high-performance organization*, Betacodex Publishing, https://www.betacodexpublishing.com/.

Pharoah, R. and Hopwood, O. (2013) *Families and hardship: In new and established communities in Southwark*, London: ESRO.

Phelps, R., Adams, R. and Bessant, J. (2007) 'Life cycles of growing organizations: a review with implications for knowledge and learning', *International Journal of Management Reviews*, 9: 1–30.

Phillimore, J. and McCabe, A. with Taylor, R. and Soteri-Proctor, A. (2010) *Understanding the distinctiveness of small scale third sector*, Working Paper 33, Birmingham: Third Sector Research Centre, University of Birmingham.

Phillimore, J., Grzymala-Kazlowska, A. and Cheung, S. (2017) 'Voluntary action for asylum seeker and refugee integration', in A. Heath (ed) *If you could do one thing: 10 local actions to promote social integration*, London: British Academy, pp 19–15.

Phillips, C. (2007) 'Ethnicity, identity and community cohesion in prison', in M. Wetherell, M. Lafleche and R. Berkeley (eds) *Identity, ethnic diversity and community cohesion*, London: Sage Publications, pp 75–86.

Phillips, R. (2005) *Community indicators measuring systems*, Aldershot: Ashgate.

Phillipson, C., Allan, G. and Morgan, D.H.J. (2004) *Social networks and social exclusion: Sociological and policy perspectives*, Aldershot: Ashgate Publishing.

Piacentini, T. (2017) 'More than a refugee community organisation: a study of African migrant associations in Glasgow', in A. McCabe and J. Phillimore (eds) *Community groups in context*, Bristol: Policy Press, pp 199-217.

Piacentini, T. (2018) 'African migrants, asylum seekers and refugees: tales of settling in Scotland, 2000–2015', in T. Devine and A. McCarthy (eds) *Scotland's immigrant communities*, Edinburgh: Edinburgh University Press.

Piketty, T. (2013) *Capitalism in the 21st century*, London: Belknap.

Pilch, D. (ed) (2006) *Neighbourliness*, London: Smith Institute.

Pine, B.J. and Korn, KC. (2011) *Infinite possibility: Creating customer value on the digital frontier*, San Francisco: Berrett-Koehler Publishers.

Pinker, S. (2009) *How the mind works*, New York: W.W. Norton & Company.

Pitchford, M. (2008) *Making spaces for community development*, Bristol: Policy Press.

Plastrik, P., Taylor, M. and Cleveland, J. (2014) *Connecting to change the world: Harnessing the power of networks for social impact*, Washington, DC: Island Press.

Platts-Fowler, D. and Robinson, D. (2013) *Neighbourhood resilience in Sheffield: Getting by in hard times*, Sheffield: Centre for Regional Economic and Social Research.

Poll, C., Kennedy, J. and Sanderson, H. (2009) *In community: Practice lessons in supporting isolated people to be part of the community*, Stockport: HAS Press in association with In Control.

Popay, J. (2017) *Big Local and health inequalities: An update from the Communities in Control study*, https://sphr.nihr.ac.uk/research/health-inequalities-research-programme-communities-in-control-study-overview/

Popple, K. (2015) *Analysing community work*, Buckingham: Open University Press.

Popple, K. (forthcoming) 'Populist politics and democracy in the UK: what are the implications for community development?', in S. Kenny, J. Ife and P. Westoby (eds) *Populism, democracy and community development*, Bristol: Policy Press.

Power, A. (2007) *Neighbourhood renewal, mixed communities and social integration*, Report to Neighbourhood Renewal Unit, Centre for Analysis of Social Exclusion, London: London School of Economics and Political Science

Prendergast, J. (2008) *Disconnected citizens: Is community empowerment the solution?*, London: Social Market Foundation.

Price, L. (2015) *Incidental connections: An analysis of platforms for community building*, London: Community Links.

Probyn, E. (2004) 'Everyday shame', *Cultural Studies*, 18 (2/3): 328–49.

Purcell, R. (2005) *Working in the community: Perspectives for change*, North Carolina: Lulu Press.

Purcell, R. (2009) 'Images for change: community development, community arts and photography', *Community Development Journal*, 44: 111–22.

Purdue, D. (2007) 'A learning approach to community empowerment', in T. Gossling, L. Oerlemans and R. Jansen (eds) *Inside networks*, Cheltenham: Edward Elgar, pp 93-114.

Purdue, D., Razzaque, K., Hambleton, R. and Stewart, M. (2000) *Community leadership in urban regeneration*, Bristol/York: The Policy Press/Joseph Rowntree Foundation.

Putnam, R. (1993) 'The prosperous community', *The American Prospect*, 13: 11–18.

Putnam, R. (2000) *Bowling alone: The collapse and revival of American community*, London: Simon and Shuster.

Putnam, R. (2007) 'E pluribus unum: diversity and community in the twenty-first century', *Scandinavian Political Studies*, 30: 137–74.

Rahman, H. (2006) *Empowering marginal communities with information networking*, Hershey, PA: Idea Group Publishers.

Rahman, M.A. (1993) *People's self-development: Perspectives on participatory action research: A journey through experience*, London: Zed Books.

Ramalingam, B., Jones, H., Reba, T. and Young, J. (2008) *Exploring the science of complexity: Ideas and implications for development and humanitarian efforts*, London: Overseas Development Institute.

Rathke, W. (2018) *Nuts and bolts: The ACORN fundamentals of organising*, https://socialpolicypress.org/ Social Policy Press.

Rattansi, A. (2002) *Who's British? Prospect and the new assimilation: Cohesion, community and citizenship*, London: Runnymede Trust.

Ray, K., Savage, M., Tampubolon, G., Warde, A., Longhurst, M. and Tomlinson, M. (2003) 'The exclusiveness of the political field: networks and political mobilisation', *Social Movement Studies*, 2: 37–60.

Reagans, R. (2011) 'Close encounters: analyzing how social similarity and propinquity contribute to strong network connections', *Organization Science*, 22: 835–49.

Rees, J. and Mullins, D. (2017) *The third sector delivering public services: Developments, innovations and challenges*, Bristol: Policy Press.

Rees, S. (1991) *Achieving power: Practice and policy in social welfare*, London: Allen and Unwin.

Rheingold, H. (2002) *Smart mobs: The next social revolution*, Cambridge, MA: Basic Books.

Rheingold, H. (2012) *Net smart: How to thrive online*, Cambridge, MA: MIT Press.

Richardson, L. (2008) *DIY community action: Neighbourhood problems and community self-help*, Bristol: Policy Press.

Richardson, L. and Durose, C. (2013) *Who is accountable in localism? Findings from theory and practice*, Swindon: AHRC.

Riedel, B. (2008) *The search for Al Qaeda: Its leadership, ideology and future*, Washington, DC: Brookings Institution Press.

Riley, E. and Wakely, P. (2005) *Communities and communication: Building urban partnerships in Colombo*, Rugby: ITDG Publishing.

Roberts, P. and Stewart, B.A. (2018) 'Defining the "generalist specialist" niche for Pleistocene Homo sapiens', *Nature Human Behaviour*, 2: 542–50.

Robertson, D., Smyth, J. and McIntosh, I. (2008) *Neighbourhood identity: Effects of time, location and social class*, York: Joseph Rowntree Foundation.

Robinson, D. (2004) *Unconditional leadership: A principle-centred approach to developing people, building teams and maximizing results*, London: Community Links.

Robinson, R. and Reeve, K. (2006) *Neighbourhood experiences of new immigration: Reflections from the evidence base*, York: Joseph Rowntree Foundation.

Rochester, C. (1999) *Juggling on a unicycle: A handbook for small voluntary agencies*, London: London School of Economics and Political Science.

Rochester, C. (2013) *Re-discovering voluntary action*, Basingstoke: Palgrave Macmillan.

Rose, S. (1998) *From brains to consciousness*, London: Allen Lane.

Ruggeri, K., Garcia Garzon, E., Maguire, A. and Huppert, F. (2016) 'Comprehensive psychological well-being', in *Looking through the kaleidoscope: Results from the European survey*, ch 1 [online only].

Russell, C. (2015) *Asset based community development (ABCD): Looking back to look forward: In conversation with John McKnight about the intellectual and practical heritage of ABCD and its place in the world today*, e-book: https://itunes.apple.com/GB/book/id1007493751?l=en

Russell, K. (2004) *Hui: A hui to discuss how to create and maintain a relationship with Māori organisations*, Dunedin, New Zealand: Department of Community and Family Studies, University of Otago.

Ryberg, T. and Larsen, M.C. (2008) 'Networked identities: understanding relationships between strong and weak ties in networked environments', *Journal of Computer Assisted Learning*, 24: 103–15.

Ryder, A. (2017) *Sites of resistance: Gypsies, Roma and Travellers in the community, school and academy*, London: Trentham Press IOE (Institute of Education).

Sampson, R. (2004) 'Networks and neighbourhoods', in H. McCarthy, P. Miller and P. Skidmore (eds) *Network logic: Who governs in an interconnected world?*, London: Demos.

Sampson, R., Morenoff, J. and Gannon-Rowley, T. (2002) 'Assessing neighbourhood effects: social processes and new directions in research', *Annual Review of Sociology*, 28: 443–78.

Sandel, A. (2014) *The place of prejudice: A case for reasoning within the world*, Cambridge, MA: Harvard University Press.

Sarason, S.B. (1974) *The psychological sense of community: Prospects for a community psychology*, San Francisco: Jossey-Bass.

Schön, D. (1990) *The reflective practitioner: How professionals think in action*, Aldershot: Avebury.

Schumann, S. and Klein, O. (2015) 'Substitute or stepping stone? Assessing the impact of low-threshold online collective actions on offline participation', *European Journal of Social Psychology*, 45 (3): 308–22.

Scott, J. (2000) *Social network analysis: A handbook* (2nd edn), London: Sage Publications.

Scott, M. (2010) *Unseen, unequal, untapped: The potential for community action at grass roots*, London: Community Sector Coalition.

Scott, M. (2011) 'Reflections on "The Big Society"', *Community Development Journal*, 46 (1): 132–7.

Scott, M. (2018) 'Reflections: 'The third sector ain't dead, it just smells funny', in A. McCabe (ed) *Ten years below the radar: Reflections on voluntary and community action 2008–2018*, Working Paper 143, Birmingham: Third Sector Research Centre, University of Birmingham, pp 47–51.

Scott, S., Houston, D. and Sterling, R. (2002) *Working together, learning together: An evaluation of the national training programme for social inclusion partnerships*, Glasgow: Department of Urban Studies, University of Glasgow.

Scott, W.R. (1992) *Organisations: Rational, natural and open systems*, Englewood Cliffs, NJ: Prentice Hall.

Seabeck, A., Rogers, B. and Srikandarajah, D. (2007) 'Living together: diversity and identity in contemporary Britain', in N. Pearce and J. Margo (eds) *Politics for a new generation: The progressive moment*, Basingstoke: Palgrave Macmillan.

Searle, B. (2008) *Well-being: In search of a good life*, Bristol: Policy Press.

Seddon, J. (2008) *Systems-thinking in the public sector*, Axminster: Triarchy Press.

Seebohm, P. and Gilchrist, A. (2008) *Connect and include: An exploratory study of community development and mental health*, London: National Social Inclusion Partnership/Community Development Foundation.

Sen, A. (2006) *Identity and violence: The illusion of destiny*, London: Allen Lane.

Sennett, R. (2012) *Together: The rituals, pleasures and politics of cooperation*, New Haven and London: Yale University Press.

Shahid, M. and Jha, M.K. (2016) 'Community development practice in India: interrogating caste and common sense', in M. Shaw and M. Mayo (eds) *Class, inequality and community development*, Bristol: Policy Press, pp 93–106.

Shaw, A. (2002) *Kinship and continuity: Pakistani families in Britain*, New York: Harwood Academic Press.

Shaw, M. (2008) 'Community development and the politics of community', *Community Development Journal*, 43: 24–36.

Shaw, M. and Martin, I. (2000) 'Community work, citizenship and democracy: remaking the connections', *Community Development Journal*, 35 (4): 401–13.

Sheffield, H. (2018) *Building wealth: How communities are re-shaping the economy from the bottom up*, http://localtrust.org.uk/library/blogs/how-comunities-are-reshaping-the-economy-from-the-bottom-up.

Shuftan, C. (1996) 'The community development dilemma: what is really empowering?' *Community Development Journal*, 31: 260–4.

Shukra, K. (1995) 'From black power to black perspectives: the reconstruction of a black political identity', *Youth and Policy*, 49: 5–17.

Singer, P. (2007) 'Give us a smile: the glow of goodwill should be a state priority. It's a cheap and effective way to improve lives', *The Guardian*, 18 April.

Sivanandan, A. (1990) 'All that melts into air is solid: the hokum of new times', *Race and Class*, 31: 1–30.

Skidmore, P. and Craig, J. (2005) *Start with people: How community organisations put citizens in the driving seat*, London: Demos.

Skidmore, P., Bound, K. and Lownsbrough, H. (2006) *Community participation: Who benefits?* York: Joseph Rowntree Foundation.

Skinner, S. (2019) *Building strong communities: Guidelines on empowering the grass roots*, London: Red Globe Press.

Skinner, S. and Wilson, M. (2002) *Assessing community strengths*, London: Community Development Foundation.

Smith, G. (1999) 'IT rams CD', *SCCD News*, 21: 9–16.

Smock, C. (2004) *Democracy in action: Community organising and urban change*, Chichester, NY: Columbia University Press.

Social Change Project (2018) *Social power: How civil society can 'play big' and truly create change*, London: Sheila McKechnie Foundation.

Social Enterprise UK (2018) *Public service mutuals: The state of the sector*, London: Department for Digital, Culture, Media and Sport.

Solnit, R. (2016) *Hope in the dark, untold histories, wild possibilities*, Edinburgh: Canongate.

Somerville, P. (2005) 'Community governance and democracy', *Policy and Politics*, 33: 117–44.

Somerville, P. (2009) '"The feeling's mutual": respect as the basis for co-operative interaction', in A. Millie (ed) *Securing respect: Behavioural expectations and anti-social behaviour in Britain*, Bristol: Policy Press, pp 139–67.

Somerville, P. (2016) *Understanding community: Politics, policy and practice* (2nd edn), Bristol: Policy Press.

Sorter, B.W. and Simpkinson, C.H. (1979) 'Coordinated networks: a method for community development', *Journal of the Community Development Society*, 10 (2): 89–100.

Soteri-Proctor, A. (2011) *Little big societies: Micro-mapping of organisations operating below the radar*, Working Paper 71, Birmingham: Third Sector Research Centre, University of Birmingham.

Soteri-Proctor, A. (2017) 'Getting below the radar? Micro-mapping hidden community activity', in A. McCabe and J. Phillimore (eds), *Community groups in context*, Bristol: Policy Press, pp 27-47.

South, J. and Stansfield, J. (2018) *Health matters: Community-centred approaches for health and wellbeing*, London: Public Health England.

South, J., White, J. and Gamsu, M. (2013) *People-centred public health*, Bristol: Policy Press.

Sprigings, N. and Allen, C. (2005) 'The communities we are re-gaining but need to lose', *Community, Work and Family*, 8: 389–411.

Stacey, M. (1969) 'The myth of community studies', *British Journal of Sociology*, 20 (2): 134–47.

Stack, C. (1974) *All our kin: Strategies for survival in a black community*, New York: Harper and Row.

Stackman, R.W. and Pinder, C.C. (1999) 'Context and sex effects on personal work networks', *Journal of Social and Personal Relationships*, 16: 39–64.

Standage, T. (2013) *Writing on the wall: Social media: The first 2,000 years*, London: Bloomsbury.

Steen, M. van (2010) *Graph theory and complex networks: An introduction*, Self-published.

Stein, M.R. (1960) *The eclipse of community: An interpretation of American studies*, Princeton, NJ: Princeton University Press.

Stephens, L., Ryan-Collins, J. and Boyle, D. (2008) *Co-production: A manifesto for growing the core economy*, London: New Economics Foundation.

Stephenson, K. (1999) 'Networks', in R. Dorf (ed) *The technology management handbook*, Boca Raton, FL: CRC Press, pp 40–5.

Stephenson, K. (2004) 'Towards a theory of government', in H. McCarthy, P. Miller and P. Skidmore (eds) *Network logic: Who governs in an inter-connected world?*, London: Demos, pp 35–48.

Stephenson, M. (2007) 'Developing community leadership through the arts in Southside, Virginia: social networks, civic identity and civic change', *Community Development Journal*, 42: 79–96.

Stewart, M. (2000) 'Community governance', in H. Barton (ed) *Sustainable communities: The potential for community neighbourhoods*, London: Earthscan, pp 176–86.

Strang, A. and Quinn, N. (2014) *Integration or isolation? Mapping social connections and well-being amongst refugees in Glasgow*, https://eresearch.qmu.ac.uk/handle/20.500.12289/4139.

Streets Alive (2008) *Older people and neighbouring: The role of street parties in promoting community cohesion*, Bristol: Streets Alive Ltd.

Strogatz, S. (2004) *Sync: The emerging science of spontaneous order*, Harmondsworth: Penguin Books.

Sullivan, H., Downe, J., Entwistle, T. and Sweeting, D. (2006) 'The three challenges of community leadership', *Local Government Studies*, 32: 489–508.

Surowiecki, J. (2004) *The wisdom of crowds: Why the many are smarter than the few and how collective wisdom shapes business, economies, societies and nations*, London: Random House.

Swales, K. and Tipping, S. (2018) *Fragmented communities? The role of cohesion, community involvement and social mixing*, London: NatCen.

Symons, B. (1981) 'Promoting participation through community work', in L. Smith and D. Jones (eds) *Deprivation, participation and community action*, London: Routledge and Kegan Paul, pp 207–24.

Szreter, S. and Woolcock, M. (2004) 'Health by association? Social capital, social theory, and the political economy of public health', *International Journal of Epidemiology*, 33: 1–18.

Tajfel, H. (1981) *Human groups and social categories: Studies in social psychology*, Cambridge: Cambridge University Press.

Tarrow, S. (2005) *The new transnational activism*, Cambridge: Cambridge University Press.

Tarrow, S. (2011) *Power in movement: Social movements, collective action and politics* (3rd edn), Cambridge: Cambridge University Press.

Tasker, L. (1975) 'Politics, theory and community work', in D. Jones and M. Mayo (eds) *Community work two*, London: Routledge and Kegan Paul.

Tattershall, A. (2010) *Power in coalition*, Ithaca and London: ILR Press.

Tayebi, A. (2013) 'Communihood: a less formal or more local form of community in the age of the internet', *Journal of Urban Technology*, 20 (2): 77–91.

Taylor, M. (1996) 'Between public and private: accountability in voluntary organisations', *Policy & Politics*, 24: 57–72.

Taylor, M. (2007) *Neighbourhood management and social capital*, London: Department for Communities and Local Government.

Taylor, M. (2008) *Transforming disadvantaged places: Effective strategies for places and people*, York: Joseph Rowntree Foundation.

Taylor, M. (2011) *Public policy in the community*, Basingstoke: Palgrave Macmillan.

Taylor, M. and Wilson, M. (2015) *Changing communities: Supporting voluntary and community organisations to adapt to local demographic and cultural change*, London: The Baring Foundation.

Taylor, M. and Wilson, M. (2016) 'Community organising for social change: the scope for class politics', in M. Shaw and M. Mayo (eds) *Class, inequality and community development*, Bristol: Policy Press, pp 209–34.

Taylor, M., Barr, A. and West, A. (2000) *Signposts to community development* (2nd edn), London: Community Development Foundation.

Taylor, M., Wilson, M., Purdue, D. and Wilde, P. (2007) *Changing neighbourhoods: Lessons from the Joseph Rowntree Foundation Neighbourhoods Programme*, Bristol: The Policy Press.

Temple, B. (2005) *Learning to live together: Developing communities with dispersed refugee people seeking asylum*, York: Joseph Rowntree Foundation.

Terry, L. (2018) *Community leadership: A literature review*, London: Local Trust.

Tett, G. (2015) *The silo effect: Why every organisation needs to disrupt itself to survive*, London: Little Brown.

Tett, L. and Fyfe, I. (2010) *Community education, learning and development*, Edinburgh: Dunedin Academic Press.

Thake, S. (2001) *Building communities, changing lives: The contribution of large independent neighbourhood regeneration organisations*, York: Joseph Rowntree Foundation.

Theocharis, Y., Lowe, W., van Deth, J.W. and García-Albacete, G. (2015) 'Using Twitter to mobilize protest action: online mobilization patterns and action repertoires in the Occupy Wall Street, Indignados, and Aganaktismenoi movements', *Information, Communication & Society*, 18 (2), 202–20.

Theodore, N. and Martin, N. (2007) 'Migrant civil society: new voices in the struggle over community development', *Journal of Urban Affairs*, 29: 269–78.

Thomas, D. (1976) *Organising for social change: A study in the theory and practice of community work*, London: Allen and Unwin.

Thomas, D. (1983) *The making of community work*, London: Allen and Unwin.

Thomas, D. (1995) *Community development at work*, London: Community Development Foundation.

Thomson, L.J., Camic, P.M. and Chatterjee, H.J. (2015) *Social prescribing: A review of Community Referral Schemes*, London: University College London.

Timms, H. and Heimans, J. (2018) *New power: How it's changing the 21st century – and why you need to know*, Basingstoke: Macmillan.

Tindall, D. (2007) 'From metaphors to mechanisms: critical issues in networks and social movements', Book review, *Social Networks*, 29: 160–8.

Tönnies, F. (1887) *Community and association*, London: Routledge and Kegan Paul.

Traynor, B. (2008) 'Community building: limitations and promise', in J. DeFilippis and S. Saegert (eds) *The community development reader*, London: Routledge, pp 214–24.

Trevillion, S. (1999) *Networking and community partnership*, Aldershot: Ashgate.

Turkle, S. (2017) *Alone together*, New York: Basic Books.

Turning Point (2010) *Navigators: A review of the evidence*, London: Turning Point.

Twelvetrees, A. (1982) *Community work* (1st edn), Basingstoke: Macmillan.

Twelvetrees, A. (2017) *Community development, social action and social planning*, Basingstoke: Palgrave Macmillan.

Twine, F. (1994) *Citizenship and social rights: The interdependence of self and society*, London: Sage Publications.

United Nations (1955) *Social progress through community development*, New York: United Nations.

Vandeventer, P. and Mandell, M. (2007) *Networks that work: A practitioner's guide to managing networked action*, Los Angeles: Community Partners.

Vaneigen, R. (2006) *The revolution of everyday life*, London: Rebel Press.

Vidyarthi, V. and Wilson, P.A. (2008) *Development from within: Facilitating reflection for sustainable change*, Herndon, VA: Apex Foundation.

Völker, B., Flap, H. and Lindenberg, S. (2007) 'When are neighbourhoods communities? Community in Dutch neighbourhoods', *European Sociological Review*, 23: 99–114.

Vollman, M. (2018) *Hyperlocal neighbourhood networks: Building social capital and empowering local urban communities*, Urbanet, www.urbanet.info/hyperlocal-neighbourhood-networks/

Wakefield, S.E.L. and Poland, B. (2005) 'Family, friend or foe: critical reflections on the relevance and role of social capital in health promotion and community development', *Social Science and Medicine*, 60: 2819–32.

Waldrop, M. (1992) *Complexity: The emerging science at the edge of order and chaos*, New York: Simon and Schuster.

Walker, P., Lewis, J., Lingayah, S. and Sommer, F. (2000) *Prove it! Measuring the effects of neighbourhood renewal on local people*, London: New Economics Foundation.

Wallace, J. (2013) *The rise of the enabling state: A review of policy and evidence across the UK and Ireland*, Fife: Carnegie UK Trust.

Wang, J. and Qixin, S. (2013) 'Short-term traffic speed forecasting hybrid model based on Chaos–Wavelet Analysis-Support Vector Machine theory', *Transportation Research Part C: Emerging Technologies*, 27: 219–32.

Warburton, D. (1998) *Community and sustainable development: Participation in the future*, London: Earthscan.

Ward, C. (1973) *Anarchy in action*, London: Allen and Unwin.

Ware, P. (2015) '*Black people don't drink tea …*': The experience of rural black and minority ethnic community groups in England*, Working Paper 130, Birmingham: Third Sector Research Centre, University of Birmingham.

Warner, W.L. and Lunt, P.G. (1942) *The status system of a modern community*, New Haven, CT: Yale University Press.

Watt, S., Lea, M. and Spears, M. (2002) 'How social is internet communication? A reappraisal of bandwidth and anonymity effects', in S. Woolgar (ed) *Virtual society? Technology, cyberbole and reality*, Oxford: Oxford University Press, pp 61–77.

Watts, D.J. (2003) *Six degrees: The new science of a connected age*, London: W.W. Norton.

Watts, D.J. (2004) *Small worlds: The dynamics of networks between order and randomness*, Princeton, NJ: Princeton University Press.

Webber, M.M. (1963) 'Order in diversity: community without propinquity', in W.J. Lowdon (ed) *Cities and space: The future use of urban land*, Baltimore, MD: Johns Hopkins Press.

Weber, M. (1947) *The theory of social and economic organisation*, New York: Free Press.

Weeks, J. (2000) *Making sexual history*, Cambridge: Polity Press.

Wei-Skillern, J., Ehrlichman, D. and Sawyer, D. (2015) 'The most impactful leaders you've never heard of', *Stanford Social Innovation Review*, 16 September.

Wellman, B. (1979) 'The community question: the intimate networks of East Yorkers', *American Journal of Sociology*, 84: 1201–31.

Wellman, B. (2000) 'Network capital in a multi-level world: getting support from personal communities', in L. Nan, K. Cook and R. Burt (eds) *Social capital: Theory and research*, Chicago, IL: Aldyne de Gruyter, pp 233–73.

Wellman, B. (2002) 'Little boxes, glocalization, and networked individualism', in M. Tanabe, P. van den Besselaar and T. Ishida (eds) *Digital cities II*, Berlin: Springer-Verlag, pp 10–25.

Wellman, B. (ed) (2006) *Personal networks in the 21st century*, special issue of *Social Networks*, 28.

Wenger, E., McDermott, R. and Snyder, W.M. (2002) *Cultivating communities of practice*, Boston, MA: Harvard Business School Press.

Werbner, P. (1988) 'Taking and giving: working women and female bonds in a Pakistani immigrant neighbourhood', in S. Westwood and P. Bhachu (eds) *Enterprising women: Ethnicity, economy and gender relations*, London: Routledge, pp 179-202.

Werbner, P. (1990) *The migration process: Capital, gifts and offerings among British Pakistanis*, Oxford: Berg.

Werth, S. (2018) 'The Tafel and food poverty in Germany', in S. Cohen, C. Fuhr and J.-J. Bock (eds), *Austerity, community action and the future of citizenship in Europe*, Bristol: Policy Press, pp 131-42.

Westoby, P. (2015) *Soul, community and social change: Theorising a soul perspective on community practice*, London: Routledge.

Westoby, P. (2017) 'A community development response to "sham" right wing populism', *Social Dialogue – Magazine of International Association of Schools of Social Work*, 17: 39-40.

Wetherell, M. (2011) *Affective practices*, London: Sage.

Wetherell, M., Lafleche, M. and Berkeley, R. (eds) (2007) *Identity, ethnic diversity and community cohesion*, London: Sage Publications.

Wheatley, M. (2006) *Leadership and the new science: Discovering order in a chaotic world* (3rd edn), San Francisco: Berrett-Koehler.

Wheatley, M. and Frieze, D. (2011) *Walk out, walk on: A learning journey into communities daring to live the future now*, San Francisco: Berrett-Koehler.

Wheeler, W.M. (1928) *Emergent evolution and the development of societies*, New York: W.W. Norton.

White, L.E. (1950) *Community or chaos*, London: National Council of Social Service.

Whitney, D. and Trosten-Bloom, A. (2010) *The power of appreciative inquiry* (2nd edn), San Francisco: Berrett- Koehler.

Wilkinson, R. and Pickett, K. (2010) *The spirit level: Why equality is better for everyone*, London: Penguin Books.

Willats, S. (2012) *Artwork as social model: A manual of questions and propositions*, Leeds: Research Group for Artists Publications.

Williams, G. (1973) 'Ways in for a community development worker', *Talking Point*, 10, Newcastle-upon-Tyne: ACW.

Williams, G. (2004) 'Towards a repoliticisation of participatory development: political capabilities and spaces of empowerment', in S. Hickey and G. Mohan (eds) *Participation: From tyranny to transformation*, London: Zed Books, pp 92–107.

Williams, P. (2002) 'The competent boundary spanner', *Public Administration*, 80: 103–24.

Williams, P. (2013) 'We are all boundary spanners now', *International Journal of Public Sector Management*, 26: 17–32.

Williams, R. (1976) *Keywords: A vocabulary of culture and society*, Glasgow: Collins.

Williams, C. and Windebank, J. (2000) 'Helping each other out? Community exchange in deprived neighbourhoods', *Community Development Journal*, 35: 146–56.

Williams, C. and Windebank, J. (2003) *Poverty and the third way*, London: Routledge.

Williamson, O.E. (1975) *Markets and hierarchies: Analysis and anti-trust implications*, New York: Free Press.

Wills, J. (2002) *Union futures: Building networked trade unionism in the UK*, London: Fabian Society.

Wills, J. and Simms, M. (2004) 'Building reciprocal community unionism in the UK', *Capital and Class*, 28: 59–82.

Wilson, E.O. (1990) *The ants*, Cambridge, MA: Harvard University Press.

Wilson, E.O. (1998) *Consilience: The unity of knowledge*, London: Little, Brown and Company.

Wilson, M. (2018) 'Reflections on change: opportunities and challenges for community led development', in A. McCabe (ed) *Ten years below the radar: Reflections on voluntary and community action 2008–2018*, Working Paper 143, Birmingham: Third Sector Research Centre, University of Birmingham.

Wilson, R., Mezey, M. and Nielsen, N. (2013) *Anti hero: The hidden revolution in leadership and change*, https://www.academia.edu/5184723/Anti_Hero__the_Hidden_Revolution_in_Leadership_and_Change

Wollebaek, D. and Selle, P. (2002) 'Does participation in voluntary associations contribute to social capital? The impact of intensity, scope and type', *Non-profit and Voluntary Sector Quarterly*, 31: 32–61.

Womankind Worldwide (2000) 'Exchanging skills and experiences', *Newsletter*, Winter.

Woodward, V. (2005) 'Engaging civil society, civil renewal and active learning for active citizenship', *Development Education Journal*, 12: 9–11.

Woolcock, M. (1998) 'Social capital and economic development: towards a theoretical synthesis and policy framework', *Theory and Society*, 27: 151–208.

Woolcock, M. (2001) 'The place of social capital in understanding social and economic outcomes', *ISUMA Canadian Journal of Policy Research*, 2: 11–17.

Worpole, K. and Knox, K. (2007) *The social value of public spaces*, York: Joseph Rowntree Foundation.

Wright, C. (2010) *Swords of justice and civic pillars: The case for greater engagement between British trade unions and community organisations*, London: Trades Union Congress.

Young, F. and Glasgow, N. (1998) 'Voluntary social participation and health', *Research on Ageing*, 20: 339–62.

Young, M. and Willmott, P. (1957) *Family and kinship in East London*, London: Routledge and Kegan Paul.

Younghusband, E. (1968) *Community work and social change: A report on training*, London: Longman.

Yunus, M. (2010) *Building social business: The new kind of capitalism that serves humanity's most pressing needs*, New York: Public Affairs.

Zeldin, T. (1994) *An intimate history of humanity*, London: Sinclair-Stevenson.

Zetter, R., Griffiths, D. and Sigona, M. (2006) *Immigration, social cohesion and social capital: What are the links?*, York: Joseph Rowntree Foundation.

Zipf, G.K. (1965) *Human behavior and the principle of least effort*, New York: Hafner.

Zipfel, T., Tunnard, J., Feeney, J., Flanagan, A., Gaffney, L., Postle, K., O'Grady, F., Young, S. and Bennett, F. (2015) *Our lives: Challenging attitudes to poverty in 2015*, RyanTunnardBrown, http://is.gd/kNBVUV

Zuber-Skerritt, O. and Teare, R. (2013) *Lifelong action learning for community development: Learning and development for a better world*, New York: Sense Publications.

Index

Printed and bound by CPI Group (UK) Ltd, Croydon, CR0 4YY

09/06/2025

14685898-0003